Rochdale's Pioneers of Worker Education

The WEA Class of 1908

Gary Heywood-Everett

This book is dedicated to the first tutorial class of the Workers Educational Association and to the hope and spirit which led working people to it, a spirit that celebrated and, through education, elevated them and their social class *'to build from within, to help men to develop their own genius, their own education, their own culture'* (R H Tawney 1914).

Acknowledgements

Thanks go to the Workers Educational Association, the Local Studies Department, Touchstones Arts and Heritage Centre in Rochdale, The British Library, The People's History Museum in Manchester, The Working Class Movement Library in Salford, Lancaster University Library, The Independent Labour Party, London Metropolitan University TUC Library, Co-operative College Library and Archive, Bolton Central Library, The John Rylands Library Manchester, Keighley Central Library, The Peace Museum, Bradford.

Personal thanks for the help with archived material to Stuart Watson at Clover Street Unitarian Church in Rochdale, Cyril Pearce for material on the conscientious objectors Hewitt and Kershaw, Glyn Hopper (Churchwarden, All Saints' Church, Pickhill) and Derek Hopper for their church archive on the Reverend Walter Stopford.

Thanks must also be recorded to the research respondents some of whom have passed away since my interviews with them : Mrs Bertha Radcliffe, Mr Ernest Thornton, Mr Phillip Elgey, Mrs Alice Taylor, Mr John and Mrs Margaret Dawson, Mrs Bracegirdle and Mrs Phyllis Meekes.

Contents

Introduction 7

Conditions and Responses 9

    Work and struggle.. 9

    A Political Response 14

Late 19th Education and Change 16

The Rise of the Labour Movement... 22

University Extension, the WEA and the Rochdale experiment 28

So Why Rochdale ? 56

    The Church, the Chapel and the WEA in Rochdale 59

    Nonconformity and Sunday Schools in Rochdale 59

    The Co-operative Movement... 68

The Rochdale Education Guild and its tutorial class............................. 72

    Organising the Tutorial class... 75

Who were the students ? 84

Sketches of the Students 86

    Occupations and social class.. 145

    Values and beliefs.. 149

    Women and the tutorial class.. 152

    Student homes and houses.. 158

Reflections on the Tutorial Class 165

    The Curriculum 165

    Teaching and learning 167

    The Teaching role of Tawney 174

    Attendance, attainment and difficulties............................... 175

    Essays and assessment 177

    Resources 178

Tutorial Class Evaluations..180

Motives and motivation...188

    Attendance at lectures as normative practice..............................189

    Social mobility 190

    The Prospect of Graduation 194

    The raising of working class students to power and influence........196

    Politics and the WEA..199

    A community of learning...204

    The search for knowledge...205

Final Reflections...208

References..220

Index 230

Introduction

I've always enjoyed browsing in libraries, you never know what you're going to find. In the days before the internet, surfing for information meant walking from shelf to shelf and picking out books to see what glimpses of other worlds they could offer. Not so much surfing as paddling. In the 1980's I was doing this in a corner of the library at Lancaster University where I was taking time away from primary school teaching to research teachers' responses to computers in the classroom, when I picked up a book on adult education. Scanning through it, I was surprised to see a photograph of what purported to be the first tutorial class of the Workers Educational Association (the WEA). The fact that this event took place in my home town of Rochdale in 1908 was extraordinary and interesting enough, but what particularly took my eye was that the photograph had been taken in front of my secondary school, the Rochdale Technical School on Nelson Street, now sadly, no longer there. The picture of the students intrigued me because of my connection to the old place, but not only that, it raised a number of questions. Were these dapper gents and ladies actually workers, and if so, why did they take on study ? What was it that they studied ? Why did such a movement have its beginnings in Rochdale ? What did these men and women go on to do after their WEA programme ? And who were they ?

There was a danger over the next few months that my interest in this group of local learners was going to hijack my own, very different, research project and I tried but without success to secure funding to conduct research into the tutorial class under the aegis of the then North-West Regional Studies at the university. I even placed an article beneath a copy of the original photograph in the Rochdale Observer accompanied by a short piece asking if any readers recognised these students or knew anything about them. The response was not long in coming from a surprising number of Rochdale people so I immediately interviewed those who had memories of relatives or friends in the class or who were simply interested in adult education from that period. I recorded the interviews and the data from these respondents provided a personal account of the WEA which largely confirms the published academic material to which I refer throughout this book.

However, some time in 1986, with no funding forthcoming to look at the WEA class and my own research to complete, I let the subject go, even though it meant a great deal to me.

Following my course of study at Lancaster University, I found lecturing work at the University of Central Lancashire in Preston and regretfully left behind the Rochdale WEA tutorial class of 1908. Twenty seven years later, however, on retirement, I dug out the cassette tapes (!), dusted down the copies of original student essays which I had collected from the WEA at Temple House in London and remembered why it had been so fascinating. The subsequent paths down which this research has since taken me has proved to be truly amazing, ranging from an interest in working class radicalism, through the dissenting voices of Thomas Paine, Samuel Bamford, John Mitchell and of course to the energies of Albert Mansbridge and R H Tawney.

I hope that you find this book as interesting to read as I did to research and write, and I offer it in all humility, as a contribution to the WEA and to a town's history which has consistently produced radical ideas and practices, one of which was this successful 'experiment' in the education of working adults.

The group assembled for the photograph in 1908 is the central focus of the book. I am interested in them because of their commitment to learning and their particular interest in politics and industrial economics at a time when both, in a period of change, impinged on their lives. I also found them intriguing because of my own working class background, the fact that I left school with very few qualifications and entered employment with an asbestos processing company from where I began my own struggle to become 'educated,' although was never clear why.

But neither my own story nor that of the individuals from the pioneering Rochdale class of 1908 is in itself important. What is more so is the motivation – perhaps Darwinian, perhaps through personal or familial desperation, perhaps to do with a moral right or a set of principles – which drives individuals to make more of their lives than they feel society has so far offered them.

Gary Heywood-Everett   October 2015

Conditions and Responses

Education systems sit within their own social and political contexts. The chicken or egg question as to whether education determines or is determined by this context has long been argued. Some maintain that the curriculum, whether in schools or in further and higher education has a determining effect on how individuals carry their thinking into the world, and that the way that they 'see' that world depends on how their minds have been attuned to it through accumulated knowledge and skills. Others see the education system as being, itself, determined by societal events. The economic climate, for example, as has been suggested by too many commentators to name, precedes institutions and provokes their reaction. Marx, of course, held that view. Bill Clinton made it famous with 'it's the economy stupid' and it certainly can be a determining lens through which to perceive and understand the students in the photograph of the first WEA tutorial class. That being said, these people were active agents who rowed against the tide of social norms, who denied the established orthodoxies of student passivity and social position. By denying their functional 'fit' they were just as much 'producers' as they were 'products' of an economic system which tried to place them in the social order as manual labourers or artisans, blue or white-collar workers. They were producers insofar as their motives for stepping into a testing educational arena identified them as 'pioneers' acting on their own initiative, perhaps on their class initiative, rather than accepting the status quo. It was a brave and potentially isolating thing to do and must have raised a degree of amusement and sometimes derision on the factory floor when it was known that they were going back to study on their precious Saturdays afternoons away from work.

In order to try to understand what stirred this group of students, it is first necessary to look at the economic and political times in which they lived and to what degree they conditioned the student's motives. They were individuals, but their individuality was inexorably touched by their economic and political moment.

Work and struggle

As with so many towns in the late 18th and 19th century, Rochdale developed in part because of its climatic conditions – damp (but not as damp as some down south would have us believe) and wet (insofar as it was served by a number of Pennine rivers) - an environment known to be perfect for processing textiles be they wool or cotton. The change in the local economy from an agriculture base through small rural manufacturing to urbanisation followed a slow and an often resisted course and the specialism of woollen treatment took time to embed into the town's industrial profile (Wiggins 1995 p27). However, as early as 1650 Rochdale was benefitting from a growing prosperity as a wool and worsted town (Berg 1994), later diversifying into bleaching and finishing with an increase and targeting of capital investment. The age of industrial expansion from the close of the 18th and through the 19th century witnessed an eightfold rise in the size and number of mills in the region (Williams and Farnie 1992 p15) although fulling mills in Rochdale had been running from the first quarter of the 17th century at Falinge, Weurdle and at Godplay with further bleach houses at Beursil, Butterworth and Spotland, (Linehan 1977). But it was the gradual and assured development of cotton manufacture and in particularly weaving in Rochdale that gave it its particular industrial profile and which set it aside from towns further to the south and east of the county which specialised in cotton spinning.

Cotton, therefore became Rochdale's mainstay and by 1906 'cotton mills found employment in Rochdale for four or five times as many people as the woollen trade' (Rochdale Municipal Borough Council 1906 p12). This particular development should, however, be seen against a backdrop of economic volatility in the late 19th century. Whilst the production of commodities such as iron, steel and coal witnessed boom times, the textile industry experienced slow but steady decline, its contribution to the national economy falling from 55% in 1870 to 34% by 1909 (Harrison 1990 pp16-17; Craik 1964 p22). And because of the instability of trade cycles and the fluctuating nature of the export markets, textiles were particularly susceptible to recession and frequently went from times of plenty to times of very little. But even in periods of plenty, worker pay was meagre, Stanley Taylor, a WEA student from Littleborough in 1911 writing in his tutorial class essay that the average earnings for loom weavers was 26/9d per week men and 27/6d a week for women (TUC Library : Ref 3/6/2) which, although roughly the national average for a male labourer (Board of Trade 1908) and slightly in excess for women, is misleading when one considers that take-home pay depended on the number of looms that each worker operated and fails to recognise the irregularities of employment and lay-off. Very few took home anything like the national average.

One social consequence of industrial vulnerability - at points fruitful and promising growth, at other times facing cut-backs – was that those who worked in the textile manufacturing and treatment industries paid a social price in the over-population of urban settlements as the population grew or people moved from the countryside as employment on the land dwindled. The associated housing and sanitation problems are well known and recorded, health being a major concern. Taylor, writing about the town concludes that 'certain localities …. possess an unenviable reputation for filthiness and untidiness of population' (Taylor in Rochdale Borough Council 1906 p26).

The Paddock, Rochdale 1910 (The Local History Centre, Touchstones)

As ever, the working and living environments of those in employment at the turn of the 20th century, as well as the health and social conditions in the town, were at the mercy of both industrial speculators and seismic shifts in the market due to overseas wars, climatic change and the attendant scarcities of raw materials, which meant that life in the growing urban environment of the North West of England was hazardous and unforgiving for many individuals and their families. The textile industry was particularly susceptible to downturn at such times because the machinery which was used in cotton manufacturing and treatment, if left completely idle, suffered mechanical depreciation and, in extreme cases, total break-down. In order to avoid this, short time operating was preferable to complete lay off but this led to further irregularities and unpredictability in working life.

Rochdale in the second half of the 19th century, as was the case with many industrial towns, produced many hard working people who, although subjected to difficult circumstances, maintained good (often gallows) humour and responded to the harshness of living and working conditions with hope and a positive outlook albeit sometimes accompanied by the violence of Luddism, sometimes in the form of direct protest as with the radical Samuel Bamford, sometimes through policy change as with John Bright or trades unionism, sometimes through the theories of a Marx, Engels, Owen or a Thomas Paine. Alternatively, the response to social hardship could be found in a retreat into religious observance and its reassurances, R H Tawney suggesting that the cause of social unrest and part of its remedy was 'not simply economic, nor party-political, but moral and spiritual.'

Although less severe, social conditions in towns such as Rochdale were also hard for many outside of the working class. Those from lower middle class communities, the sector which produced the clerks, the dressmakers and some of the semi-skilled, often endured poor pay and conditions, long hours and unhealthy lodgings. They were not, however, at the bitter end of the social spectrum. Extreme poverty, especially amongst the elderly, was common in the late 19th century and surveys at the time showed that between 30% and 40% of those over 65 were categorised as paupers for many of whom the grim salvation of the workhouse was the only prospect. That was if they survived to that age, life expectancy for men being 47 and for women 50 (Office for National Statistics 2012).

Notwithstanding these conditions, the turn of a new century may have held out a glimmering promise of better days to come for many and it was true that there were positive demographic transitions alongside the social and industrial changes taking place in daily life. A decrease in the death rate and a slowing of population growth (Jefferies 2005) characterised the time and Harrison writes that national fertility rates showed a fall from 6.16 children per family in the 1860's to 5.27 by 1881 and then to 2.73 in 1914 (1990 p14).

The picture was the same in Rochdale. The population had more than doubled to 83,112 between the years 1861 and 1901 (Lee 1987 p6) and by 1891 17,600 habitable houses were standing in the town with an average of 4.1 people per house. 1900 saw this number rising again to 19,600 but with a lower average of 3.8 people to each household (Rochdale Borough Council 1900). Whilst it could be argued that conditions were improving, this figure was still above the national average and a 1911 Housing Reform Council survey cast a further shadow over the town by reporting that 22% of Rochdale's housing was in a poor condition or worse, whilst 88% was 'good or merely passable' (Moran no date).

Objectively though, wages throughout the late Victorian years were rising nationally and this was the case even in the cotton industry with skilled operatives earning 20 shillings in 1850 but in some cases 35 shillings by the turn of the century. Again, care should be taken here, as this only applied to those lucky enough to be in work and even then, for many, low wages meant marginal poverty. Those without employment fell into desperation. It is alarming indeed to read Charles Booth or the social research of Rowntree concerning the hardships that many people faced with their 'life lived under chronic want' (Rowntree 1899 p39) or the large sections of the population who did not earn enough to buy food to constitute an adequate diet. Many relied on neighbours in times of sickness or for help with cooking and cleaning and some of the lowest class in Rowntree's study were either living in actual poverty or liable to sink into it at any time : 'They live constantly from hand to mouth' (ibid p54). By 1909 poverty had been recognised as an endemic problem in the inner cities and small towns of the North West of England. The Manchester and Salford Co-operative Herald (1909 p122) reported that there had been an increase in those seeking poor relief, a trend that had been growing steadily for some time, and the same newspaper records that in Manchester 'on March 13th there were 853,129 persons on the relief lists…. The rate of increase was 3.3% from 1908…. The rate of pauperism stood at 23.8 per 1000'.

Workers in a weaving shed circa 1910 (The Local History Centre, Touchstones)

Sanitation was a related and on-going problem and had a particular Rochdale angle. Abendstern (1986 p63), writing about conditions into the 1930's, notes that '2300 houses occupied in Rochdale had been classed as 'unfit and unhealthy' by the local Health Inspector' and that there were '3000 pail closets still in use in the town though they were later replaced by water closets.' The pail system, deployed in 79% of the houses in the town in 1911 (Rochdale Housing Reform Council), with closets often shared between three or four families, was a way of disposing of human waste using a tub under an outdoor toilet which was emptied (every so often) by the local authority and nationally referred to as the 'Rochdale system' due to its widespread use across the town. One closet toilet within three feet of a back door (ibid p4) was recorded and condemned by the Chief Medical Officer for the borough.

Unsurprisingly then, the death rate in Rochdale was above the national average due in the main to poor sanitation, poor drainage and un-sewered and un-cleaned streets (Moran : no date; Rochdale Housing Reform Council 1911 p86). Roads and footpaths which were unpaved, accounting for 31% of all roads and 50% of those abutting onto others (ibid p2), were so commonplace in some areas that the Medical Officer wrote : 'I know of no town in Lancashire where the requirement (for paved streets) has been so laxly observed as in Rochdale' (ibid). This was no insignificant civil engineering issue. Unpaved roads meant that they could not be cleaned effectively and so litter and refuse would build-up on the outside of housing, inviting vermin and disease. The inside of houses was little better in many cases. Scant water supply (one in four houses in the town was without water in the mid 19th century), overcrowding and dampness seeping through the walls and paved floors contributed to the risks to health. Typhus was common into the early 20th century, one of the causes being the build-up and proximity to living quarters of human and domestic waste. With the removal of night soil remaining a problem into the 1870's (ibid p31) and the changing of ash pits only occurring every two weeks, airtight vans were seen as a solution and later introduced to take away excrement. Gradually therefore, for some areas of the town, matters improved and when the Great Public Health Act of 1875 set up a Code of Sanitary Regulations, standards were again raised in sewerage, scavenging, housing and the purity of the water supply (Hall and Watkins (1937).

In passing, it is important to note, with Rowntree (1899), that one major cause of poverty within a family was the death of the main wage earner, usually the father, and even though mortality rates at the time were in decline, the UK national census data reveals many families becoming dependent on children going out to work at the earliest possible moment due to a death in the household.

A Political response

Joyce (1982) highlights the crucial role of the cotton industry in Lancashire in the lives of many individuals, not simply in providing a wage for a week's work, but also in the framing, if not the dictation, of political sensitivities. Living within a paternalistic system in both negative and positive senses, the relationship of the cotton worker to the owners and even the under-managers, the over-lookers, the foremen etc., could lead - in extremis - to either deference or resistance. In the final decades of the 19th century the experience was of a growing sense of inequity from the lower social classes and a willingness amongst many of them, to protest about it. As to the contrary response, some historians (Savage 1988 ; Nordinger 1967) have identified an established deference amongst working class communities, a dogged paternalism in the industrial base and an occupational 'caste system' (Clarke 1899 pp27-8) which separated labouring poor from artisans, business class from merchants and the majority from what remained of the local gentry. Acquiescence through deference was as much the case in some Rochdale communities as elsewhere.

However, the patterns of social life and stratification in the second half of the 19th century were changing in this respect and ripples from these changes beginning to be felt across all sectors of society – from a decline in the effective power of the aristocracy, from the rise of the middle classes through business ownership, finance and control and from the emergence of white collar occupational groups. At a systemic and political level, emergent power bases were beginning to erode the old and challenges arising from newly-empowered sections of the population. Deference was becoming less likely as a consequence. One catalyst for this was a new and skilled workforce with reformist if not radical political ideals pressing for power to be placed into the hands of the many and not simply the few, with unforgiving economic forces stimulating these demands. Rising prices, pressures on the productivity of the labour force and fixed wages with little or no bargaining power fermented discontent which was bubbling up and provoking action from large sections of the population.

And as a wider political consensus was promoting incrementally greater power for working people, the question was starting to be asked as to how this power was to be operationalised. The vote would have been one answer and although the size and social constituency of the electorate had grown with an extension of the United Kingdom franchise in 1867 and 1884, by 1903 it remained the case that not all men (and no women at all) were allowed the ballot box and in 1911 there were still only 8 million citizens with the eligibility to vote, or 29% of the adult population.

Yet from the 1860's to the end of the century, rising social resentment at the levels of poverty, the dire living standards experienced by many people and an under-representation at the highest tables of power, was not so easily ameliorated by incrementally increasing the right to vote. What had to change in order to make a difference was the nature of representation itself and thereby the empowerment of the working population. The suggestion at the opening of Tom Paine's book 'Crisis' that 'these are the times that try men's souls….' could also be legitimately claimed for the late decades of 19th century Britain, or as Albert Mansbridge and Robert Halstead put it in 1903 : 'working men today are all afire to act politically.' One of the original members of the WEA tutorial class, Fred Hall, later to become Principal of the Co-operative College and author of many books on Co-operation, reflected in 1937 that the 1880's were lean years creating a climate of dissent and a growing critique of the standing of capitalist industry. In a later book he, with Watkins (1937 p135) suggested that the root cause of this political unrest had been social and that 'the real magnitude of the problem of poverty' had suddenly been made clear to them. In the final years of the 19th century, such sentiments were given theoretical and political muscle with an interest in the works of Marx and Engels whose texts had been translated into English in 1883.

Late 19th century Education and Change

So, a new and vital consciousness was emerging, one driven by adverse social conditions that had for some time been fermenting anxiety and pressure in the manufacturing towns across Europe. It was fuelled by new industrial technologies, communication and transportation systems which served both to aggravate these conditions but also to raise awareness of them through their more effective dissemination in national newspapers and mass circulation periodicals. Furthermore, because a greater section of the population was now better educated following the Education Act of 1870 and with the spread of public libraries in the late 19th century, more people than ever before were reading, discussing and thinking about the nature of their lives, their history and culture. This included an increasing awareness of their class' exploitation.

However, for the working population in the United Kingdom the role of education in raising this political awareness had been a long time coming and Thompson (1991) in his seminal book on the English working class records many a stalled 19th century initiative in the extension of education to workers through Bible Societies and Sunday Schools which, although largely focusing on scriptures, also set their sights on developing basic reading skills so that they might learn for themselves. These initiatives stalled because access to learning and knowledge lacked the institutionalisation and organisation that would come 80 years later.

The tide of change could not, however, be held back indefinitely, and especially regarding the education of young children it was recognised that the situation had become critical. The nature of education for the majority throughout the 19th century tended to be based not on the needs of the child but on the demands of the local economy and – in the North West of England - on the daily requirements of a system which predicated educational opportunity within the balance sheet of loom, foundry or farm productivity. A succession of Factory Acts from 1833 onwards attempted to change this repressive situation although employers throughout the country, apart from the odd liberal, fought hard to maintain the working hour's flexibility, and therefore the educational subjugation of a young workforce.

Nonetheless, what the 1833 Act achieved was to highlight the importance of education for child workers by ensuring that at least part of their day was allocated to the development of the basic skills of reading, writing and arithmetic. This, half-time system officially persisted until the implementation of state education in 1870, Simon (1965 p138) suggesting that it had been particularly prevalent in the Lancashire and Yorkshire textile industries because it offered mill owners the flexibility, with child labour support, to operate six looms rather than four and thereby sustain high productivity. Change was, however, in the air although a Royal Commission of 1892 reported that many of Rochdale's children were still subject to the rigours and restrictions of the half-time system. The Borough 'Return' on the Employment of Children in 1913 confirms this with its report that 6.7% of the 14000 children of school age being 11 years or over were half-timers and excused 5-10 school sessions per week to work 'in mills, in shops or at home' (Rochdale Touchstones archives : Education Provision in Rochdale and District) provided that they held a certificate to show that they had reached a minimum educational level of Standard IV.

Child workers in the Cotton Industry 1900 (courtesy of maggieblanck.com)

Craik (1964 p23) has written that as a consequence of technological developments in the work place and the political pressures and changes that followed in their wake, government was eventually forced to give serious consideration to the education of children (and adults), and so the Education Act of 1870 was made law in order to provide elementary education wherever local and existing facilities for its implementation were available. Prior to this, the curriculum and therefore learning, had been under the control of religious bodies, the elementary curriculum gradually being enriched as the 19th century went by (Martin 1997) and as literacy and numeracy demands upon the workforce became so manifest that they could no longer be ignored. The Forster Education Act of 1870 was not, however, without its critics – and for familiar economic reasons - an example being the novelist, socialist and social reformer H G Wells (in Harrison 1990 p200) who felt that the Act had been designed in order to make productive workers ever more productive. And even with this legislation, it was not until 1881 that attendance in an elementary school was made compulsory, challenging, as it did the old Factory Acts and Child Labour Regulations, although employers – and families in need of an extra wage – continued to find ways of avoiding compulsory attendance. Furthermore it was not until a decade later that the Elementary Education Act of 1891 made this phase of education free. Up to that point, for the privilege of learning, children had to give 'school pence' which varied according to ability to pay. A local history group from Rochdale recalled (Living History Group 1975 p46) that fees in the ordinary elementary schools ranged from 2d to 4d per week, Mrs Edwards remembering paying every Monday morning and Mrs Woodhead paying 2d instead of the regular 4d because her mother was widowed.

Notwithstanding the advances in elementary education and a corresponding focus on teacher training, by the close of the century education at a secondary level had changed very little, and was still primarily available to serve a middle class looking to find routes into the professions for its young people, the Samuelson Report (1884) making this clear with a plea that 'intelligent youths of the artisan classes should have easier access to secondary and technical schools by numerous scholarships.' But working class scholarships were the exception rather than the rule. Those fortunate enough to progress in school beyond Standard V by the age of twelve or thirteen and were bright enough *and* had parents who were not forced by immediate circumstance to have them earning for the family, could win a scholarship towards the end of the 19th century and go on to a Higher Grade School, but these were in the minority.

Educational policy makers were, however, anxious for change. In attempting to implement new teaching and learning pathways within schools and to distinguish curricula in order to meet developmental needs as well as age-appropriate labour requirements, the Cross Commission of 1887 set firm a distinction between elementary and secondary education and did so with progressive ideas about a suitable curriculum for each sector within a school leaving age of 11 years. Indicating the growing political presence of the working class as a pressure group at the time, Thomas Smyth, a plasterer who spoke for the London Trades Council and described as 'a representative of the working class,' was asked to give evidence to this Commission about the existing policies and practices of Board and Voluntary schools. His views in arguing the case for Board Schools, which he describes as 'the people's schools' (Report of the Royal Commission 1887), had been supported by his own research with teachers as well as by his experiences as a manager of evening classes. The fact that he was allowed to give evidence at all and that working people were now placed on School Boards (Simon 1965 p123) was a testament to shifts in policy determination and to the rise, within the accepted ranks of influence, of the working man and woman. It is clear from these policy changes, therefore, that education was by no means closed off from reform.

Regardless of change however, the experience of school for many at the end of the 19th century remained harsh and learning haphazard, with an emphasis on rote learning and unsympathetic discipline all set within the structure of half-time schooling and a monitorial system where older children 'taught' the young, a system condemned by the Cross Report as 'the worst possible system of supply.' Charles Dickens in many of his novels but particularly in Dombey and Sons (1848), Hard Times (1854) and Our Mutual Friend (1864) was critical of the school provision of his time. He writes in Dombey and Sons that it was 'part of Mrs. Pipchin's system not to encourage a child's mind to develop and expand itself like a young flower, but to open it by force like an oyster,' and in Hard Times he lampoons the pupil-teacher system (in a letter of 1856 he called it Kayshuttleworthian nonsense) by presenting Mr M'Choakumchild as a product of the monitorial system in teacher education as 'one of those who had been lately turned at the same time, in the same factory, on the same principles, like so many pianoforte legs' (Dickens 1854 p13).

What some saw as the industrialisation of education was under attack, although Rose (2010 pp158ff) in his vivid account of the intellectual life of the working class of the 19th century finds positive counter arguments in the words of those who benefited from their time in elementary schools. And whilst it is true that many derived something from it in basic skills and a rudimentary knowledge of history and geography, many others (Maclure 1970) recorded the reality of passive learning, exhaustion within the part-time system and an unnecessary deployment of corporal punishment.

Nor was Dickens the only critic. In the 1890s the Independent Labour Party (ILP) urged reform of the curriculum and an investigation into teaching standards and styles as well as calling for the raising of the school leaving age to the mid teens. School Boards could only compel child attendance up to the age of 14 as late as 1900 although demands for its rise continued into the early decades of the 20th century as can be seen with an SDF plea for 'elementary education to be free, secular, industrial and compulsory for all classes…. the age of obligatory school attendance to be raised to 16' (Editorial in Justice 16/11/07), and similarly a speech by R H Tawney in Rochdale urged support for a trades union resolution to raise the school leaving age to 16 (Rochdale Observer 22/10/09).

Demands for the reform of secondary education from many sources began to be acceded to by policy makers in the early years of the 20th century with the nascent Trade Union movement pressing for change to remove secondary school fees. Simon (1965 p270) writes that in 1907 the unions continued their attack on these charges whilst, at the same time targeting the inadequate scholarship system which allowed too few working class children progression into higher education. In response to these pressures, the grammar schools closed ranks (Simon 1965 p271), perceiving jeopardy to themselves in a potential influx of children from working families and thereby a threat to their standards and independence.

Change, though, had its own momentum for adult learners as well, with growing numbers of an older population beginning to see the benefits of a widening educational provision and greater access to knowledge, information and skills. Tom Price (1924), a member of the first WEA tutorial class in Rochdale comments that 'imperfect as it was, compulsory elementary education had provoked a working class reading public for the flood of pamphlets, cheap books, newspapers and periodicals which marked the closing years of the (19th) century' (p13), and elsewhere that (p8) 'the social ferment of the last 2 decades (1900-1920's) …… produced a spontaneous outburst of educational idealism, on a scale which neither Chartists nor Co-operators could have dreamed to be possible'. A few years earlier, in the WEA's house publication, The Highway (February 1909), the same author writes that 'an educated democracy will alone make the freest expression of popular will consistent with sound government'.

Price's words resonate with the political sentiment – often raised defensively by those fearful of change – that alongside wider educational access would come new and dangerous ideas, both political and social. This is hinted at in one of Tom Price's essays for the WEA when he suggests that 'the time has come for the working man to demand a share in liberal education' and where he makes a call for 'admitting the workers freely to a share in their treasures' (TUC Library : Ref 3/6/7). And this enthusiasm for learning amongst large sections of the working population was palpable as can be sensed from workers such as Tom Bell (1941 p97) :

> 'We read feverishly, discussed fiercely, and walked the streets, often after midnight, in an effort to sort out for ourselves the problems of man and the universe. We experimented psychologically on everything and everybody and eagerly watched for the results.'

Similarly 'CRV' (1908) writing in Justice magazine maintained that :

> 'the man of toil is at last becoming the man of knowledge, reflection and action in the interests of his class and in antagonism to both of the sections (Liberal and Tory) who have continued to keep him in subjection by the ownership of the means of his life.'

And so it was against this backdrop of change in basic educational provision that a vitalised labour movement began to test its growing political muscle and make claims for education in each of the sectors – even the one catering for adults of working class communities. Furthermore, the widening of the political franchise sent waves in another direction and demanded that if more people could vote, then more people should have the knowledge to vote.

Policy tremors in favour of a wider educational franchise were also being felt at university level. The authors of the Joint Report of 1908 (WEA/University of Oxford) concerned as they were with national pressures for reform, highlighted possible change for the universities :

> 'This demand that the universities shall serve all classes derives much additional significance from changes which are taking place in the constitution of English society and in the distribution of political power. The most conspicuous symptoms of such changes to which we refer, have been the growth of Labour representatives in the House of Commons and our municipal bodies, the great increase in the membership of political associations …. the increasing interest taken by trade unions …. and the growing demand for a widening in the sphere of social organisations.'

The Rise of the Labour Movement

The momentum towards a labour movement purporting to represent the lives and hopes of workers especially through the 1880s and 1890s, presented ordinary people with an idealism and a hope for change which was unstoppable not just in Britain but across the industrialised world. In the United Kingdom the social and economic conditions towards the end of the 19th century provided fertile soil for political reform and saw the emergence of new political parties such as Hyndman's Social Democratic Federation in 1881 and the Independent Labour Party, set up in Bradford in 1893. It also produced, at the industrial and commercial level, the rise of organised trade unionism.

Unlike the Chartists half a century before, this movement advanced and offered power and influence to striking figures such as William Morris, Keir Hardie, George Lansbury, Albert Mansbridge, R H Tawney and many others, although Simon (1965) suggests that early 20th century socialism became divided because there were <u>too many</u> personalities and that there subsequently arose no strong and unifying leadership to steer a clear direction from undoubted and committed political energies.

At the same moment, and for the same reasons, institutions either grew by affiliation with others or contested space and power in the name of a demand for social justice, with pressure groups and agencies emerging such as Toynbee Hall in 1884, Socialist Sunday Schools, the Adult Schools, the Fabian Society, the Central Labour College and the Plebs League, and the Clarion. The sweep of these political and quasi-political initiatives from the mid 19th century represented a challenge to a weakening Liberalism and a test of strength with the established hierarchies of church, state and industry. This meant that the period from 1870 onwards was one in which change itself, socially, economically, but most of all politically, was tangible. William Morris, drawing from Marx's focus on labour and the possibilities of human development (Simon 1965 p53) recognised this and called, specifically, for the transforming power of education to be the critical engine by which working people would be carried towards political decision-making and thereby to a determination of their own destinies. Morris went on to write that such a redistributive change should be led by the intelligent and well-informed from every social class.

Election Poster for Kier Hardie 1892 (The Working Class Movement Library, Salford)

And the call for such political change came not only from individuals or newly established political parties but was channelled through publications such as The Clarion with its philosophy of a socialism rooted in fellowship rather than in overt political theory and in its own way, indicating the grassroots reach of its idealism. By no means was it the only one. Other publications sprang up to herald this new dawn such as Labour Leader, The Socialist, Commonweal, Justice and the Clarion Magazine itself launched in 1891, The Bee Hive underscoring trades union activism - all periodicals which joined the earlier radicalism of the Manchester Observer and Black Dwarf. Rose (2010 p10) celebrates this new readership and notes that the working class, as never before, was turning to print media for their information, for their attitudes and for a reinforcement of emerging values. He quotes Bourne (1912) : 'Thanks to the cheap press, ideas and information about the whole world are finding their way into the cottages of the village,' and if this was the case in the countryside, so much more was it the case in the town.

As a result of collective organisation and the amplification of their voices through such publications, leverage from reformers increased around particular issues, one being child labour and the restrictions imposed by it upon the education of the young. Articles, speeches and direct action mounted for a reduction in children's working hours in order to set aside time for education, and groups on the political left of centre gathered and canvassed accordingly for an 8 hour day and for changes in child labour policies.

However, on a party political level, the General Election of 1900 frustrated those wishing to see a political breakthrough that reflected this groundswell for an improvement in working peoples' lives as only Keir Hardie and Richard Bell were returned to Westminster. Successful representation, however, was not long in coming with Labour gains in the wake of a Liberal landslide victory of 1906 when 29 socialist members were elected on the back of anger at the Taff Vale judgement and a pacifist and anti-imperialist clamour for reform (Cole 1948 p253). Parliamentary progress led to an expectation that there would be a fundamental, if not a radical, set of policy changes and that this direction of travel – perhaps a socialist direction – would have its educational corollary in a renewed call 'to educate men to understand the need for social change and the means to bring it about' (Simon 1965 p296).

This, then, was a moment of anticipated political reform at grassroots level, a time when those with idealism looked towards new socialist horizons for a more inclusive world and a better life for working people. It was a moment when hope and fellowship and political idealism met, as in the Clarion movement, with its cycling and rambling clubs and its political/cultural activities, and when new optimism for a government intent on social equity seemed to be within reach, promoted through new journals and pamphlets : 'it was a period of confidence, of high optimism and enthusiastic conviction on the part of the militants in the certainty of victory, and of a new socialist society' (Bell 1944 p8).

Working people in the United Kingdom found themselves for the first time at the vanguard of a demand for the representation of their interests, with groups to carry their voice and more MPs in tune with their needs.

Rochdale wasn't going to be left out. As a town, it had enjoyed a long and colourful radical history. It had returned Liberal representation at the elections of 1832, 1837, 1841, 1847 and 1852 principally as a response to pressure following the Reform Act of 1832. Operationally, it had a relatively open system of township, parish, ward and council meetings around a pluralistic and contested pattern of party politics (Garrard 1983 p109) which made it possible to sustain lively political debate. Not only was Rochdale the cradle of Co-operation with the Rochdale Pioneers of 1844 but before that it had been a garrison centre for Parliamentary forces in the Civil War, a bastion of Chartism and a town known for its fierce opposition to the Corn Laws, Factory Acts and Poor Laws. Thomas Livsey – a disciple of Cobbett – was an example of the town's radicalism and lived as a towering influence in Rochdale in the period up to 1860, supporting measures to curb child labour, attacking the Poor Law and supporting the Charter, all with militant conviction. Garrard (1983) records William Nassau Molesworth's recollection that when Livsey died, thousands turned out to honour the cortege whilst the Parish Church bells tolled in mourning over the town.

Other examples of a radical town history include a procession in June 1817 led by 8,000 women followed by 30,000 men which met at Cronkeyshaw Common carrying banners demanding Universal Suffrage and 'Destruction to all Governments,' Samuel Bamford's march on St Peter's Field Manchester two years later picked up 6000 individuals (including 200 women) from the Rochdale districts (Bamford 2005 p147) some of whom were killed at what became known as Peterloo, or in 1844 the Manchester Guardian being 'appalled' to discover that those elected to Rochdale's Board of Guardians 'are nearly all of them Chartists' (Manchester Guardian 1844).

Bamford (1843) records public disorder at one of many outdoor meetings held at the time on Cronkeyshaw Common to which speakers had been invited, including Bamford himself. Perhaps it had been the freezing cold or the rain, but he was the only speaker who turned up for it although promised four shillings for doing so provided that he spoke to the assembled, which he did to some effect. The organisers of the demonstration met beforehand in the Rose Tavern on Yorkshire Street whilst a company of soldiers (redcoats carrying arms) was placed on alert in the town, preparing for trouble. Bamford's memoir records that the rain had been torrential all day and that the radicals thought that there would be so much water in the soldiers' gun barrels that they would squirt them rather than shoot them ! Comedy, however, later turned to tragedy when a young boy was killed during the protest meeting. Two decades later in August of 1867, a demonstration against the inadequacies of the Reform Bill witnessed 10,000 citizens of Rochdale marching on the town hall in torch-lit procession, and in the months of July to August of 1872 regular meetings were held in the town centre, attended by 3000, protesting at the price of meat and milk (Garrard 1983 p130).

So, political agitation had been common in Rochdale throughout the 19th century, there being regular organised and enthusiastic demands for working class representation and policy reform. One such in April 1874 saw a procession and meeting in the town by workmen from 16 leading industries demanding that their workforce be represented in parliament (Coneys no date).

However, notwithstanding this enthusiasm for social justice and representation, the reform of key policy and decision-making areas was politically resisted by the Liberal majority on Rochdale town council, a majority which was sustained into the 20th century with 78% of councillors from that party returned in 1902 (Lee 1987 p43). Liberalism at this official, council level acted as a brake to rapid change and served to preserve the vested interests of church and industrial leaders. For example, it took many years before trade unionism took hold in what was a rather paternalistic and conservative textile industry, one which found its champions amongst the Liberals of the time. It has been suggested (Coneys no date p19) that weaving itself was slow to unionise and take a radical stance due to the fact that many women worked in the industry but Burgess (1975 p247) sees it more systemically : 'a sense of congratulation [and apathy] isolated the textile industries from the labour movement in the late 19th century,' even going so far as to recognise its resistance to a reduction of the working day to 8 hours in Rochdale on the grounds of efficiency and output. This position was attacked by the Social Democratic Federation (SDF), a Rochdale branch of which was formed in 1887 and met thereafter on the last Tuesday of every month at the Social Democratic Club near to Parish Church steps.

Politically then, the later years of the 19th century in Rochdale might be characterised as Liberal defensiveness in the face of an emerging Labour momentum, the SDF putting up candidates supported by the Trades Unions in the municipal elections of 1890 and 1891 but failing to be elected and then facing fierce critical comment from the (Liberal) Rochdale Observer which accused the SDF of 'deliberately making and widening the gulf between themselves and the democratic (Liberal) party' (Rochdale Observer 24/9/1890). Even though they failed to elect, the strength of Labour votes increased with each subsequent ballot and on the crest of this (small) wave, the Rochdale branch of the Independent Labour Party (ILP) – supported by the Trades Council in the town - was established following a meeting in November of 1892 in The Coffee House at 42 Drake Street. From around this date the Liberals, seeing which way the wind was blowing nationally and locally (the Rochdale Times of 1894 noted that 'workingmen are forsaking Liberalism'), courted the rising tide of the labour vote with social justice policies of their own and it was only their better organisation and established power in the town that resisted any immediate success for the Labour movement.

However, the General Election of 1895 was seen as a chance for socialism to break the mould, and to that end the National Secretary of the ILP, Tom Mann, leant his considerable weight to the Rochdale candidates by appearing and speaking to an audience of 500 and then 1000 in the town. Hailed as the 'John Bright of the ILP' his speeches were enthusiastically received and although the Liberals held onto power with Clement Royds' small majority, the Labour and socialist tide was now flowing in the town with not only clear defections from the Liberal vote but a growing voice of its own. As if to reinforce the material and ideological foundations being set, The Rochdale Times reported that by April of 1895 new premises for the SDF and the ILP had been opened on George Street and 'the Red Flag of revolt against capitalism seemed to be gathering to it an increasing army of men and women day by day.'

It is no surprise then, with a history of reform in the town, that the years up to the beginning of the 20th century should witness passionate and organised political activity and that Rochdale should be known as a 'progressive town' (John Rylands Library : letters and documents of A P Wadsworth) by many in the Labour movement. Interestingly however, and in line with the town's idiosyncratic nature, the form that reform took was through education rather than direct revolutionary action. Rochdale had its militants in the past and would have them in the future such as the Marxist alternatives to the WEA, but its revolt as the new century unfolded would take its immediate lead from a demand for knowledge and a reaching out to widening horizons through worker education.

University Extension, the WEA and the Rochdale experiment

Perhaps it was because of the Chartists' experiences of defeat, perhaps because some of them tasted the fruits of a recovering economy from the 1840's, whatever the reason, groups of workers (especially the skilled) in the second half of the 19th century resisted direct political action on the streets in order to achieve social reform, and instead turned 'towards the more limited objective of building up and consolidating the strength of their organisations within the confines of the system' (Kirk 1985). In this way, reform rather than revolt provided the impetus for the Weavers Society (with its own library) established in 1832, the Oddfellows Literary Institution and of course the Trades Union Movement. Foster (1977) maintains that such reform could not have been instigated or developed were it not for the social sub-group which Bronterre O'Brien called the 'labour aristocracy' and in an educational context by collectives which Rose (2010 p36) identified as 'knowledge Chartists.'

And although the Mechanics Institutes had led the way for workers' education in the 1820's and to some degree laid the foundations for the Co-operative movement's education activities, their organisational inadequacies could do nothing to sustain a consistent national presence and this resulted in a gradual dwindling of participation by those studying under them. Furthermore, and most damningly, the Institutes were increasingly attracting the middle rather than the working classes and were eventually riven by ideological conflict rooted in a dispute about different objectives that was echoed 100 years later in the debates between the WEA and the Central Labour College.

Developing the same theme, Thompson (1991) writes that there had been a strain of socialist thought emanating from Robert Owen that anticipated reform rather than revolution as an effective way forward and a particular reform at that - through education as an institutional foundation incorporating principles of social justice. For Owen :

> 'the new society would offer a balance between intellectual and physical labour, entertainment and the cultivation of the physical powers as in Greece and Rome. All citizens should abandon ambition, envy, jealousy, and other named vices' (in Thompson 1991 p867).

Apart from the references to the classical world, this idealism had much in common with the educational vision of Christian Socialism and in that sense would have recommended itself to Albert Mansbridge, the founder of the WEA and R H Tawney one of its earliest champions, who recognised 'the religion of the Incarnation in its bearing on the social and economic life of man' (Tawney 1940).

Mansbridge, as a young man at the end of the 19th century, had been aware of the shortcomings of adult education in reaching all classes of people in a 'new society' and later reflected that 'the education services which were devised on the behalf of working men and women, but not in co-operation with them, tended to be utilized by others' (Mansbridge 1920 xviii). His remedy for this, as with the Fabian Society, was incremental reform, permeation and change *within* the established structures of society, a model of Christian democratic protest.

In clearing a path for the WEA and the realisation of this change, a number of earlier initiatives had been put in place which attempted to promote the education of the working man and woman. William Lovett's London Working Man's Association in the 1830's and the work and theoretical texts of Frederick Denison Maurice had been pioneering projects (albeit with limited success) in bringing education to a wider and disenfranchised constituency. Some of Maurice's ideas had been more successfully realised by the Reverend Robert Slater Bayley, Minister of Howard Street Congregational Chapel who, in 1842, set up the Sheffield People's College for children, young people and adults of working communities. By insisting on the name 'College' Maurice was suggesting that it was similar to study taking place in the universities although a key attribute of the Sheffield venture was that it was organised and democratically governed by working people themselves. It achieved some success until educational policy changes at a national level in 1870 led to its decline and closure.

In the development of such initiatives, Maurice received support from the Co-operative movement which had similar ideological and policy objectives, Hall and Watkins (1937 p102) writing that such was the Co-op's determination to raise its adult education profile and activities, that by 1854 they employed Maurice himself to draw up a constitution for their organisation in Rochdale. The vision was to 'promote humane education amongst adults, combined with a training in the fundamental principles of Co-operation' (Joint Committee of University and Working Class Representatives 1909 p4).

Building on these earlier projects, James Stuart, Professor of Mechanism and Applied Mechanics at Cambridge University, attempted to draw together the universities and a working population separated from them. Initially his vision was to bring the university experience within reach of women and 'those with lesser means,' but this was soon extended to all adults in educational need. In the 1870's Stuart tested what he perceived to be a demand for university-level education by setting up in Rochdale a series of experimental lectures on science subjects hosted by the Rochdale Pioneers : 'Stuart was greatly influenced by his contact with the intelligent artisans of Rochdale, at whose promoting he added a discussion class to his original scheme of formal lectures' (Jennings

1992; Twigg 1924 p19). Stuart was convinced that 'the highest class of education, if properly adapted, was capable of being appreciated by, and of real use to, the general mass of people' (Jennings 1992).

James Stuart 1843-1913 (from Vanity Fair October 1899)

Success followed this initiative and by 1871 Stuart was attracting an audience for his lectures in Rochdale of nearly 1000, later recalling that :

> 'it was my experience at Rochdale that not only greatly encouraged me, but that determined me to go on – that opened my eyes in fact, to what was needed, and that gave me confidence, never since shaken, that the demand existed if the supply was only forthcoming' (Harrison 1961 pp222-223).

In the following year, Stuart was sending lecturers out to provincial centres across the country focusing on history, economics and social sciences following the model pioneered in Rochdale (Hall and Watkins 1937 p135).

Given Stuart's success with outreach lectures, the universities saw this as a way to raise their profile and fulfil their moral and democratic mission by re-energising University Extension lectures, the first presentations of which had been given in 1867 under the auspices of the University of Cambridge. They also saw it as a way in which younger lecturers might sharpen their skills before returning to their 'home' teaching establishments. Within the University Extension movement a certain amount of devolved power was possible in that local centres were free, to a point, to decide their own subjects for study after consultation with a local committee. Following such a decision, funds would be raised to implement and support the programme at the close of which would be an examination for the students as was the case at university proper. The combining of established institutions with voluntary action was a balance which worked well and would later pave the way for the WEA.

University Extension proved popular, certainly with women and notably (see Simon 1965 p89) with miners, achieving its high water mark in the 1880s and 1890s with 60,000 students attending lectures set up by Oxford and Cambridge. Regular attendances were recorded particularly in the North-East coalfield and the industrial North of England, many colliery and mill owners supporting these lectures for their workforce. In some areas and for some subjects up to 1000 men attended them in the winter of 1883 (ibid), missing shifts and losing wages in doing so. Historians such as Jennings (in Roberts 2003 p12) however, demur from this as representing a socially inclusive initiative, feeling that there was only a limited worker response to university extension for two reasons : one, that the lectures had to be self-supporting and thereby incurred quite high fees, and two, that they alienated a working class community suspicious of middle class benevolence and university control. These views, however, may have differed from place to place, from subject to subject and may have depended on the subtleties of the tutor's teaching style as was seen in the Rochdale experience.

The University Extension movement was not the only enterprise to try to reach a wider, working population though, as parallel institutions were concurrently attempting to meet the same needs. Although having no formal ties to the university, Ruskin College in Oxford had been founded in 1899 by the American Christian Socialists Walter Vrooman and Charles A Beard with the aim of training young workers to become leaders in the working class movement from within the university sector 'so that in place of talking against the world, they will begin methodically and scientifically to possess the world' (Barnard 1971 p276). They offered study partly by correspondence course but also through residential programmes in the social sciences, industrial history and politics to student workers which included, in 1902, miners, compositors, brush-makers joiners, engineers and weavers (Ruskin College 1949).

Another institution with a similar, albeit more localised mission was the Co-operative movement. In Rochdale, as early as 1871, the Pioneers (the Co-op) had approached Cambridge University with a request to develop in the town what eventually became University Extension work and Twigg (1924) writes that adult classes under those auspices were available in the 1870's in Maths, Geometry, Mechanical Drawing, Physiology, Botany, Magnetism, Electricity, Chemistry, Geography, French and Art' with Molesworth, the Anglican radical and supporter of the Co-operative Movement in Rochdale being particularly active in their organisation.

But it was in the last decade of the 19th century that a young clerk, working in the Tea Department of the Co-operative Wholesale Society, began to take up in earnest the cause of extending educational opportunities for working people. By the age of 14 in 1890, Albert Mansbridge was attending University Extension courses himself, enrolling on 'The Chemistry of Everyday Life' at the end of which he was awarded a certificate with distinction. At 20 he had been employed in the civil service but 'failed to progress' (Marsh 2002). During these years he attended a number of Extension courses and, as one of its employees, became involved in the development of the Co-operative movement's own educational work. These early experiences must have stimulated his vision of an organisation which could deliver worker education more effectively and on a larger scale.

Mansbridge was ambitious too, and in 1894 he applied for a Co-operative Society Scholarship to Oxford University but was rejected, Jennings noting that he found some consolation shortly afterwards in passing the examination to become a licensed lay reader. These formative years of struggle and disappointment for Mansbridge were stimulated by ideology, Creighton (in Roberts 2003 p26) pointing out that the ideas for worker education which were crystallising in his mind constituted a fusing together of the spirituality of his early membership of the Congregational Chapel at which he was a Sunday School teacher, and his experiences of the Co-operative Movement. In time this led him to a progressive Anglicanism and an abiding sympathy for others belonging to a social class less advantaged than his own. Christian Socialism (he was a lay preacher in the Church of England for many years) in these terms, invoked a spirituality which took its 'text' as much from ideas of social morality and the earthly dilemmas of Bunyan's Pilgrim's Progress as it did from Biblical sources, although one might hypothesise that Mansbridge was a Christian first and a Socialist as a consequence. 'Justice', the journal of the SDF, ran with a claim from an un-named Christian Socialist that their manifesto 'involves the public ownership and management of the means of production and exchange' and maintained that 'our Socialism is not less earnest nor less complete because it is inspired by Christianity' (Justice 25/1/08). These sentiments suggest that the separation of Christian and Socialist, even Christian and Marxist was, at that time, and always has been, blurred according to an individual's standpoint. Mansbridge started to see a way to bring these elements together for adult worker education and in this he may well have been influenced by his mother, herself a reformer and a member of the Women's Co-operative Guild.

Mansbridge was invited in 1899, to bring his theories to Oxford University in the form of a paper entitled 'Co-operation and the Education of Citizens' which he presented at a Co-operative Conference held during the University Extension Delegacy Summer School. Unfortunately he took an overly aggressive stance in his text against the shortcomings of the University Extension movement, placing the blame for them on an inadequate partnership between the Co-operative Society and the universities. This was not well-received by either.

Albert Mansbridge (Workers Educational Association)

Around this time however, a key partnership was formed when Mansbridge invited Charles Gore, the Bishop of Birmingham and another radical Anglican, to submit an article to The Union Observer. Although Gore declined the invitation, a dialogue was opened thereafter with Mansbridge which was to last for many years and which helped build the foundations of the WEA.

Given Albert Mansbridge's dual background in the Co-operative associations and in the church, it is unsurprising that an initiative which brought the two together in the name of social inclusion and equality – the WEA – should later be seized upon by church-going nonconformists in Rochdale. Others too, but from an Anglican standpoint - Gore, Temple and Tawney - were similarly driven by a sense of social justice from a Christian Socialist standpoint and a decade later in 1918, in the same vein, George Lansbury would write 'socialism is to me the finest and fullest expression of religion' (in Evans 1966 p84).

This stream of Christian Socialism took its 19th century spring from both the church, but also, Hall and Watkins suggest (1937 p91), from the remnants and narratives of revolutionary France. Principles espoused by the Rev J F D Maurice, Professor of Theology at Kings College, saw the gospel not so much spreading the word of 'individual' but of 'social' salvation. Fellowship therefore was a central emphasis in Christian Socialist thinking and critical in its mission 'to preserve this fellowship and to protest against the selfishness that was disintegrating the nation and plunging the working class into misery' (Ibid p91). 'Practical Christianity' was to be the watchword for the personal and moral responsibilities of 'charity, equality and doing good' which formed 'the consensus theology of British working people whether or not they attended church' (McLeod 1986).

Building a bridge between faith and education may have seemed a clear objective to the early fathers of the WEA, but the question soon arose as to whether the path from this bridge was towards the overthrow of a harsh and uncaring capitalism or to find a way of reforming capitalism from within whilst regretfully accepting that this would entail social injustice on the way. To expel the money-lenders from the temple or to educate them ? R H Tawney's search was to find a formula 'expressing the attitude of all good men to social questions, which should be so entrenched in public conviction as to be drawn into dispute by no party' (Tawney 1912). It may have been, of course, that 'good men' were those whose Christian faith coincided with his own.

R H Tawney circa 1908 (Workers Educational Association)

Although his proposals had received a setback at the 1899 Conference, Mansbridge was undeterred and over the next four years continued to develop his ideas for university-level study for working people and in 1903 published the first of three articles which presented them in greater detail. At the same time, and based again on his dual religious and social beliefs, he formed the Christian Economic Society and then, significantly, the 'Association to Promote the Higher Education of Working Men' which later became the WEA. His proposals, it seems, were coming to maturity at the right time in that the Cockerton Judgement of 1901 was changing national regulations for funding and for adult educational opportunities by proscribing rate expenditure across all sectors except for elementary education. An unforeseen consequence of this was that adult day or evening classes would not, from that date, be paid for by the local School Board or from the rates, and this opened the way for the consideration of new and innovative funding streams for adult education. Mansbridge's own evening classes for the London School Board were similarly placed in jeopardy.

It now is clear that Mansbridge's motivation for educational development came from the emergence of a social and political consciousness in the late 19th century and he believed that an educated workforce was crucial in maintaining and progressing on-going reform. In order for this to happen, he knew that he would have to enlist the support of four key groups ; the Co-operative Society, the church, the trades union movement and the universities. His ultimate goal was to enable greater access to worker-relevant adult education which he envisaged running alongside what already existed. The fact that he did not want to destroy what was available, for example the work of the Co-operative Education programmes, is suggested by Mansbridge (an ex Co-op employee) along with Robert Halstead (the Secretary of the Co-operative Production Federation) being jointly responsible for drawing up the WEA's inaugural plans.

A central principle for Mansbridge was that education and culture should not be the private preserve of the wealthy and that all people, born equal, inherited them as a human right. Nor did he believe that adult education should simply be a way of alleviating poverty through social mobility, Smith (1956 p15) suggesting that the same view was quite widespread at the time and uses the voice of a student involved in early adult education in the North East of England to that effect :
'Miners don't give tuppence for increasing their wages but …. want to discuss Greek history with Alfred Zimmern, poetry with Gilbert Murray and philosophy with W H Hadow.'

But to discuss these matters for what ? And accessing culture to what end ? Was there an ulterior reason ? Mansbridge's answers to these questions at some moments invoke values which promote education as an intrinsic 'good,' seeing education for its own sake, whilst at other moments he writes from a pragmatic-benevolent point of view about the purpose of the WEA being to educate in order to enhance political abilities, intending the working class to 'lift itself up through higher knowledge' (Mansbridge 1944) and that this 'higher knowledge and these higher pleasures ... bring about right and sound action upon municipal, national and imperial affairs' (Ibid p2).

Some years later and looking back at Mansbridge's original intentions, Tawney (1914 p3) encapsulates the aims of the early proponents of the WEA by writing that it was set up

> 'to articulate the educational aspirations of Labour, to represent them to the proper authorities, to stimulate into activity, when it exists, the organisation through which they can be satisfied, and create it when it does not….. To build from within, to help men to develop their own genius, their own education, their own culture.'

Around this time, Tawney overheard a comment by Mansbridge (TUC Library : undated Ref 3/6/4) : 'What we want to strive to provide is not bread but the opportunity to win it.' But in addition, and significantly, Mansbridge believed moral and spiritual development to be just as important in an individual's growth in order that they would raise men, and working men in particular, out from under mere material considerations :

> 'Deep draughts of knowledge will divert the strong movements of the people from narrow paths of immediate interests to the broad way of that rightly ordered social life of which only glimpses have yet to be seen even by the greatest of the world's seers' (Mansbridge 1944 p6)

and he believed that, notwithstanding the Christian moralistic tone of such a statement, the a-political and non-sectarian nature of his vision located an educational position for it to take place. But what is the 'rightly ordered social life' ?

The Horrabins in 1924, never amongst Mansbridge's staunchest supporters, reflected approvingly on the young Mansbridge's undeniable passion for education and his heavily-guarded promotion of the University Extension Movement whilst acknowledging that he had the insight to recognise its two main flaws in not reaching working people effectively and that its resources, curricula and practices were 'too disjointed, too scrappy to have much educational effect.' It was partly as a response to such failings that Mansbridge envisaged a new educational association which would engage more immediately with the workers whilst retaining its ultimate objective as a link to the cultural life and possibilities of the university. He proposed that such an institution would 'make ready the Democratic Mind for the operations of University Extension' (Craik 1964 p47).

So the ideology which lay behind Mansbridge's thinking and action was based on social justice projected through a Christian Socialist lens intent on individual and social salvation. He writes (Mansbridge 1913 p129) that there should be a Highway :

> ' which leads directly to a state of society in which people will do the work for which they are best fitted and which they are happiest in doing – when men and women will be no longer the slaves of convention, but having broken free from hampering tradition and the bonds of their serfdom, will rise to the plane of things which endure; when, captains of their own destiny, whatever their intellectual capacities may be, they will enter with power and spirit upon education as upon joyous adventure or splendid exploration.'

Davies (1975) writes that what Mansbridge wanted to do was to bring the loose federations of university teaching and learning, the Co-operative movement and the church 'into closer communion' and the choice of language here is again apt as it touches the religious zeal which sought to bond together this aspiration. It is unsurprising then, that Mansbridge should find amongst his closest allies the aforementioned Bishop Gore who provided political support through his influence in the House of Lords, but also Dr William Temple, then a lecturer in philosophy at Queens College Oxford but later to become the WEA's first President and then the Archbishop of Canterbury.

William Temple 1881-1944 (Workers Educational Association)

Temple, Gore and Alfred Zimmern had previously formed the Catiline Club, a Christian Socialist society of tutors at Oxford University, and individuals from this group provided the foundations needed to lend establishment credibility to Mansbridge's proposals. As if in recognition of this sacred-secular synergy, Mansbridge offers his imprimatur to the values held by Temple, claiming that he 'lived on terms of intimate friendship with all types of men and women in fields, mines and workshops, as in universities, palaces and cathedrals' (Jackson, no date), later giving him the epithet of 'the people's archbishop.' This vein of political Christianity should not be underestimated in supporting early WEA initiatives nor should the pitch of Mansbridge's evangelism to the universities and to nonconformist working people be overlooked.

Charles Gore 1853-1932 (Great Thoughts Treasury)

An initial stage in the formation of the WEA was reached on May 6th 1903 when Mansbridge launched 'The Association to Promote the Higher Education of Working Men' in the most domestic of circumstances with his wife offering him 2/6d as a treasury start-up and a small group of friends, which became a provisional committee, appointing him its Honorary Secretary. Advised that £50,000 would be needed to secure such a venture (Jennings in Roberts 2003 p15), urgent and formal financial progress was required to avoid immediate and crippling debt. So in order to publicise the initiative and to draw interested and potential funding parties together, the new organisation's First National Delegate Conference was called at Toynbee Hall on August 22nd 1903 with representatives invited from the church, the trade unions and the universities. In addition, and providing an essential insight into the principles which were being promulgated, a constituency of workers was also present to meet with the University Extension personnel, the Bishop of Hereford and the Dean of Durham.

Progress from that point was swift with the First National Meeting of the new organisation taking place at the Palmer Hall in Reading on October 1st 1904, the town in which the initial WEA branch was established. In the same month a meeting of University Vice Chancellors from Manchester and Liverpool and the Presidents of the Women's Co-operative Guild and the Manchester Trades Council agreed, in the Whitworth Hall, Manchester, to form a North West District of the association (ibid p16). By the end of 1905 seven more branches had been set up across the United Kingdom.

Under pressure from the Women's Co-operative Guild amongst others, the name – which alluded to the education of working 'men' - was changed in 1905 to the Workers Educational Association and in the spirit of worker inclusion Price (1924 p16) records that a Provisional Committee was formed to oversee its development that included George Alcock, F Rockwell, Leonard Idle, W R Slater, A S H Thomas, W H Berry and J W Cole – all of them Co-operators or trades unionists.

For years Rochdale had maintained a lively University Extension programme and Albert Mansbridge recognised this as early as 1905 when he sent good wishes and financial assistance to support its commitment to worker education (Rochdale Education Guild Minutes May 2005) whilst offering the opportunity for local students to attend Summer School at Oxford (Rochdale Education Guild Minutes July 2005). A University Extension (evening) Lecture Committee had been set up in the town in 1903 and two years later was carrying a range of presentations including two Winter programmes of lectures, although a later Report (Rochdale Education Guild 1906) pointed out that many people from working class communities – those which the universities were targeting - were not attending in numbers anticipated. This was a serious concern, the Mechanics Institute having succumbed to decline through similar middle class hegemony, so in order to attract more working people, those managing and organising adult education in Rochdale directed their attention to the ideas coming from Mansbridge and his new association.

At the aforementioned October meeting at Manchester University, L V Gill and Alec Carter who were Honorary Secretaries of the Rochdale University Extension Committee, arranged to meet with the then Association to Promote the Higher Education of Working Men and specifically Albert Mansbridge and Mr Y Pickles, the Secretary of its North West Committee. It was put to them that

Rochdale was not only in a position to form a local branch of the Association but was well-placed to act as a hub for further developments across the North West.

Mansbridge agreed to these proposals and in order to take advantage of the momentum gathering around Rochdale's heightened role, conferences were immediately arranged in the town in March and April of 1905 which attracted the attention of trades unionists, Co-operative and educational societies plus adult classes from local Sunday Schools. At the second of these conferences, Walter Neild and Sidney Chapman presented the case for Rochdale's prominence in adult education, Sidney Waterlow from Manchester University also speaking in support of the town's readiness to take a regional lead. Never ones to let important details slip, the Rochdale committee raised a criticism about the name to be adopted by the town's association, the local contingent feeling it to be too long and smacking of patronage, proposing that the 'Rochdale Education Guild' would be more appropriate. Tom Price writes that 'the committee thought that the name 'Guild' conveyed the fraternal spirit and idealism of the new movement' and this was the name by which the branch began. It is a mark of the eagerness that Mansbridge must have felt in getting Rochdale on board that this important change was conceded so readily, and from this point instead of being part of an 'Association', Rochdale, though affiliated to the WEA, was now a 'Guild.'

Although formally inaugurated within the national Association at that conference (resolution proposed by J H Brittain and seconded by James Firth, the Secretary of Rochdale's Trades Council), it was at a further meeting at The Lyceum on Baillie Street on April 10th ('Working Men and Co-operators are specially invited') that the new name was officially adopted. Jennings (2002 p32) writes that the former evening class Committee was then dissolved and its assets and responsibilities transferred to the new Guild, L V Gill and Fred Greenwood to act as secretaries with Alec Carter as treasurer. One can imagine the interested, perhaps heated debate around the non-sectarian and non-political principles held by the Association given the strength of feeling on both of these matters in the town, but any qualms that might have been raised were answered readily and the first payment of one guinea made as an affiliate from the Guild to the national Association. It then fell to the Rochdale Education Guild to find its own funder-affiliates, the earliest of these being Clover Street Unitarian Church and the existing Ruskin Hall classes.

ROCHDALE EDUCATION GUILD.

CONSTITUTION AND RULES.

1.—The Society shall be called "THE ROCHDALE EDUCATION GUILD."

2.—The object of the Guild shall be to assist in promoting higher education amongst the people of Rochdale and district.

3.—The Guild shall endeavour to fulfil its object in the following principal ways:—

(a) By organising—
  (i.) University Extension and (if thought desirable) other Lectures.
  (ii.) Reading Circles and Discussion Classes.
  (iii.) Visits and Excursions of an educational character.

(b) By encouraging attendance at Evening Classes.

(c) By making such suggestions to the various local educational bodies as, in the opinion of the Guild, may seem desirable.

(d) By sending to its members in the autumn of each year a short calendar of the chief Educational Fixtures in the district for the ensuing winter.

4.—Any person, not under 18 years of age, may become an ordinary member of the Guild on payment of a minimum annual subscription of one shilling.

5.—Any person, not under 18 years of age, may become an honorary member of the Guild on payment of a minimum annual subscription of five shillings.

6.—*All members shall be entitled to admission to the Guild's Lectures at reduced terms.*

7.—Co-operative, Trade and other Organisations within the Rochdale district may, with the consent of the Council, become affiliated to the Guild on payment of a minimum annual subscription of two shillings and sixpence. Any Organisation paying such subscription shall be entitled to send one representative to the Council of the Guild, but *affiliation does not entitle individual members* of the Organisation to be members of the Guild except upon payment of the usual subscription (see Rules 4 and 5).

8.—The Officers of the Guild shall be a President, Vice-Presidents, Treasurer, and Secretary (or Secretaries).

9.—The management of the Guild shall be vested in a Council and an Executive Committee.

10.—The Council of the Guild shall consist of the Officers, together with one delegate from each of the affiliated Organisations (see Rule 7), and one representative for every 25 individual members of the Guild. In addition, the Chairman, Vice-Chairman, and Secretary of the Rochdale Education Committee, and also of the County (Area 26) Education Committee, shall be *ex-officio* members of the Council.

11.—The Council shall meet at least twice in each year.

12.—*The Executive Committee shall be appointed by the Council* at its first meeting after the Annual General Meeting, and shall consist of the President, Treasurer, Secretary (or Secretaries), and eight other members of the Guild or Council.

13.—The Annual General Meeting of the Guild shall be held in or about the month of April. At that meeting the Officers, Council, and Auditors shall be elected, and the Council shall present a report on the work of the Guild, together with a duly audited balance sheet.

14.—A Special General Meeting of the Guild may be called by the Executive Committee, which shall also convene such a meeting upon receipt of a requisition signed by not fewer than twelve members.

15.—Alterations of these rules may be made only at an Annual General Meeting of the Guild, or at a Special General Meeting called for the purpose. Notice of any proposed alteration must be sent to one of the Secretaries not later than three days before the date of such meeting.

Rochdale Education Guild Constitution and Rules 1905 (The Local History Centre, Touchstones)

The newly-formed Guild's work was not only to build educational provision and to evaluate incoming proposals for lecture courses, but to carry forward successes from the existing University Extension programme which continued to draw large audiences, some of them 'travelling miles on foot to the lecture room, retiring again to burn the midnight oil' (Dobbs in Parry 1920 p48). No shortage then, of individuals interested in Extension classes and mostly engaged for all the right reasons, for self-improvement. One tutor for the Ruskin Hall sessions records that he had been waiting for a group like this for 20 years and, by request, extra classes were organised in the town as supplementary study before and after some of the lectures. So the Guild planned to run its own WEA lectures alongside these programmes and funded scholarships to send students to University Summer Schools. The fact that additional local WEA branches were set up almost immediately, Littleborough being the first, consolidated this momentum.

WEA Group at the 1909 Summer School, Balliol College (Workers Educational Association)

In retrospect it should have been of little surprise that the Guild venture took off as well as it did in Rochdale as its management and organisation seems to have been second to none. Lawrence Vincent Gill and Alec Carter in particular, both being teachers, knew the education system well and, as Guild secretaries, had built up impressive networks within the local and national education authorities as well as being adept at organising adult and worker education through their strong community leadership. One example of this educational entrepreneurialism may be seen in Jennings (2002 p6) who writes that the Guild's Committee managed to persuade the local education authority to pay for a lecturer for a supplementary studies class over and above a customary entitlement. Their efficiency in terms of financial management was confirmed too when, within 9 months, by the Summer of 1905, there was local support for the town's Guild from 62 affiliating societies in the area including 22 Trade Unions, Co-operative Agencies, churches and individual subscribers. The minutes of the Guild (June 29th 1905) suggests an effective level of practical organisation in the preparation, printing and distribution of 2000 handbills, the same with 200 window bills, the printing of tickets and lectures being advertised in local newspapers. Interestingly, and as an indicator of where students might be found, an early meeting suggested that lectures should be targeted 'through the Sunday Schools' (Rochdale Education Guild minutes November 28th 1905).

L V Gill Honorary Secretary of the Rochdale Education Guild (Workers Educational Association)

The affiliation of the Guild to the WEA was indeed an important step towards delivering successful adult education in Rochdale although it was never intended to eliminate what had gone before. In fact, a synergy of the various education groups was soon achieved with University Extension students joining any new (WEA) classes, as did some from the Ruskin Hall Correspondence Class and students from two classes organised by the Clover Street Sunday School. Jennings notes that 'one of the latter studied Psychology under a Unitarian minister' whilst others followed courses in Sociology and Economics under the leadership of T W Price, a warehouseman who was both a member of the

SDF and a student in the first WEA tutorial class. A French visitor (Riboud 1910) to the Guild noted that 'societies flourish in such numbers, are so intermingled that it is not a rare thing to meet with workmen who belong to seven organisations at one time : co-operative society, trade union, friendly society, political organisation, religious body, temperance society and athletic club.'

So although 1906 was the year that the Rochdale Education Guild took over the work of the University Extension Lectures Committee, it organised and promoted many other six-meeting programmes on Literary and Historical subjects. University Extension classes themselves continued, students attending Hudson-Shaw's lectures on 'Ruskin' for example, with attendees satisfied enough to comment at the end that 'the world is bigger for us than it was before.' In the heady years between 1888 and 1896 Hudson Shaw's Extension lectures proved immensely popular with large audiences not just in Rochdale but in most of the towns in the region with Co-operative Education Societies having to find seats at his talks for up to 1000 in Oldham and 600 in Hebden Bridge (Harrison 1961 p236).

Reverend George William Hudson-Shaw (1859–1944) himself was charismatic, a distinguished teacher and seen by some as 'the father of Oxford Extension' (Rochdale Education Guild 1909). He was Rector of the church at South Luffenham but combined his ministry in Rutland with peripatetic work for the University Extension programme, lecturing in History under such titles as 'Heroes of the Nations' in which he presented – amongst others - the life, opinions and times of King Alfred, Luther and Cromwell. One of his mainstay subjects was John Ruskin.

Michael Sadler, then Professor of History at Manchester University, writing to him in 1909 suggested that 'for more than twenty years you have been one of the great moving forces for good in English life,' and 'more than any other man you have made Ruskin's words live and bear fruit' (in Royden 1947 p33). He did not, however, always get his own way in Rochdale. Hudson Shaw proposed a lecture programme for the Guild on 'Italian Cities' but the Committee rejected it, possibly because it was thought irrelevant to many potential attendees and insisted on him presenting his sessions on 'Heroes of the Nations' instead. Certainly, attendances were impressive for such lectures, often attracting upward of 500-600 students from the town, many of whom expressed a wish to stay on for more discussion once it had finished in such numbers, that student enthusiasm itself became a problem, Tom Price, as a Guild Official, commenting that dealing with such demands had become an impossible proposition for the lecturer.

Nor were these the only lectures available to the townsfolk. Elementary and Advanced English language classes flourished across Rochdale as did Saturday evening lectures, Ruskin lectures, Pioneer lectures from the Co-op (single talks or short courses on history, industrial history, economics, literature and natural history), discussion groups at the Art Gallery and Museum, the Gilman Study Circle concerned with educational work for women – all were running in parallel. Cultural activities were taking place alongside as well, one example of their popularity being a Guild outing to Manchester to see Shakespeare's Cymbeline which attracted 122 individuals on a freezing February evening in 1906 (Rochdale Education Guild Minutes). In addition to the extensive educational and cultural provision and for an additional fee there were Reading Circles which became well-attended in support of lecture programmes, plays and orchestral concerts. Informal, supplementary group sessions following lectures, often organised by students themselves, were considered to be aspects of good practice and some churches ran a Ruskin Hall group (The Monthly Messenger 1902) for the 'systematic reading' of useful books, again in support of their studies.

Just how it must have felt to attend one of these lectures is impossible to know with any certainty and we have little recourse except to go to the few commentaries that have survived. Certainly it would seem that independent thinking was promoted through all of the adult classes and those students suspected of mechanistically following a talk without critical thought, or merely 'pasting' presentational materials into an essay, would have been frowned upon as the tutor comments on student essays made clear. The rapt attention given to the first hour's lecture seems to have been balanced by a clamour of questioning in the second. Attendance at most of these events – even for the church and chapel meetings - was keenly monitored and in some cases a register of attendance was critical in ensuring continuation and individual progress. With the WEA, for example, in order to be entered for the examination, students had to be seen to have attended two thirds of the programme.

Other, telling indications as to the atmosphere at the lectures exist. As an observance of the protocols expected by the universities, according to the private (for lecturers only) 'Outlines' or Tutor Guidance for the Oxford University External Lectures (TUC Library : Ref 4/2/2/4), gowns were required to be worn by teaching staff unless there were special reasons to the contrary. In this, and in other ways, although the Extension lectures were popular amongst certain sections of the public, others saw them as elitist (Simon 1965 p87), catering for middle class audience expectations of what the academy should be and often presenting themselves as inappropriately 'academic' and 'lacking human interest' to worker-students in their language and delivery (The Daily Chronicle 1903). J M Mactavish spoke for many at the 1907 Oxford Conference when he said that 'I believe that one of the …. great reasons why University Extension lectures have not been successful is due to the fact that the average…. lecturer is decidedly middle and upper class in his outlook.' In the same year Jack Lawson, a worker student attending Ruskin College Oxford, expressed his experience whilst at that institution as being akin to living in a 'hostile centre' when he and his fellow workers were permitted access to university lectures, often wearing their dingiest clothes to play up to the discrimination that they felt and tacitly referring to 'Oxford University' as their code for the capitalist class (Lawson 1946). Prynn (1976 p74) adds to this when he writes about University Extension that 'attempts by intellectuals to 'improve' the working class resulted in resentment by the latter, even if this was not always fully conscious' and in his pamphlet for the North West WEA William Temple (no date) recounts the story of a miner who, affronted by the tone and aloofness of an Extension tutor walked up to him in the hall saying 'Young man. I have no quarrel with you for you're doing your best ; but them as sent you 'ere ought to be 'ung.'

J M Mactavish (Workers Educational Association)

Comments such as these should neither be dismissed as apocryphal nor inconsequential, for there was a clear prospect that what had happened to the Mechanics Institutes with its eventual inclination to recruit and meet the needs of the middle class, was repeating itself with the University Extension programmes. Simon (1965 p91) confirms this when he writes that 'of the 29 Oxford Extension courses in Yorkshire during 1885-1902, only 6 had an actual majority of working class students' and throughout the country worker-students accounted for only 25% of the classes, instead attracting 'ladies of leisure and pupil teachers' rather than being drawn from the heavy industries and the bulk of the working population. Carpenter (1903 p72) makes a similar point, claiming that University Extension took audiences (and their experiences) from 'the commercial classes' rather than reflecting upon the working conditions of the many, writing that the majority of pupils were of the 'young lady class' (Ibid p79).

A further criticism centred on finance and the curriculum. As University Extension lectures relied for their continuation on fees paid by the students, questions were raised about the relationship between charges and the syllabus. In order to attract and enrol enough students to keep down the cost to the attendee, the subject matter of the lectures had to be popular if not populist, thereby guaranteeing a full class. Evaluating the 'success' of the sessions then became a matter of quantity (numbers through the door) rather than quality. As a result, lectures approved by the universities tended to cater for short courses and subjects appealing to a lowest common denominator, and local authorities (who, to some degree subsidized them) supported courses that were going to attract most students, but in so doing potentially neglected innovative or difficult subjects for lecture programmes. As a result, University Extension courses began to carry the joint stigma (Thompson in Parry 1920 pp175-6) of low-level study whilst attracting students with least ability.

Any success of the University Extension class also depended on the profile and ability of the lecturer and in many instances these qualities were reported to be falling short of university standard –some academics saw these classes as useful practice for the real thing - and as a consequence, the student experience was not one that might be expected in a traditional university community.

Albert Mansbridge, as early as 1902, had been only too aware of all of these issues and in particular the gap (in Doyle 2003 pp7-8) between workers and the university in terms of a relevant curriculum, appropriate design and worker-friendly delivery. He felt that Extension programmes represented 'undemocratic methods of organisation' in that the universities ended up making decisions which others – those paying fees – were made to follow. He also knew that resources from the universities to support outreach lectures were minimal and felt it regrettable that tutors received inadequate salaries for the important work that they were doing. Furthermore, the Extension lectures had to be largely self-supporting with fees drawn from the students and this flew in the face of the philosophy of the WEA which was to promote and provide egalitarian and relevant educational experiences for all working people regardless of their ability to pay.

Notwithstanding these problems, the Extension classes in Rochdale were maintained through into the early years of the 20th century, the lecture programmes across the town being focused mainly on literature and science. In its first year of existence as an affiliate of the WEA, the Rochdale Education Guild continued to promote them as policy, relying on such stalwarts as Hudson Shaw and his sessions on 'The Life and Teaching of Ruskin' and J C Powys' 'English Social Reformers' and 'Imperial Rome.'

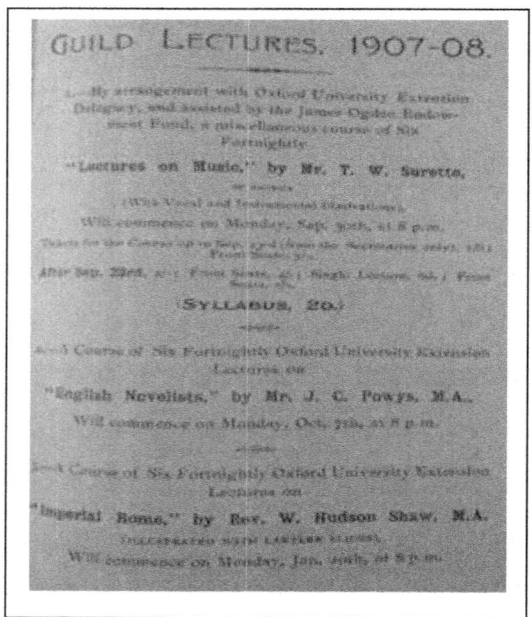

Rochdale Education Guild Extension Lecture Programme for September to January (The Local History Centre, Touchstones)

In addition to these presentations, other lectures were taking place across Rochdale, for example talks at the Rochdale Rambling Club on 'Birds' and evening classes in Castleton, Shawclough and Littleborough dealing with Citizenship, Zoology and Botany (Rochdale Education Guild Calendar 1905-06).

Rev. Hudson Shaw (Workers Educational Association)

At one point around 1906 however, a different note was struck by the lecturer E L S Horsburgh who was attracting many students from across the town to a social science class. His 'Politics and Social Problems' series drew a large and enthusiastic audience as well as such a commitment from them that the students set up their own Summer school in Rochdale before the lectures started in order to prepare themselves for it. Price wrote that whilst all subjects were popular, the Horsburgh sessions were striking for the eagerness of the students, many of whom expressed a strong desire to stay on after the lecture, ready to extend the presentation with discussion with the tutor and talk through the finer points of the set books. Horsburgh himself commented upon this (Jennings 2002 p37) adding that 'a larger number than ever before wrote papers.' The WEA Report on the First Year's Work of the Rochdale Education Guild (1906 p1) similarly reported that Mr Horsburgh's sessions were characterised by excellent discussions, 'many shades of opinion and much knowledge' and that the students' work had been 'really admirable.'

It would seem then, that there were two issues arising for the Guild at this time ; first that the nature and relevance of the lecture subject was a crucial reason why people – and working people in particular - attended, and second that there was a presentational problem in that students wanted more than was being provided in a straightforward talk or in over-crowded lecture theatres which limited both discussion as well as the opportunity for the student to bring his or her experience to any debate. Two hundred and fifty miles away a similar critical note was being sounded by the Barry branch of the Amalgamated Society of Railway Servants with its protest that the existing University Extension lectures had been given to audiences that were too big and therefore restrictive of individual attention (Joint Committee of University and Working Class Representatives 1909 p57). Furthermore, they said that the sessions had been 'discontinuous' and out of touch with the needs of working people.

These became such points of contention that they were placed at the top of the agenda at the WEA's Annual Conference in 1906. The specific concerns were : pedagogical effectiveness, the randomness of curricular design and lack of progression, the 'optional' regulation of written work, the under-engagement of working people and the inadequate connection to the universities for further certification or diploma studies.

Key to the discussion, and attending this conference, was John Marriott who had succeeded Michael Sadler as Secretary of the Oxford University Extension Delegacy and as a new broom was looking for developments which might revitalise the flagging Extension movement. Mansbridge was, of course having parallel discussions with Hudson Shaw amongst others about the failure of the universities to reach working people and was trying to find a more effective and appropriate way to engage with them.

Given the pervasiveness and urgency of these questions, the universities responded, and in 1907 a Conference was organised to focus on one specific topic : 'What Oxford can do for Working People.' In so doing, it attracted the attention of Sir Robert Morant the Permanent Secretary to the Board of Education who had developed friendly but formal links with Mansbridge partly because he admired him for his 'combination of evangelical zeal and reverence for Oxford and Cambridge' (Jennings in Roberts 2003 p18). The Conference chair was taken by Charles Gore and he welcomed in his opening speech over 430 delegates from 210 organisations including trades unions and trades councils. Papers by the Fellow of St John's College Sidney Ball and by the distinguished Co-operator Walter Neild were prominent in addressing the inadequacies of worker education. A letter from Ball to R H Tawney before the conference (21st March) suggested that 'a tide was rising again which should be taken at the flood,' and asked him for supplementary notes for his speech to the Conference to further their case.

At the Conference, the SDF called for the educational programme of the trades unions to be implemented as a publically-controlled, free and secular programme from elementary to higher education, but following some debate Gore ruled this out of order (Quinney 1983 p62). Then the presentations by Ball and Neild suggested that a solution to the problems would be to set up, within the WEA, tutorial classes of significant length, academic depth and student-identified relevance which would lead on, for selected students, to further study at the university. Issues of student decision-making, participation and curriculum relevance were essential if it was to succeed. Working people deserved and were demanding a voice.

Such impassioned pleas were responded to with a degree of concerned dissent from Marriott, a prominent Tory and here representing the Oxford Extension Delegacy, who foresaw the danger to the universities of a tutorial class movement forming a separatist working class faction in adult education (Marriott 1998 p20). He also wondered whether it was going too far to give worker students the right to choose both the subjects AND the lecturers as was being suggested, objecting to the possibility that WEA students should 'if not tune the pulpits, at least choose the preachers' (Jennings in Roberts 2003 p19). As an angry and direct counter to this, Mactavish felt that the universities would, if they were allowed the chance, carry on selecting only middle class students and that this ran contrary to WEA principles. Power and access was consistently being preserved by the few. Mansbridge also saw the dangers of university entrenchment and wrote on the subject of

Marriott : 'We do not fear him at all. He will not be allowed to even put his little finger in the new arrangements' (ibid).

In the face of the education establishment's anxiety at the new 'muscle' of the working class, Walter Neild, then President of the North West Co-operative Education Committees' Association, reminded the conference forcibly that the founding of Ruskin College itself was an example of letting 'Oxford open wide its doors' (Neild 1907) and Sidney Ball's paper reinforced this with a desire to see a more profound dissemination of intellectual activity from the universities to working people as part of their moral mission. He noted that 25 years had passed since these ideas were first mooted by Sadler, and 60 years since William Lovett's London Working Men's Association. The time was right to act.

But the universities still harboured doubts. There was the concern that tutors would lower their academic sights with a working class group and that as a consequence, standards would fall and reflect negatively on the universities. And were worker students able to cope with the rigours of intense study ? For the conference then, the problems remained : how could working men and women be reached equitably and effectively by university education whilst preserving its quality ? How could, in Marriott's phrase, an 'educated democracy' be achieved ? Repeatedly came the claim from the floor that there was too much power from above, too little from below and that if workers were to receive 'liberal' and 'humane' education, they should be trusted and empowered to do so. But therein lay the problems of quality, values and control.

Ball raised the stakes by suggesting that the WEA was the organisation to make it work for the universities and whilst doing so maintain their high standards. He claimed that the Co-operative Education movement had cleared the ground already in affording the working man the opportunity to receive enough higher education to 'raise his class but not necessarily to raise him out of his class.' Furthermore the WEA had laid foundations for such study groups – small in size, with district autonomy but in conjunction with the universities and run in industrial settings. Surely the same could be done in tutorial groups with highly qualified, university-appointed staff. 'Why should a definite experiment not be made in this direction ?' It was also suggested that the universities might be called upon to support such a venture financially as it would be prestigious for them to press forward with their espoused objective of 'a University co-extensive with the nation' (from Doyle 2003).

But it fell to Mactavish, a Scottish shipwright and a later President of the WEA, to capture the hearts of all at this conference with his impassioned speech in favour of making worker education a reality.

He spoke of his determination in favour of a social science 'that will teach us the true relationship between production and consumption; that will teach us the true economic relationship in which men ought to stand to men, and men to women' (WEA/University of Oxford 1908). At all costs an educational direction needed to come from the people themselves, and speaking from a position of slight distrust of the universities he rose to the occasion by declaring 'I decline to sit at the rich man's gate praying for crumbs. I am not here as a suppliant of my class …. I claim for my class all the best that Oxford has to give' (ibid).

To some extent, the day was won in terms of re-examining the purpose and the delivery of the universities' commitment to extramural worker education and as an immediate commitment a Joint Committee was set up to look again at the questions raised and design a workable model for a tutorial class. In line with the ideals of equality and inclusion, the new Joint Committee consisted of 14 individuals, 7 representing working class institutions and organisations appointed by the WEA, 7 from the universities including Berry, Bowerman and Shackleton from the Council of Ruskin College and 2 secretaries, one of whom was Albert Mansbridge.

It was not too long before critics from the far left came forward, the SDF challenging the representativeness of this committee in purporting to carry the voice of working people and bemoaning the fact (in 1908) that no report had been forthcoming from them to confirm that they were pushing forward on much-needed and radical change. They saw the Committee as a vehicle for what they called the 'mischievous proposals of the WEA,' into the coffers of which Morant, they felt, would pour capitalist gold (Justice 15/8/08 p7), an argument which continued for another two decades and which factionalised the left around worker education. Tom Price was quick to defend the Joint Committee's democratic intentions and its structure, claiming that it would 'wrest back those educational rights that have been stolen from the people' (Justice 5/9/08 p10). He repudiated the SDF's assertion that members of the committee were capitalist puppets, although Henry Adkins came back at him (ibid) to declare that the Committee consisted of 'seven wise and seven Pickwickianally foolish fellows.'

The early proposals from this Committee were that tutorial classes should build on, but be more substantial in content than University Extension lectures, should allow for student progression and carry the objective of preparing individuals for future careers. To this end, the curriculum must be suitable (to give an example) for the training of Labour leaders. There had also been a problem about the somewhat detached interaction of some Extension tutors to the student body, the

Joint Committee : Albert Mansbridge front second from right (Workers Educational Association)

question arising as to whether there might not be a better way to capture the undoubted interest of the worker student and to deal with subjects interactively whilst, at the same time, maintaining relevance, affordability and quality.

The model they settled upon was a locally-chosen programme for an interactive tutorial class of two years duration with the possibility of successful students going on to a university-recognised Certificate or Diploma. This would, then, provide a solution to some of the difficulties voiced about the Extension programmes and was acceptable to the universities with three provisos : that there should be no more than 30 students in any class, that they should be set up in industrial towns where there existed a working class organising body, and that they should be designed – in content and delivery - by workpeople alongside personnel from the University.

The proponents saw this as an 'experiment in adult education' and Rochdale was, from an early point, singled out as being an ideal town in which it should be based as Mansbridge knew that it had been a well-managed centre for University Extension lectures and an effective hub of WEA study. Mansbridge himself had visited the Rochdale Education Guild in April 1906 and addressed an Annual Meeting there at the Temperance Hall, being impressed by the Guild's proliferation of events and its effective administration. From a vantage point very close to the proceedings, Price (1924 p31) suggests that it was, in fact, Rochdale that made the first move with proposals to Albert Mansbridge for a worker-directed set of lectures, curriculum-relevant and with a low fee-base and not – as some have suggested - the other way around. This may have been so as Mansbridge, it seems, replied immediately and positively to the offer, recognising in Rochdale a town with a good educational

Discussants around the Tutorial Groups circa 1908 (Workers Educational Association)

Gill (top left), Price (top right), Mansbridge (front left), Temple (front middle)

base, effective leadership and a history of educational innovation, commenting that the place had been 'a sort of educational clearing house' for many years and revealing something of his Christian Socialist foundations in seeing the townspeople as 'missionaries' for this new form of adult education.

As has been seen, the lectures of Hudson Shaw, Powys and Horsburgh had been attracting part of their audiences from working class communities in addition to which the Co-operative movement continued to drill down into that constituency with vital educational roots. The town, now, had a lively Educational Guild which was not only innovative and inclusive but also had the infrastructure to handle a new administrative load. Albert Mansbridge recognised all of these elements and was sure of his faith in the town : 'I came to the conclusion that the best thing to do would be to ask Rochdale to get 30 students to pledge themselves to make every attendance for 2 years and to write regular essays. If they would do this we would get the best tutor in England' (Mansbridge 1944 p37).

In order to operationalise activities in the town, it was agreed that there should be a secretary to act as correspondent with bodies such as the universities, the Board of Education and the local authority and to shoulder the general burden of management. Again, Rochdale was well-prepared for this with L V Gill and Alec Carter already in place. Finally, a tutor was to be appointed, Oxford agreeing to pay half of his or her fees.

Before anything could happen however, as had been re-emphasised by the 1907 Conference (WEA/Oxford University 1908 p59), to carry the support of local people, not only should fees be as low as possible but the students themselves should make the prior decision as to what was to be studied. Hudson Shaw was particularly adamant on this latter point, being set firm against any suggestion that Oxford should 'tune her pupils' to suit a particular social class by making all the curricular decisions (Price 1907 p37). Furthermore at the Conference it was suggested that the students should choose their own tutor but in the event this decision was made by the university. Some years later in 1910 at the Annual WEA Conference, Bishop Gore revisited the principle of worker decision-making by saying that the simple passion of the working man would achieve nothing without knowledge and that 'you will be trodden down again under the feet of knowledge if you leave knowledge in the hands of privilege' (from Smith 1956 p59). So there was real determination that the decision about the title and nature of the tutorial programme was to be taken, at a subsequent conference, by working people from the chosen town - Rochdale – with any necessary assistance from staff at the WEA. The subject would be selected and then put to the university for formal approval although it was felt at an early point by many witnesses to the success of Horsburgh's lectures, that subjects such as Political Science, Economics or History would best suit the needs of the new class. This view, in line with a Benthamite tradition of public enlightenment, elevated the study of subjects such as politics and economics to prominence in the discharge of civic duties (Dobbs in Parry 1920 p41).

A call therefore went out from the Rochdale Education Guild in early Summer 1907 for 30 working men and women who were ready to pledge themselves over 2 years to a new sort of tutorial class and Price records that Rochdale answered in typical fashion, between 60 and 70 potential students responding immediately and with enthusiasm !

So Why Rochdale ?

As has been made clear, there had been lectures under the University Extension programme in Rochdale for some time, holding presentations in the hall of the Co-operative Stores in Toad Lane as early as 1868 (Price 1924) so the sort of tutorial arrangement proposed was nothing new to the working people of the town, nor, as Rose (2010) suggests, to the populations of many others in Britain at the time. And yet a special case can be made for Rochdale – the town's organisation, management and enthusiasm for ventures characterised by independence and self-help were highlighted by Michael Rose in his piece suitably entitled 'Rochdale Man and the Stalybridge Riot : the Relief and Control of the Unemployed during the Lancashire Cotton Famine' (in Donajgrodzki (ed) 1977). Rose felt that for many reasons Rochdale as a town had particular characteristics which gave rise to a working man or woman being 'respectable, self-helping, self-educating …. with his/her co-operative society, savings bank and chapel'. This is far from any notion of 'embourgoisement' as it did not necessarily enrich or materially empower the individuals concerned, rather it suggested a self-sufficiency demanding that its own will and energy serve and determine the individual's life-experiences and outcomes. Stubborn perhaps, self-motivated certainly.

And Albert Mansbridge, choosing Rochdale as a town for his great worker education experiment, might have had the wisdom of his choice confirmed had he taken note of evidence from Parliamentary debates from the 19th century. In the House of Commons on the 12th March 1866 for example, Gladstone said that 'Rochdale has probably done more than any other town in making good to practical minds a case for some enfranchisement of the working classes,' and Royden Harrison (1965 p133) framed this radical characteristic as the 'Rochdale argument,' suggesting that the town was a municipal symbol of 'all the advances made by Labour since 1832.' Even in the late 18th century a radical perspective on education was in evidence and Thompson (1991 p186) recognises it by writing that Rochdale and Royton appear to have been pre-eminently linked with a centre in Manchester calling itself the 'Institute for the Promulgation of Knowledge amongst the Working People of Manchester and its Vicinity.' Certainly by the 1840's Rochdale could boast a number of independent centres for education amongst which were the Equitable Pioneers, the Literary and Philosophical Society, the Debating and Conversation Society, the Botanical Society, the Church Institute and the People's Institute (Aspin 1969 p121).

Educational commitment, however, arose also from a political and social oppression tempered by a good humour that was noted by Thompson (1991 pp462-3) when recording Cooke Taylor's astonishment at the degree to which working people in Lancashire bore extreme social conditions

> 'with a high tone of moral dignity, a marked sense of propriety, a decency, cleanliness and order …. which does not merit the intense suffering I have witnessed. I was beholding the gradual immolation of the noblest and most valuable population that ever existed in this country or in any other under heaven.'

And this spirit nurtured a collective consciousness, a class consciousness, which gathered force through the 18th and 19th century and was not only recognised in the revolt against industrial working conditions in the towns of the North West of England but also found a voice in calls for policy changes in health, housing and education. Social reformers and radicals such as William Morris, J L Joynes and H M Hyndman were regular speakers at rallies and meetings on a northern political circuit which was fertile soil for agitation and reform. Thompson (1991 p914) sees the independence of mind and action that made this possible as a clear mark of the industrial radical who, in 'one direction of the great agitations of the artisans and outworkers, continued over 50 years, was to resist being turned into a proletariat.' Stirrings of working class consciousness and independence of mind were cast in the same socio-economic fire.

Deep well-springs of radicalism in Rochdale have already been noted. The early movement for reform of the Charter, the eminence of the Co-operative Society and the early take-up of the Labour movement through the ILP and the SDF of which many in the first cohort of the WEA were members, made Rochdale a Labour if not a socialist town with education as its banner. Cole's sentiment that mid-Victorian 'sensible capitalists were prepared to find it within their interests to come to terms with 'sensible' workmen' (Cole 1948 p165) may well have been the case with policy development in Rochdale. Many would see this as a reforming rather than a revolutionary characteristic reflected in the town, emblematic of a response to social injustices more widely felt.

And the coming together of various institutional strands across Rochdale enhanced these political and educational stirrings. Even an establishment figure such as Colonel G Kemp MP, Vice-President of the Rochdale Education Guild, was a virulent advocate for more accessible education above all other social questions by maintaining that the town's institutions had a part to play in its development. He said that 'classes connected to churches, chapels and Co-operative Societies ought to be centres for educational work….. there, they should discuss intellectual subjects with the same enthusiasm as a discussion about the football match' (WEA 1905 pp11, 23).

From another perspective, some historians, in attempting to explain its radical nature have looked at Rochdale's geographical size and location and, in relation to these, its industrial contribution to the local and national economy. Garrard (in Gill 1986 p3) for example notes that the smaller size of

Rochdale's factories and workshops may explain in part why it was that the town's working class was 'more frequent, more autonomous and welcome participants in the political process.' The hypothesis continues that the skilled artisans of the industrial North West, because of their independence of mind and their critical position in the chain of labour – workers such as cotton spinners, calico printers, pattern makers, mill-wrights, shipwrights, croppers, wool-combers and outworkers such as weavers and framework-knitters – were amongst the most prominent of voices in pushing for industrial reform. This would make sense in this case as, occupationally, 44% of Rochdale's working population at the turn of the 20th century were artisans, shopkeepers, engineers and machine makers (Inkster no date p12). The proximity to the centre of production of skilled artisan labour involved rather than dissociated that section of the working class from local decision-making. A related argument is put by Cole (1948 p205) in reference to the radicalism of mining villages and towns, claiming that workers' houses belonged to the coal-owners, shops were stocked by the same group and 'if they transgressed the law they were brought up before a magistrate's bench consisting of coal owners.' This close inter-locking of work and ownership, no doubt strained by sharp economic differences between the two sections of society, made for a visibility of inequity and a simmering sense of injustice especially in small to medium sized settlements. Thompson (1991 p571) writes that the croppers controlled the finishing processes and like the wool-combers maintained a strong position from which they could organise and rebut unskilled labour : 'They made up the aristocracy of the West Riding cloth workers' and as such had distinctive and powerful voices for or against change. Rochdale from the mid 19th century was a town built on a combination of skilled artisan and unskilled labour close enough to the ownership of production to rail against any inequities and powerful enough in its skill-set to wield influence of its own.

Furthermore, it has been suggested that Rochdale was always a two-class town due the absence of a landed aristocracy (Foster 1977). In its place, the economic and social stratification rested on the industrial middle class on the one hand and the working artisan and labouring class on the other. This situation thrust the two groups together in a classic capitalist dualism, one that the Liberal party capitalised upon until the rise of Labour in the late 19th century.

So, although the political foundations were present in the town for such educational reform as was being suggested by the WEA, other contributory elements were necessary. In Rochdale, these elements were a moral core through the role of the church and particularly nonconformity, and a social binding through an active communitarian ethic. This second element was present due to the town being hard-wired to the Co-operative movement, Beatrice Webb catching the significance of these two elements when she visited Rochdale in the 1870's and observing the extent to which the town's 'whole social life depended on t'owd store and the chapel' (Webb 1926).

The Church, the Chapel and the WEA in Rochdale

As was the case with the Co-operative movement, the WEA emerged as a response to questions of social justice and it seems clear that this response had, in the lives of both the organisers and the students, a moral or religious foundation. Notwithstanding a gap of over half a century between them, there are interesting and direct denominational connections between the two radical reforms which historically took place in Rochdale, McLeod (1984 pp46-7) noting that at least half of the original Rochdale Co-operators in 1844 belonged to nonconformist chapels, this proportion also found amongst the first WEA tutorial class. Roper (1993 p36) goes further and claims that six members of the original Pioneers had a known connection to Clover Street Unitarian Church whilst four others were also nonconformists, the remainder being Anglican. Significantly, this is reflected in the first tutorial class, many of the WEA students being Clover Street Unitarians.

Although church attendance had been in slow but general decline throughout Victoria's reign (an average congregation at church or chapel represented, with regional variations, only 38% of the UK population in 1881 - Currie et al 1977), religious belief, especially amongst the poor, remained strong. Baptism was held onto as an important life-ritual, Harrison citing statistics to the effect that 65.8% of children born in 1902 were baptised into the Church of England, the rest into a Catholic or nonconformist church. Across the United Kingdom, the ratio of attendance between the Anglican Church and non-conformist chapels was approximately 4:3, with Roman Catholic attendance at 1.5, again with regional variations. However, in Rochdale at the turn of the 20th century the proportions in church attendance and available services were significantly different as Table 1 (overleaf) suggests.

Nonconformity and Sunday Schools in Rochdale

An analysis of the statistics in Table 1 concerning nonconformist churches and the rest (Anglican and Roman Catholic) reveals a surprising figure of 74% of the 1898 sittings in Rochdale being nonconformist, with Methodism alone, in all its forms, at 38.2 %.

And the significance of the figures becomes even clearer when seen in its effect on social affairs. The importance of nonconformity to grass roots political movements cannot be understated and Thompson (1991 p45) – with a number of important caveats - points to the central role that

Denomination	Number of Annual sittings	Percentage of sittings
Church of England	8299	22.4
Wesleyan Methodist	4393	11.8
United Methodist Free Church	7313	19.7
Congregationalist	3540	9.5
Baptist	3150	8.5
Primitive Methodist	1866	5.0
Methodist New Connection	600	1.6
Presbyterian	1050	2.8
Unitarian	670	1.8
Roman Catholic	1350	3.6
Other	4800	12.9

Table 1 : Denominational Activity in Rochdale 1898 (source : The Rochdale Nonconformist 1898)

Methodism played in social change, being 'indirectly responsible for a growth in the self-confidence and capacity for the organisation of working people'. Methodism, however, contained within it the embryonic authoritarian tendencies (Hempton 2006) which William Blake represented with **Thou shalt not**, written over the Chapel door in the 'Garden of Love,' so it tended to be those sects seceding from Methodism that carried the more liberal cause of reform. In Rochdale as elsewhere, Primitive Methodists, Congregationalists, Baptists, Quakers and most of all Unitarians rose to meet this challenge of change. Harrison (1990) supports this but with a subtle distinction in his note that the congregations of these nonconformist chapels tended to come from the middle or 'respectable' working class, which confirms the idea of a reform-oriented labour 'aristocracy' at prayer. Jonathan Rose (2010 p34) takes a different perspective on the chapel's propensity for social concern by identifying a particular set of practices in the nonconformist church which encourage 'the habits of close reading, interpretive analysis and intellectual self-improvement through scriptural scrutiny and debate' (ibid p74).

Repudiating the rigidity of Calvinist Puritanism, turning away from some of the hellfire strictures of Methodism as well as refusing to be drawn into the established conservatism of the High Anglican church, these breakaway nonconformists looked to the social and political alongside or, in some cases, instead of the scriptural for their cue for effective Christianity. It is significant that one of the points of the Unitarian 'Credimus' – principles by which they live - is a belief 'in truthfulness, honesty of conduct, integrity of character, wise and generous giving, purity of thought and life' and such plain speaking would have recommended itself to many working people who found in it an overlap between faith, social conditions and policy. It also allowed, in Rochdale, questions which often began in the chapel to reach the deliberations of the town's decision-makers, whether these were the Board of Guardians, the police or the borough committees.

So, relative to Anglicanism, a type of nonconformity in the town was fortified in its attempt to construct an intellectual bridge between the sacred and the secular, between the highest in Heaven and the poorest on Earth. For many in Rochdale, these were connected. Writing about the emotional intensity of his father in relating both of these realms, Michael Foot (1980 p15) suggested that in the Wesleyan chapel of his childhood 'laughter was always mixed with righteous fury, whether he spoke from the platform or the pulpit ; too fine a distinction, he thought, should not be drawn between the two'.

And the many Christians who professed to be Socialists at that time looked to chapel as the house of political and social debate, organising discussion groups there, often in the school room, around issues of the day which would spill over into the more overt political activity of party recruitment or the distribution of secular pamphlets. Ideas would spark and spread from chapel meetings, debates through fellowship groups and Bible classes, education through mutual improvement societies, socials and adult schools - all contributing to a fervent link between faith and social justice which Simon (1965 p39) saw as an important support for the working population with churches running 'adult classes for the study of ethics, economic history, social history and religion.'

This 'educational' role was increasingly in evidence as part of a church 'mission,' the Sunday School acting as a basic skills unit for many for whom the formal education system had been either a disappointment or had been a closed institution to them. Nonconformist chapels and their Sunday Schools in particular acted as mutual improvement societies or temperance organisations, the membership of which was drawn largely from the working class. Earlier in the 19th century Bamford (1843) notes that one Rochdale chapel – Lowerfield Methodist - had a regular meeting which emphasised 'getting on' as part of its 'improvement class'.

In fact the Sunday Schools had a critical part to play in 'getting on.' Having its origins in the late 18th century, the Sunday School Movement took up the challenge of teaching basic literacy and numeracy whilst maintaining an underlying note of moral rescue. Robert Raikes, often thought to have been a significant figure in the history of the Sunday Schools, combined the spiritual concern of resisting the on-going desecration of the Sabbath and the positive development of a Christian mission, with a secular effort in fighting the educational poverty that he saw building around him. He did this by promoting the teaching of reading, writing and the catechism by 'decent well-disposed women' (Maltby 1882 p8) who nonetheless insisted on regular attendance and were often overly-strict in their demands on their charges. Early initiatives were sporadic in their success however, and without a national body to draw aspects of charity and social improvement together, 'educational', not to mention 'salvation' results were unpredictable and inconsistent. The Nonconformist churches were, in their very essence, never the vehicles to garner such a national body.

However, the Sunday Schools Movement continued its work with children in making up for the shortcomings of elementary education as many of them, as well as their parents, were functionally illiterate. And whilst the movement can be seen as an essential educational stop-gap, some commentators view its earlier incarnations as 'a dreadful exchange even for village dame schools' (Thompson 1991 p414) with poor or no teaching and little individual development. Thompson goes even further (ibid p441) in suggesting that the hidden curriculum of the Sunday School cherished in the children of the poor 'a spirit of industry, commerce and piety' which played out more as social control than enlightenment. Not that Sunday School teaching for the poor was an easy task, as a publication by a Midlands Chapel (in Binns 2013 p43) makes clear :

> 'the (Sunday School) teachers are expected to exercise much patience towards those who may be dull and stupid ; to be particularly attentive to servants and apprentices whose time of instruction is far advanced or uncertain and who are deficient in their reading' (Rules for the Management of the Methodist Sunday School 1812).

Thompson (1991 p414) finds another example of Sunday School control at Caistor, Lincolnshire where the teachers were instructed to

> 'tame the ferocity of their un-subdued passions – to repress the excessive rudeness of their manners – to chasten the disgusting and demoralising obscenity of their language – to subdue the stubborn rebellion of their wills – to render them honest, obedient, courteous, industrious, submissive and orderly.'

Given the prevalence of such social and political concerns as poverty, industrial exploitation and high mortality through poor living conditions, it is unsurprising to see an emergent Socialist Sunday Schools Movement attaching itself to those nonconformist chapels and churches with embedded and prominent social concerns. As an alternative to orthodox Christian Sunday Schools this was an international movement coming out of the 1880s which attempted to bring children to radical thinking within a Christian ideology. Taking socialism as a basic Christian virtue, the classes at

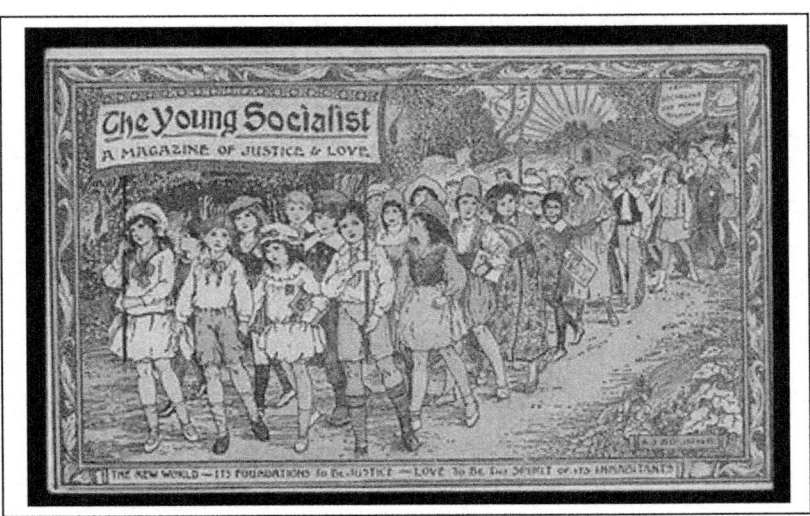

Promotional Postcard for the Socialist Sunday School magazine (Young Socialist)

Socialist Sunday Schools countered the hegemony of established faith at the time, but they went further. Nowhere in their 'Precepts' is God mentioned for example. Instead their language reflects other emphases such as that they would 'work for the day when all men and women will be free citizens of one Fatherland, and live together as brothers and sisters in peace and righteousness' (precept 10). Their Declaration too, repeated at the end of every meeting, is replete with socialist humanism :

> 'We desire to be just and loving to all our fellow men and women, to work together as brothers and sisters, to be kind to every living creature and so help to form a New Society, with Justice as its foundation and Love its Law.'

Rochdale, from the beginning of the 19th century, had been a dissenting town, Inkster (no date p8) recording that by 1848 there were 23 places of worship with the Church of England representing only a third of them offering services, and this was the same 50 years later (see Table 1 above). By

1861 the number had grown to 32 churches and chapels. Nonconformist influence was not simply one of number, Rochdale for many years having been a town where religious affiliation found a place in political circles. Garrard (1983 p110) noted that in the 19th century the political elite of the town

> 'was not united but continuously and often bitterly divided along overlapping lines of religion and party. The religious conflict was fought out between Nonconformists and churchmen….. The church owned approximately one third of the land within the 1872 boundaries …. and so was drawn into many key local issues.'

This is important in that the wealth of the Anglican Church in the town was not proportionate to its leverage. Although it stood as a major landlord in Rochdale, the political momentum in the town ran counter to its quiet Toryism with a nonconformist majority prominent in positions of council influence.

In addition to the denominational-political associations, many of the local mill owners were practicing nonconformists and perhaps because of the anti-hierarchical structures in their chapels, held more power through them than they would have had done in the established church. Be that as it may, Gowland points out (1979 p70) that in Rochdale 'the conformist was the nonconformist' and independence and self-help were endemic to the town's psyche. Birchall confirms this image when he writes (1994 p40) that from the mid 19th century there had been in Rochdale 'a bewildering variety of nonconformist sects to choose from.'

Politically, the Liberal party in the town was almost exclusively nonconformist whereas the Conservatives, more often than not the minority in the local council, generally allied themselves to the Anglican Church. More specifically, according to Bamford (1843) the Liberals formed a pivotal element of the Wesleyan-Methodist Association in the 19th century which had established itself in Baillie Street and became in effect 'the centre of local government …. dominating legal and council proceedings,' (ibid) a situation which continued into the 20th century.

One of the more prominent radical chapels to emerge was that of the Unitarians which had an intellectual tradition dating back to the 18th century with such luminaries 'as William Frend, Benjamin Flower, George Dyer, Dr. Estlin, Gilbert Wakefield – with whom young Coleridge was associated' (Inkster no date p8). At the local level, the Rochdale Unitarian ministry had never been politically or theologically submissive. The same author writes of Rochdale that

> 'a very special place was won by the Unitarians. The emergence of the Cookites and Providence Chapel at the turn of the (19th) century, were products of an unusual movement

from an intellectual brand of Methodism towards true Unitarianism with energetic lay preachers such as the woollen weaver John Ashworth, the shoemaker James Wilkinson and the lay preacher James Taylor, who not only stood as a radical candidate for Rochdale in 1832 but also led a torchlight political procession in Todmorden in 1837' (Ibid).

Determined to declare as an alternative to the Methodist church, Joseph Cooke, an itinerant preacher on the circuit, set up a Unitarian chapel on Blackwater Street where it was to become the most prominent dissenting body in the town (Travers Herford and Priestley 1909).

Blackwater Street Unitarian Church (Clover Street Unitarian Church)

Although trained as a Methodist minister, Cooke opposed its refuge in emotionalism and it's anti-intellectual, uncritical stance on social issues and was not shy in making this known. In publishing two sermons to that effect, 'Justification by Faith' and 'Witness of the Spirit,' he angered members of the Methodist hierarchy who felt them to be 'unscriptural and un-methodistical' (Methodist Preachers 1807) and in 1806 expelled him for what they saw as the clash of his Unitarian views with the mother church (Roper 1993 p3). His congregation was, however, loyal, and followed him into a new ministry at the Blackwater Street Church where he set up as a demi-sect. Cooke was charismatic enough for Ashworth (1817 p26), writing soon after this event, to record that 'there never was a preacher in this country so universally admired and beloved.'

Many in his congregation, as well as Cooke himself, became Chartists and Co-operators (McLeod 1984 pp46-7) and Ditchfield (1991 p56) saw Unitarianism representing not simply a sub-sect of the Methodist church but heirs to the dissent which stretched back to Jacobinism : 'Its pastors were highly erudite men, many of whom made a reputation for their theological scholarship, whose sermons were what then amounted to the academic level of a university'. Furthermore, their mission was one focused on the congregation and the community rather than the individual. In 1890 Blackwater St and Clover St Unitarians amalgamated and eventually Blackwater St Church closed its doors.

Attendance at Clover Street Unitarian Church was strong albeit in slow decline throughout the 19th century, the average attendance at services being 73 in 1873 and 67 in 1875 (from Bolton Central Library : Attendance Register for Mission Churches 1872-76) although Sunday School teachers at the church numbered 39 individuals at the end of that period, teaching 140 Scholars. This suggests a lively, family-oriented congregation and the finances of the church reflected this, being secure enough for recourse to Central Mission funding to be resisted in 1875. This picture of a congregation built around working class communities, of social and fiscal responsibility sitting alongside Christian faith and hope is replicated in the novel of 1881 'Hiram Greg' by Joseph Crowther Hirst with its 'Heather Street Church' modelled directly on Rochdale's Clover Street Unitarians.

A sketch of the first Clover Street Unitarian Chapel 1850 (Clover Street Unitarian Church)

One aspect of Unitarianism which might have appealed to the radically-minded of the town was the organisation and constitution of the church itself with its officials directly elected from the congregation, each church having its own Chair, Vice Chair, Treasurer, two auditors, two secretaries and a Committee which included a Minister and two lay people also drawn from the congregation (Bolton Central Library : Constitution and by-Laws for North and East Lancashire Unitarian Mission 1897). McLachan (1919 p113) has written that in the early days the Unitarian ministers were referred to as lay preachers, the term 'ministers' being resisted on the grounds that it was hierarchical and only came into authorisation in 1818 before which there was 'no difference between pulpit and pew.' The organisational structure of the Unitarians resembles a Trade Union meeting or company rather than a church - perhaps a Co-operative Society.

Little wonder then, given the church's democratic structure, its grass-roots affiliation and the translation of faith into social concerns, that the links between this church and politics had been so strong, characterised as they were by an intellectual outlook and a commitment to theological and political radicalism. Thompson suggests the same when he writes (1991 p55) that 'the Unitarians or independents, with a small but influential artisan following, (were) nurtured in a strenuous intellectual tradition of social reform.' Inkster links these facets together within the local context when he notes that the Rochdale Literary and Philosophical Society was inaugurated in 1833 by a group of dissenting clergymen and liberal manufacturers, teaching subjects which included science, astronomy, politics and literature. It should be of little surprise that the classes were held at the Blackwater Street Unitarian Chapel (Inkster no date p11).

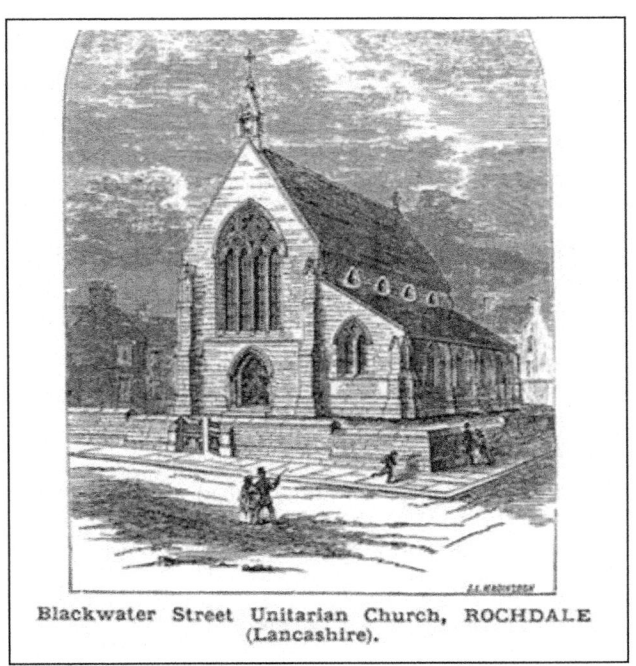

Blackwater Street Unitarian Church (Manchester Libraries, Information and Archives, Manchester City Council)

As a further mark of the political nature of this church, Cole (1984 p13) records that the radical MP for Oldham, John Fielden, chose Clover Street Unitarians as a venue from which to speak against the

Registration Act of 1836 and Clover Street was one of the first affiliates to the Rochdale Education Guild (and thereby to the WEA) in November 1909.

So, education for the Unitarians was a project for both faith and politics spoken in the language of the weaver and the artisan. On weekdays or Saturdays the church doors were open to classes dealing with such secular subjects as popular geology and other sciences, fine art, literature and leisure pursuits, and church records from Clover Street (from the 'Monthly Messenger') show Men's Classes running every Sunday at 9.00am and 1.45pm on the 'improving' subjects of Arithmetic and Composition. This church, then, can be seen as a critical exemplar of the way nonconformity impacted upon the educational policies of the town, another, the fact that by 1908 the Socialist Sunday School in Rochdale, although only opened for nine months in November, was already attracting 200 adult and juvenile scholars (Justice 21/11/08 p9).

The Co-operative Movement

Complementing the role of the church and chapel in policy debate, Rochdale had a pivot point in the Co-operative Movement, not simply from a sentimental and historical perspective but through its networks and organisation in the town. Whilst others have pointed to Rochdale's industrial profile, the size of its factories, the prominence of its artisans etc., as being the catalyst for political enthusiasm, others have seen the mass membership and grass roots strength and establishment of the Co-operative Movement as being decisive in driving policy change, particularly in education.

Certainly the Co-op's connection with teaching and learning has a formidable history. From its beginnings it was crucial in underpinning the Co-operative enterprise, in fact 'Education' stood as the seventh of eight Rochdale Pioneers Principles of Co-operation (Birchall 1994 p61). The Co-operative Society organised educational activities, classes and lectures throughout the 19th century, had its own Education Fund in 1844 and by 1899 was spending £60,000 a year on education, using its own Co-operative Halls as lecture rooms and meeting places (Simon 1965 p46). Garrard (1983 p133) points out that the Society had, by the 1870's, eleven newsrooms, a public lecture hall which could seat 1400 and a library with over 9000 books.

This was, however, neither the first co-operative educational initiative nor was it an exclusively Rochdale phenomenon. Robert Owen in his New View of Society, held men's character to be best formed by an environment planned 'not upon lines of oppression but of mutual co-operation, forbearance and understanding' (Cole 1948 p73) and Co-operative Unions before the Rochdale Pioneers had been active nationwide outside of food merchandising, Twigg offering an example

(1924 p1 and 2) in the 1825 London Co-operative Society which held weekly debates and circulated literature to promote its own co-operative cause as well as wider policy issues. Brighton Co-operative Society held science classes in 1828 and as (at the same time) the Mechanics Institutes were catering more for the middle classes than for 'mechanics,' this experiment was successful in attracting and educating a wider, working class, constituency. However, these early attempts at co-operation struggled in large part because of their local, if not parochial nature and their limited aspirations.

With individuals in Rochdale such as John Mitchell however, there was a broader message to articulate and organise in support of co-operation : 'The three great forces for improvement of mankind are religion, temperance and co-operation' (Mitchell 1892). Mitchell, born out of wedlock to a poor Rochdale working woman and educated at the National School in Red Cross Street, was a life-long nonconformist, initially attending Milton Church in the town and then the Provident Independent Chapel where he was a Sunday School teacher. His first employment, before his twelfth birthday, was as a little piecer at the Townshend Cotton Mill but, as with the WEA class 50 years later, he looked to education to raise his sights and prospects. In the 1850's he joined the Rochdale Equitable Pioneers and influenced their education provision in the town.

John Mitchell 1828-1895 (The Local History Centre, Touchstones)

By the mid 19th century the Education section of Rochdale's Co-operative movement was receiving individual subscriptions of 2d per month and finding premises for classes in the old store that had previously been used by the Bethel Chapel community, the second floor being taken over as meeting rooms. In addition to teaching spaces, the same location was used as a combined newsroom and shop where newspapers, books and periodicals could be bought, the profits from such sales going back into the growing library (Twigg 1924 p59). Statutes within the Co-operative Society of 1854 set up a separate fund for the 'intellectual improvement of members' and by 1856 discussion groups were meeting in the Toad Lane store on Saturday afternoons with further classes held on Sundays expressly to help the poor to read and write. Two years later a Co-operative school and adult education classes were also running (Birchall 1994 p61), the Rochdale Pioneers committing 2.5% of their own trading surplus to education.

Part of the 2d a month levy was set aside to fund a stock of newspapers which could be read on-site including the three Rochdale papers – The Observer, The Star and the Times – and periodicals such as 'The Moral World,' 'The Northern Star' and 'Reynolds' Newspaper' (Rochdale Touchstones : Co-operative Society News). By 1862 a librarian was employed for 7 hours a day by which time the library was supporting, with books and other resources, classes in physiography, botany, magnetism, electricity, maths and French. Not exclusively book-based either, the Co-operative Library had wider educational purposes as an almanac of 1868 suggests :

> 'If a working man wishes to borrow a microscope to examine fine work, or insects, or flowers gathered in his walks afield, or an opera glass to scan the features of some distinguished lecturer or speaker, or a stereoscope to amuse and instruct the children, he can obtain the loan of them for a trifling fee' (All The Year Round Almanac February 29 1868).

The North West of England, by the end of the 19th century, seems to have become a centre for the Co-op's educational activities with almost 90% of its national expenditure on books, reference facilities, periodical, classes and libraries committed to that region. The fact that this was not the case nationwide was recorded in 1882 by Arthur Ackland, an Oxford don and pioneer of University Extension who, reporting for the United Board of the Co-operative Union, noted that in contrast to Rochdale, most (local) societies were doing very little (Birchill 1994 p94).

Whilst the Co-operative Education section set out to promote cultural, educational and basic skills and knowledge amongst adults towards the turn of the century, there grew – alongside the political changes already alluded to – an interest in economics and industrial/constitutional history 'as they have a bearing on co-operation and the opportunity to train men and women for industrial and social reforms' (Hall and Watkins 1937 p4). So, making a link to national programmes which were focusing on social and political matters, the Co-operative movement became active in adult and higher education, particularly in the social sciences, and it gave solid support – financial and organisational - for these subjects under the University Extension scheme, providing lecture and meeting rooms, books and human resources, Davies (1975) even suggesting that the Co-operative Society paid, in part, individual student fees for those suffering greatest hardship.

By 1907 grants made by the Co-op for educational purposes amounted to £ 93000. Mansbridge and Halstead (1903 p7) – being good Co-operators themselves - had noted the enthusiasm and commitment alongside the University Extension programme for the propagation of the Co-op's own educational activities in Rochdale, although this was probably more reciprocal than Mansbridge realised with groups of Co-operative scholarship holders attending Extension classes from 1891 onwards and going on to Oxford or Cambridge Summer Schools. More importantly, the Rochdale Pioneers, because of their material influence through local networking was able to carry decision-making into the heart of the town and provide a viable bridge between grass roots political and economic thought, the moral edifice of the church and an extension of higher education. Price notes (1924 p14) that 'it was with the Co-operative Movement chiefly that relations were established' between themselves (the WEA), the Trade Unions and the Universities in promoting worker education.

The Rochdale Education Guild and its tutorial class

Before affiliating to the WEA as the Rochdale Education Guild, those organising and managing adult education met regularly as the Rochdale University Extension (evening) Lecture Committee. They were a formidable group of individuals with an effective structure and close working relationships and this was maintained when authority was transferred to the Education Guild with the continued support of its President, Lieutenant-Colonel Henry Fishwick FSA, JP., a local historian and a Conservative who held the presidency until his death in 1914, and with two Colonels (Kemp and Royds) as vice presidents. Aldermen and councillors were also key executive members of the Guild Committee along with the powerhouse Honorary Secretaries Lawrence Gill, Fred Greenwood and Alec Carter. When, as in 1905, a full council meeting took place, the main Guild officers were augmented by representatives from no fewer than 50 affiliated organisations across the town and Doyle (2003 p18) offers a profile of such meetings when he writes that the Guild council in 1911 consisted of 57% working men, 28% teachers plus one ex-teacher and one employer.

Executive Committee of the Rochdale Education Guild 1911 (Workers Educational Association)

By the time the Education Guild took on the organization of the University Extension classes in the early years of the 20th century they were mobilising 'the teaching and lecturing power in the town' (Price 1924 p25). Financially, the Guild grew and by 1905 there were already 70 affiliates which can be broken down into the following :

Type of affiliate	Percentage of overall affiliation
Church	35
Trades related and trades unions	31
Education	10.9
Socialist groups	5.5
Other political groups	4
Literary and Scientific groups	4
The Co-operative movement	2.8
Sundry affiliation	6.8

Table 2 : 1905 Affiliation to the Rochdale Education Guild (The Local History Centre, Touchstones)

It is clear from Table 2 that the main support for the Guild's work in 1905 came from religious and from labour organisations, with education groups also contributing not only funding but proposals for new presentations, lectures and venues. Such was the success of the Guild that by 1907 an 'Education Handbook and Calendar' had to be launched to publicize its forthcoming activities across the town and over the years this publication grew as more and more events took place. Not that the Guild was simply concerned with face to face classes. Reading circles, library stock and links to churches, chapels and national bodies were important aspects of the Guild's work and these too were announced in the Handbook.

However, it was the range of lectures that was most impressive with Jennings (2002 p156) writing that the Guild by 1905-06 was organising presentations that ranged from events at the Chrysanthemum Society to 'The Care of the Horse' which drew 100 attendees, from the Gilchrist lectures (started in 1880) on such subjects as 'Origins of the Minutest Forms of Life' by Rev W H Dallinger to a lecture for the Women's Social and Political Union on 'Ruskin on Women' (Working Class Movement Library 1909) and the Castleton Literary and Scientific Society organising discussion groups on Literature, Music and Art. Outside of the town centre, a great deal was taking place in the affiliated districts. The Guild Calendar 1909-10 for example, lists lectures on Economics by Fred Hall

(B.Com) at the Co-operative Society, University Extension lectures from Powys and Hudson-Shaw and presentations at Smallbridge, Castleton (Literary and Scientific groups), Shawclough (Institute), Whitworth (Popular Lecture Society), Norden, Milnrow and Newhey (separate Education Guilds), Hamer (Church Institute), Spotland (Men's Institute) and Lowerplace, (Wesleyan Men's Club).

Sessions such as these were so successful that by 1907 up to 900 tickets were being sold on subjects as diverse as Art and Nature, Politics and Economics. An issue of the university magazine 'Young Oxford' in 1902 publicized a range of University Extension lectures taking place across the country, but notably in Rochdale, where two classes had been organised for the Winter of 1902 to meet in rooms at the Toad Lane Stores, yet another example of the links between worker education and the Co-operative Society.

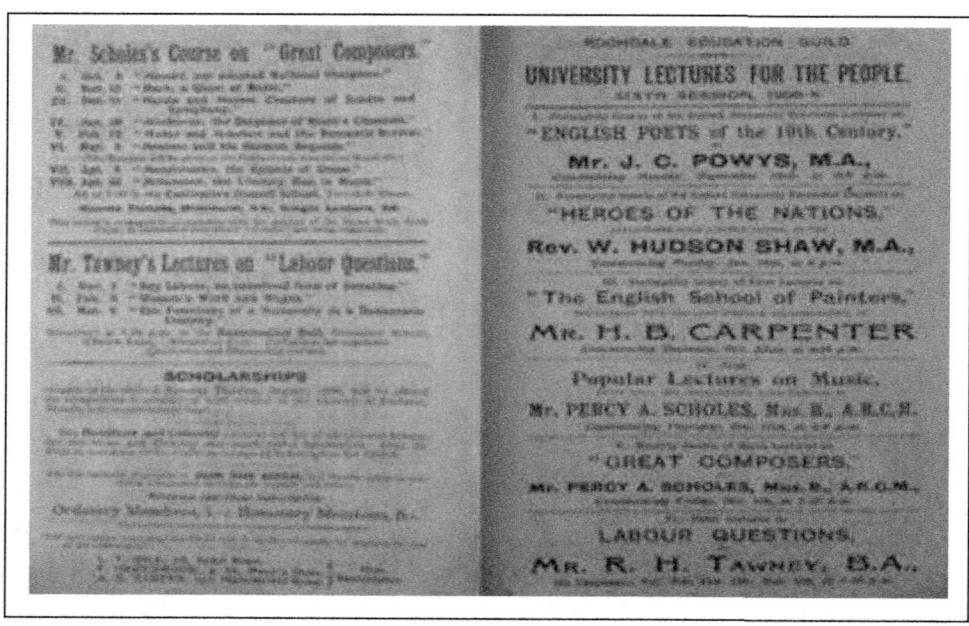

University Extension sessions 1908-09 (The Local History Centre, Touchstones)

Further classes dealing with Psychology were running in 1907 under the Reverend T P Spedding, the Minister at Clover Street Unitarians, and yet another group meeting in the same place on Friday evenings studying Sociology and later Economics with Tom Price. The intermingling of students from the various study classes was noteworthy with members of the same church congregation often attending University Extension lectures and also the Ruskin College classes which ran on Sunday mornings at 10.30 (TUC Library : Ref 3/6/1).

Not that the various programmes were accessible to all potential students. Price (1924) makes a distinction concerning access to this provision in terms of expense, pointing out that the University Extension classes were neither subsidised nor endowed and therefore relatively expensive for working men and women. He warned that (p30)

> 'Extension courses must not be so high as to debar the average working man, or else, that a very large number of tickets must be sold, in which the latter case there was a strong temptation, when arranging the course, to pay more regard to its attractiveness than to its educational value.'

Organising the Tutorial Class

Reacting to the problems associated with University Extension courses and the demands for curricular and pedagogical change which were raised at the Conference of 1907, and then following the identification of Rochdale as a place for a new 'experiment' in worker education, Mansbridge arranged meetings in March and April in the town to discuss the potential for a fresh start in the form of a tutorial class, and invited Gill, Fred Greenwood and Carter to organise things to that end.

From its beginnings, the WEA enjoyed federal status and district autonomy and this voluntarism gave Rochdale – in theory at least - the opportunity to decide for itself what it wanted to do. So, a sub-committee of the Rochdale Education Guild was set up and W J Lawson and J Hall from its Executive Committee were approached to consider what arrangements would be advisable with respect to a class being formed for a 2 year programme under an Oxford tutor and what subject it should study (Rochdale Education Guild Minutes 28/3/07). The decision was reached to put it to the people, so Gill and Carter announced that there was to be a special meeting at The Lyceum in Rochdale on Saturday July 18th - an afternoon event – hopefully to be attended by up to 40-50 interested individuals, the agenda being to determine the nature, subject and operational organisation of their own tutorial class (Rochdale Education Guild minutes July 18th 1907).

At the meeting there was general agreement that the best time for the proposed class was a Saturday afternoon and although this clashed with attendance at the football match, it at least avoided overtime demands and student fatigue in the evenings. Textile workers, through Parliamentary legislation of 1874 had been granted a 56.5 hour working week with a one o'clock finishing time on Saturdays, so this suited many of the potential worker-students. Then the subject for the tutorial class came under discussion, the view strongly held that <u>they</u> should be the ones to make the decision, that only if the workers had a clear voice in such matters – matters of curriculum, teaching and learning - would the experiment be a success. Higher education, it was felt, could no longer be imposed upon the working man and woman by those within established power and so there had to be a partnership of concern, an equitable co-operation between the individual learner and the university, otherwise, the tutorial class would go the way of the Mechanics Institutes and the University Extension movement. This issue, more than any other at the time, encapsulates the direction of travel in linking social class, education and politics.

At the meeting, the Unitarian and Co-operator Fred Hall spoke, suggesting (Price 1924 p31) that economic history would be the most appropriate course of study for the class. Although there was some agreement about this, there then came counter-claims for subjects covering art and literature but these were immediately contested, many feeling that there were plenty of lectures on those subjects already, that social and economic history was nearer to people's lives and that 'more ornamental' subjects might follow at a later date if the experiment with tutorials was a success. This was eventually agreed and a course linking historical and socio-political issues deemed to be most acceptable.

It was then proposed that a fee for this new class should be no more than 1/- per session which was the normal price of a University Extension single lecture 'to meet local expenses' (to give one comparison, admission to football matches in 1908 was 6d) and the course should be 'open to all who will undertake to give the subject serious and systematic study.' A loan of the travelling library from Oxford University should be on hand to support study.

For Rochdale, the finer points of operationalising the programme had to be completed such as finding a suitable venue, identifying resources for the class and keeping down student fees. Furthermore the curriculum, syllabus and working details of the experiment, which had been determined at the meeting in the town, had to be presented to the universities for formal agreement. To do this, a further meeting was arranged by Mansbridge, bringing together the Dean of Christ Church Oxford (Chair of the University Extension Delegacy) with a small deputation of those students from Rochdale who had attended the most recent Summer School (Mansbridge 1913 p19). Brooks (2000) has shown that Mansbridge used the presence of working people to personalise his appeal to establishment figures, having had a party of workers meet dignitaries from the train at the 1907 Conference. At the meeting with the Dean, a lunch was arranged at the university and after a worker presentation offering a rationale for the subject of their proposed class, the Dean confessed to being so impressed with 'their hunger' for knowledge that he was willing to give his blessing for the tutorial programme and grant them a tutor.

WEA and Rochdale Guild circa 1908 (Workers Educational Association)
(end at top right Zimmern, Temple and Hudson Shaw, front from left Mansbridge, Price and Gill)

It then fell to Mansbridge to find a suitable academic figure to tutor the Rochdale class and he knew that his choice would be critical to its success. The Joint Committee required that such a person should be currently practicing at university level, be prepared to teach at Oxford University at the same time (in order that university students would benefit from knowledge gathered from worker-students) and, most importantly, 'have sufficient knowledge of working class life and habits of thought to be able to understand the lines along which students have reached their conclusions' (1909 p65), this last suggestion being one of an almost anthropological nature. Mansbridge's immediate thought was to approach R H Tawney, at that time unhappily teaching theoretical Economics at the University of Glasgow (Rusoff in Roberts 2003 p64) but soon to move to the History Department at Manchester University. Letters passed between the two which found Tawney interested enough to want to know more about the arrangements for the class, the curriculum and his role in its delivery.

In one letter to Tawney (19th September 1907), Mansbridge relayed the message regarding the day, the time and the subject, describing it again as 'experimental work' and in the same letter suggesting that the setting up of this class was important in terms of the WEA's 'prestige,' that it was a bold venture and that he (Tawney) would be recognised by the WEA as their special advisor in their experiment in worker education. There is no record of Tawney's immediate response, but an official invitation on 18th November was sent by Marriott from Oxford University asking if he 'would be free to undertake a tutorial class for this delegacy in Rochdale ?' Tawney's positive reply must have come at once as Marriott writes again to him within a week with : 'I wish you had been able and willing to accept other invitations in the neighbourhood.'

With the promise of Tawney to act as tutor, the Rochdale Education Guild moved apace with arrangements of its own and contacted him to say that they were 'in a state of extreme delight' at the thought of his arrival and that he should stay the weekend in the town ! 'You will find warm hearts in Rochdale,' Mansbridge wrote in a letter of the 26th November 1907. 'Not only warm hearts, but hearts anxious to beat,' Gill assured Tawney on December 1st. In the same letter Gill offered food and comfort for him after his journey to the town, reminding the distinguished academic that the classes would be from 2.30 – 4.30pm on Saturdays, and that a list of books had already been requested by one of the students from Harvey Pearse, the booksellers on Yorkshire Street ! He also reminded him that Marriott was going to send books for the students to use in the class.

The amount of work in organising all of this, communicating by hand-written letter to Rochdale and the universities, travelling to both sites to chair meetings in order to finalise curriculum design, not to mention sorting out resourcing and financial backing, seems to have put a great strain on Mansbridge who writes in one letter 'I am often in despair.' Despair or not, the official invitation had gone out to Tawney in a letter of 30th November 1907 following a meeting of the Oxford Delegacy on the previous evening. The class arrangements would be for three lots of twelve sessions which would run as 'Social and Economic History' with Tawney as tutor. The Rochdale Education Guild had agreed that essays would be required of the students once a fortnight and that there should be a final examination at Easter 1909. A further suggestion was that students could be tested at the end of each of Tawney's sessions although this does not appear to have happened. One feels throughout all of this a sense of trialling something new reflected in excitement in Rochdale, nervous anticipation from Mansbridge and a cautious watching brief by the universities and by other WEA centres across the United Kingdom.

R H Tawney 1908 (Workers Educational Association)

Marriott's immediate concerns were those of the University Extension Delegacy and largely concerned finalising the details of the tutorial course. He informed Tawney (TUC Library : Ref 3/6/1) that the Rochdale people 'are anxious to begin as early as possible' and sent him, in the same letter, a specimen syllabus, urging him to come up with his lecture titles as soon as he could. At the same time and in another place, the formalities and administrative protocols for the university had to be settled and Oxford, again through Marriott, its Extension Delegacy Secretary, pressed urgency in confirming the details of the programme, writing again to Tawney on 3rd December and requiring, in the strongest of terms, his submission of a detailed syllabus by 10th January 1908, two weeks before the start of the classes.

There then followed a flurry of correspondence between Mansbridge and Tawney, the latter beginning to question the appointment and the details of his fee. The points raised were seen as 'considerable inconveniences' by Mansbridge (1913 p2) and there seems to have been a risk that progress might be hampered because of them. In a letter of reassurance from Temple to Tawney of the 29th January, the suggestion was that he would receive £40, the Oxford Delegacy contributing £20, the rest coming 'from the folk of Rochdale or Stoke' (Longton in the Potteries, by that time, having arranged a class for the same weekend). It would appear from their communications that there was some concern on Tawney's part about his contract and the longevity of his commitment : 'You place me in a difficult position,' Mansbridge writes. 'This is a new kind of class (and) we have got in you the proper teacher. If you throw up the work at the end of the present course at Rochdale and Longton, as far as I can see our plans fall to the ground.' Mansbridge is desperate to keep Tawney involved for the long term : 'I do not know any one person who can supply the connecting link unless we can induce Zimmern or Temple to maintain at Rochdale and then try to get Zimmern to go on with it for a time until the younger men are developed.' This appears to be Tawney suggesting a short tenure, holding out for a higher fee or concerned at the amount of work he was required to do. Perhaps all three. Mansbridge makes an appeal to his ambition : 'I have no right to speculate with your career,' and in a terse note to Tawney points out that 'if your letters increase in acidity, you will find me knocking at your door one morning before many days are over.'

All did not seem to be well with the eminent and proposed tutor. Notwithstanding the issues concerning tenure, Tawney was also indicating a certain amount of anxiety about Marriott's role in the detailed organisation of the class, Mansbridge being forced to write back to Tawney on the 4th December 1907 suggesting that he should 'be aware that Marriott is trying to manage everything,' doubtless referring to the Oxford man's continued suggestions as to the nature of the course and his views on an appropriate teaching style. In a letter to Tawney on November 30th for example,

Marriott writes 'I should imagine that the greater part of your time would be devoted to the Mercantile system, the history of enclosures ….. and perhaps to chartered companies' and then adds 'I trust that these will fit in with your inclinations,' signing off the same letter by offering to give Tawney 'hints as to the conduct of the work.' Mansbridge writes to Tawney on December 3rd asking 'what on earth can we do with a man like Marriott ?' and on December 4th again that 'I am glad you are taking no notice of Marriott, he wants to manage everything. Keep your eye on Gill. He is the best man in the world.'

Meanwhile in Rochdale, a public announcement had been made by Gill as to the practical arrangements for the class, that there were to be 12 sessions before Easter and a further 24 between October 1908 and Easter 1909 on the subject of 'The History of England – social, industrial and economic'. There would be 36 instead of 48 lectures because the start had to be delayed, the sessions running January-Easter (12) October-Christmas (12) and January-Easter 1909 (12) with an examination at the end. It was announced that the classes would begin on January 25th 1908 and the tutor would be R H Tawney, formerly of Balliol College Oxford but now of Glasgow University. The fee to be charged for lectures would be 1/- per session and it was stipulated that those applying should be prepared to undertake the WHOLE course. An attachment to the announcement helpfully suggested that

> 'If Saturday afternoon is impossible for you, perhaps you could join the Ruskin Hall Class on the same subject that is being held on Sunday morning at 10.30am commencing today. The Secretary (Mr T Lee) will send particulars.'

At the close of the announcement there was regret that there had been an 'unavoidable delay in starting the class,' the delay, behind the scenes, having been due to two issues. Firstly the negotiations between the Board of Education and Rochdale LEA had to be finalised over student finance and whether the programme should be two or three years in duration as this had implications for possible grants paid to students. The Board of Education responded quickly by issuing Regulations which meant that a grant would be paid if the definition of a tutorial class met two main criteria – that it was three years of study following a university syllabus and that it was under a recognised and appointed tutor.

Price (1924 p47) writes that grants were paid according to the number of hours attended although this took no account of the effectiveness of the class in terms of learning. The Memorandum of Arrangements for the first tutorial class from the Oxford University Extension Office for the period January 25th 1908 to April 11th 1909 required that a block grant of £30 per session per class subject be paid and that a fee of £20 should go to the tutor plus 5 shillings expenses per lecture and 3rd class rail fare from Manchester. The cost of each class was to be shared between the universities (50%), the Board of Education (33%) and the remainder coming from the local authority. Classes were to take place in the new Technical School and the Rochdale Education Committee agreed to provide free accommodation on the premises including the heating and lighting of lecture rooms.

Central School/Rochdale Technical School 1909 (The Local History Centre, Touchstones)

The second issue to be settled concerned the number of students in the class, the Guild organisers attempting to reduce the numbers to a manageable size which in the end was 43 students, 39 men and 4 women. The Guild anticipated that students engaging with the tutorial class would be young and energetic members of the manual working class 'who are keenly alive to civic questions and with a desire to improve their knowledge of them by impartial study' (Smith 1956 p71-2). One interested student, Charlie Pearce, who had been a talented amateur footballer, clearly felt that it was worth sacrificing his sporting prospects as he was one of those enrolling.

At the same moment, the University was finalising its own regulations in official recognition of the class and over the course of two meetings on November 25th and December 16th set up an award to recognise successful study by students who have 'entered the ordinary occupations of life' but who required university education. They knew that in the past that different bodies had attempted to deal with the same 'problem' of the university failing to reach working people, but now they felt to be in sight of a solution by offering a 'Chancellors University Extension Diploma' – but not a Certificate - for study, to be completed by students within three years.

> Schoolroom, Shawclough) commencing Friday, September 13th. For subsequent dates see Calendar. Guild Members are invited.
>
> Societies desiring to make use of either of the above Courses should apply to the Guild Secretaries.
>
> ### OXFORD UNIVERSITY TUTORIAL CLASS.
>
> *[handwritten: R H Tawney]*
>
> Arrangements are being made for a tutor from Oxford University to conduct a Tutorial Class in Rochdale, extending over two winter sessions, of about 24 meetings each.
>
> *[handwritten: It began Jan 1908, & ran for 4 years]*
>
> SUBJECT—The History of England, mainly Social, Industrial and Economic, and particularly dealing with the 17th, 18th and 19th centuries.
>
> The class will meet on Saturday afternoons for two hours.
>
> The time and date of meeting will be announced later.
>
> The class will be limited to about 30 students.
>
> Men or women wishing to join should apply at once to the Guild Secretaries.
>
> ### LADIES' AFTERNOON LECTURES COMMITTEE.
>
> A course of Six Lectures on
>
> "Browning" by Miss A. M. Royden,
>
> on alternate Tuesdays, at 3 p.m., commencing January 14th, 1908, in the Lecture Theatre, Technical School. Course Tickets, 6/6. Two Tickets for Subscription of 10/6.
>
> Hon. Secretary, Miss A. W. Heap, Eversleigh.

Publicity piece from The Rochdale Education Guild Handbook 1907-08

(with Gill's handwritten additions) (Workers Educational Association)

There remained the question as to who would monitor the tutorial sessions as, although the WEA was built upon a devolved system of autonomous districts, the classes had official subvention from the universities and they would inevitably wish to exercise scrutiny and control over aspects of teaching and learning. In line with this, Simon notes (1965 p327) that the classes were required to be inspected by the Board of Education and a Report submitted by them to the universities commensurate with education at the same level. This mandated inspectors to observe the management and practices of each class, and Jennings (in Roberts 2003 p22) writes that the Board of Education approached Her Majesty's Inspectorate and they in turn asked J W Headlam and Prof L T Hobhouse to undertake the earliest inspections.

So, in February 1908 the tutorial classes were up and running, Hudson Shaw recommending and promoting them from within his existing University Extension groups so that there was, again, overlap between student pathways. Notwithstanding the excitement about the new tutorial class, the University Extension lectures continued to thrive as did other adult educational provision in the town. The Rochdale Education Guild Handbook of 1909-10 for example announced continuing lectures at the Literary and Scientific Societies, at church and chapel groups, libraries and Debating Societies, at Lay Helpers Associations and with Popular Lecture Societies. In that year presentations continued with E L S Horsburgh's six lectures on 'The French Revolution,' Saturday night talks were held by Tawney and Kolthammer both of whom also lectured for the Milnrow and Newhey Education Guild, and there were other presentations such as Margaret McMillan's on 'Education Tomorrow.' Discussion classes to support wider study were organised and presented by Theopholus David Tuton Hall, the Deputy Head at Rochdale Grammar School, and new WEA tutorial class students Henighan, Hall and Greenwood committed themselves to presenting Winter lectures across the town, Fred Hall lecturing in Norden on 'Charles Kingsley', Charlie Pearce at Castleton on 'Germany and Municipal Government' and Harold Holt to a group in Shawclough on 'Dickens and Social Reform.'

Nested within this range of lectures and talks was the tutorial class. Its students might have been from other groups, its tutor almost from another world, but they came together as part of this great experiment. So what brought them together ? And who were they ?

Who were the students ?

There have been a number of histories of the WEA which have outlined its beginnings, its development and its formative figures such as Mansbridge, Gore and Temple. Whilst this is important in understanding event chronology, it runs the risk of being about the nation's leading figures as heroes and omitting the story of the worker-students themselves and historians, for example Rose (2010), have regretted that in many accounts a grounded portrait of those at the centre of worker education is ignored or glossed over. Here, I wish to contribute to a re-balancing of this history by using what little evidence survives to sketch portraits of some of the students who took part in the tutorial class and their living conditions in Rochdale, and project from these sketches their likely motives in undertaking study, the challenges that faced them in doing so and their eventual careers. Without the students' vital energies, curiosities and aspirations, there would have been no WEA and no tutorial classes and it is to these individuals I now turn my attention.

Two points should be made in advance, however. Whilst championing the history of the individual, it is a point of regret that the material which survives does so in abundance for those who made an indelible mark on the world in the years following the tutorial class and who became known on a national or international stage, whilst the workmen and women who continued in the mill or the iron foundry following their tutorial experience, became history's vapour, disappearing from sight. So, it is not possible to trace all of the students with equal measure as some have left little record of their time with the WEA or with Rochdale's Education Guild after 1908. Given their enthusiasm and courage in attending the initial class however, most of them deserve at least a note or two to mark it.

Secondly, in presenting this part of the story on a person by person basis, by no means do I wish to suggest an individualist ethos. The camaraderie suggested by after-class activity, the evidence of family members attending together, the neighbours who made their way to the classes from the same streets, the fact that they knew each other through chapel or club – all are testament to a communality that is an important part of this story. Alfred Zimmern, close to the WEA hierarchy, made just such a distinction in this regard, suggesting in 1914 (cited in Doyle 2003 p45) that :

> 'unlike the middle class, the working class is habituated to corporate modes of life. The Trade Union, the club, the chapel, the Co-operative Society have kept alive for working people the instinct and habit of association.'

Individual characteristics do appear though, and as many as possible are presented in these pages.

First however, a list of the students portrayed :

Thomas Bailey	George E Greenwood	Eugene Kiernan	Arthur Shore
Joseph Binns	Fred Hall	Livsey Lees	Walter Ernest Stopford
Harold Briggs	James Henighan	Benjamin Lord	Fanny Taylor
Arthur Collinge	Charles Hewitt	Joseph Nuttall	Frederick Turner
Joseph Cryer	Charles Herbert Hilton	Charles H Pearce	A P Wadsworth
Stanley Dawson	James Edmund Hilton	Leonard Plant	Alfred Wilkinson
Amy Fozard	Ethel Kershaw	T W Price	Albert Wilson
Frederick Greenwood	Harold Kershaw	Eleanor Redshaw	Joseph Wormald

The Rochdale WEA Tutorial class of 1908 (Workers Educational Association)

Sketches of the Students (in alphabetical order)

Thomas Bailey

One of the many cotton workers in the class, Thomas Bailey was born in 1887 and lived at 27 Hope Street near to Rochdale Infirmary subsequently moving to Duke Street in Wardleworth where his family lived as next-door neighbour to a carpet weaver and a boiler maker.

Rear view of Hope Street 1912 (The Local History Centre, Touchstones)

Thomas' father was a cotton operative and by the age of thirteen he was already in the mill working in the ring room which suggests that he left school or was made to leave school at the earliest opportunity. The family had, by that time, moved to a house on Bury Road. After the tutorial class, in 1911, the census records show that he was still in the mill, now working as a mule piecer, in fact every one of Thomas' working family were employed in textiles, all five of the children still at home in 1911.

Thomas was a member of the Clover Street Unitarian Church and its Vice President between 1908 and 1909. By 1911 he had married and moved to 30 Oak Street, neighbour to a cardroom worker in a cotton factory. Thomas seems to have been less active than some in the class, achieving no recorded scholarships and taking no part in the organisation of the Guild once the class was completed. Nor does he seem to have been involved politically in the town.

Thomas served in the Great War in the Shropshire Light Infantry, enlisting in December 1914, at the time still at 30 Oak Street. There is no record as to his later life although most students who did not continue in education, stayed on in the cotton industry.

Joseph Binns

Born in 1876, Joseph Binns lived at 25 Hanover Street in Rochdale, a street of carters, iron workers and cotton weavers. In 1901 the census shows that Joseph was a cotton scutcher, a job in the mill for which he earned about £1 per week (Wood 1910). In the same year he married and within the following decade the couple had three children. Another member of the Clover Street Unitarian Church, there are records of his (five shillings) subscription to church upkeep in June 1900 and an announcement of his presenting a Band of Hope lecture at the church in 1904 entitled 'Drink : its use and abuse in health and disease.' By 1911 he was living at 6 Warwick Street and lived at that address through to his death.

6 Warwick St in 2015

The census records suggest that by 1911 Joseph was a cotton operative at Messrs Holt and Ogden's Brotherod Mill, later working again as scutcher at Mitchell Hey Mill and then in the same job at the Eclipse.

Joseph was elected President of the Cardroom Association and then became the Association's representative (later Executive Committee member) on the Rochdale Insurer's Committee. He was a keen sportsman and a member of Rochdale AFC for many years although he was another who seemed to make few academic waves in the tutorial class, neither going on to Summer schools nor receiving awards for his coursework. His name does not appear in the minutes of the Rochdale Education Guild but he did hold important office in the textile industry, becoming President of the Blowing Room and Ring Spinner's Association and then its Secretary from 1918, representing some of the lowest paid workers in the textile industry.

**Ornate doorway to the Blowing Room and Ring Spinner's Association in Rochdale
(The Local History Centre, Touchstones)**

Following a short illness, Joseph died in March 1937 aged 61 although he had – against all advice it seems - been at his office two days previously. His obituary describes him as 'quiet and unassuming… and of likeable temperament.' He may well have taken a political path had he not suffered from extreme deafness in later years which some say held him back in that respect. At the time of his death he left a wife and a son and was 'one of the oldest and most revered trade union officials in Rochdale' (Rochdale Observer March 1937).

Harold Briggs

Born in 1886, Harold spent his childhood near to the town centre at 42 St Mary's Gate Rochdale on either side of the family home being a tailor and a 'tripe dresser.' This area was one of the poorest in the town but Harold was still living there on his 25th birthday in 1911. In 1891 the family group was father, mother and Harold. His father – in 1901 – worked from home as a clogger and his mother likewise dressmaking. Harold, at 15 years of age had become a commercial clerk which suggests that he may have been accepted at Higher Grade School after elementary education but left at an early age to take up that position.

Yet another prominent member of the Clover Street Unitarian Church, Harold held many posts of office at the church including Committee member for the Young Men's Social Union, Steward for the Unitarian Church Messenger magazine, Assistant Secretary to the Sunday School Committee and, in 1907 in charge of the church football team. By 1910 he was representing the church at a Band of Hope Forward Demonstration at Manchester's Free Trade Hall in favour of universal temperance.

Clover Street Unitarian Chapel 1908 (The Local History Centre, Touchstones)

By 1911, Harold was still single but by now employed as an accounts clerk, passing his final accountancy examination in July 1914. The fact that he did this at 28 years of age suggests that he was ambitious enough to achieve certification incrementally through a series of evening classes. Accountancy was a skill he seems to have put to good use as he acted as auditor for many of the Unitarian church committees. By 1915 he seems still to have been living at home in an upstairs flat although by 1935 he was at 125 Bellshill Crescent between Smallbridge and Firgrove.

Harold died in September of 1974 aged 89. His is another name from the class which disappears from the record at the end of the class' existence, he took no part in the running of the Guild thereafter, nor did he present lectures in the town.

Arthur Collinge

Arthur Collinge continued his connections with the Rochdale Education Guild following his experience with Tawney's tutorial class and represented the 'Co-operation' group on the Guild Committee in 1909. Born in 1873, Arthur's father was a mill worker in the woollen industry, first as an operative and then as a warehouse porter. At the age of eight, Arthur was living as one of four children with his parents and his maternal grandfather at 115 Durham Street, his neighbours being grocers and a cotton winder, but the family (he had two brothers and two sisters) moved in the late 1880s to 16 Walsh Street from where Arthur would set off in the morning for the mill to work as a warp twister. His early working suggests that he had only an elementary education.

The next move for Arthur, following his marriage in 1894, was to be head of his own household at 35 Bedford Street with a timber worker living on one side and a labourer on the other, and it was around this time that he decided to become self-employed as a house painter. By 1901 he had a working wife, Mary Collinge, who was active in the suffragette movement and a member of the Rochdale Branch of the Women's Social and Political Union, attending the London demonstration for the vote in June 1908 (Working Class Movement Library, Salford). At the turn of the century, the Collinge family had one son to support. The early 1910's saw them move twice, once to a four bedroom house at 12 Pioneer Street and then back at Durham Street at number 72 from where his nephew ran a bookbinders and printers business, moving there no doubt due to a growing family – now two children and one sister in law at the house.

In the year previous to the tutorial class in 1908, Arthur gained an examination distinction in the subject of 'Political and Social Problems' the course run by E L S Horsburgh and in 1909 he was selected by the Guild to visit Germany on a fact-finding educational tour which Arthur did under the auspices of the Union of Co-operative Employees, the organisation which part-funded his place. Not only was Arthur in the Rochdale ILP but he was also an active member of the Rochdale Adult School and an Honorary Secretary of the Rochdale Education Guild.

In 1910 he organised a Student Fellowship under the Co-operative Union for their alumni, intending for it to provide co-operative support for new students and which ran as such for many years.

Pioneer Street in 2015

Arthur died aged 64 on 6th November 1936 although he had been working as a painter and decorator up to that date, advertising his business in the Rochdale Observer the week before his death from 24 Hare Street although he also had a business address in 1935 at 10 Norwich Street. At his death, the obituary in the Rochdale Observer noted that he had been a prominent figure in the town's Socialist movement, a founder member of the ILP and chairman of the local branch. He had also been a supporter of the Adult School which met at the Friends Meeting House in George Street and, as a Quaker he and his family were lifelong advocates of peace. A committed pacifist, although too old for conscription himself, his son, Joseph was a conscientious objector in 1916 and was court martialled and imprisoned in Strangeways for his religious and political beliefs. It was felt that had Arthur been called up, he too would have been imprisoned as an objector on moral grounds. His wife was also a pacifist with evidence of her demonstrating against the war (Working Class Movement Library, Salford) in Rochdale, Manchester and London.

Arthur stood on one occasion for town council as a Socialist, contesting Wardleworth East but failed to be elected. At his death he left 2 sons, one living in Scotland the other working as a partner in his painting and decorating business. Stanley Dawson (see below) conducted the funeral service at the Collinge house and Ethel Kershaw (see below) attended the internment. It was a mark of the stature of Arthur Collinge in the politics of the town that attending his funeral was the Lord Mayor of the day, representatives from the Adult School, Rochdale Trades and Labour Council and from the Society of Friends with whom he had a long association. The Independent Labour Party inscribed a wreath with 'our companion has remained steadfast and faithful unto death.'

Joseph Cryer

Joseph Cryer, born in 1881, was active in the Rochdale Education Guild until he moved from the town in 1909 to live in Todmorden. However, even from that distance he kept in touch with the key figures of the movement, writing one letter to Tawney in 1912 in which he discusses the causes of poverty in society and the subjugation of the working classes, feeling that the physical machinery of capitalism and its skill demands had done much to drive a wedge between those who have and those who have nothing. He adds that he is disappointed in the current socialist response to such issues and discusses the rise of syndicalism before suggesting that Tawney 'look into these matters !' Interestingly Joseph must have been running a WEA class of his own in Burnley at the time, as he comments on the poor turn-out for his tutorials. He ends the letter with a note that suggests that he had a close relationship with his old tutor by offering his best wishes to Tawney's wife. A second letter was written by Joseph Cryer to his former tutor in 1914 from an address in Burnley, critical of aspects of his new book.

When he was growing up, Joseph's father was a mechanic in the cotton industry, rising to foreman machine fitter by 1901, a mechanic in the mill earning about 24/- per week in 1906 (Wood 1901). A decade before, the household consisted of mother, father, two sons, one daughter and a live-in uncle all in the four roomed house on Copenhagen Street (number 16) where they lived for many years, their neighbours being a chemist/druggist and a commercial traveller. Joseph married in 1906 and by 1912 was living at 8 Gill Street in Burnley, the couple later having two children.

16 Copenhagen Street in 2015

Joseph himself had entered the cotton industry as an apprentice shuttle-maker, suggesting a short school education, and continued in the joinery department in the mill.

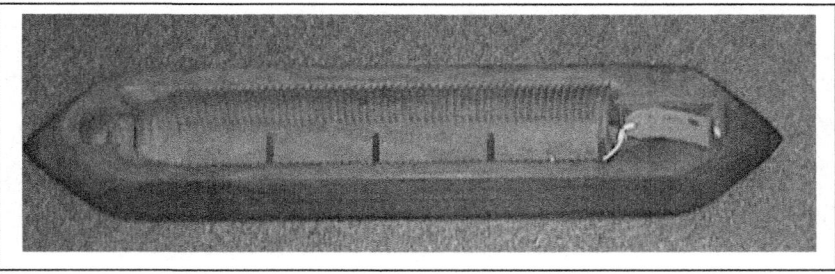

Wooden shuttle (The Local History Centre, Touchstones)

He did well in his later studies as an adult and passed examinations in Politics and Social Problems in 1907 as part of the University Extension programme under Horsburgh. In addition he gained a Waller Scholarship (1908-09) under the Education Guild, presented lectures in the town and at Castleton Literary and Scientific Society on 'The Manorial System' and attended a Summer School at the University of Oxford under the auspices of the Guild in 1908.

Joseph died at his home in Ennerdale Road in Nelson on November 10th 1952.

Stanley Dawson

Stanley Dawson's father ran a small letterpress printing company and it appears that he decided to – or was persuaded to - take the same career path from an early age. Born in 1890, by the age of 11 Stanley was living in a six roomed house with grandparents, an aunt, parents and a brother – seven in all. The family stayed at the same house – 323 Halifax Road - for more than twenty years with – in 1901 - a clogger living to one side and a dental assistant to the other. In the census return of the same year Stanley is recorded as working from home, his mother by that time missing from the record, and in 1911 Stanley was a letterpress printer in his own right, still a single man and living in the first floor front bedroom at the same address which he also used as a study. In 1914 Stanley married and in 1935 was living at 286 Halifax Road, not far from the house of his childhood.

Outside of his substantial educational and occupational activities, Stanley was a Methodist lay-preacher and conducted many baptisms, marriages and funeral, one baptism recorded in 1920 at Shawclough United Free Methodist Church and several others in a number of chapels in the town through the 1930's and 1940's. He was called upon to officiate at the funeral of Arthur Collinge in 1936.

Stanley appears to have done well in his studies with the WEA and in other classes, gaining a Pass in 1908 in a course on Imperial Rome with Hudson Shaw.

Later in his life Stanley moved to Cumbria and died in Ulverston in 1971 aged 81. His son John, with his wife Margaret became curators of the Ruskin Museum at Coniston and James Spates (2012) wrote of Stanley's son that he was 'a *giant* of the Ruskin world'. John Dawson himself died in 2011, still a great advocate of Ruskin and of the kind of socialism that his father felt and represented with the WEA almost a century before.

John Dawson (curator of the Ruskin Museum), son of Stanley Dawson, with his wife Margaret

Riley Duckworth

Born in Rochdale in 1881, Riley had no connection that can be found to the Duckworth family which owned the large grocery chain in the town. Riley's father was a cotton warper, a semi-skilled job earning about 27/- per week (Wood 1910) and the 1881 census reveals that his mother also worked in the mill as a cotton winder (13/- per week for women) although by 1901 she was no longer employed. The three lived with an aunt at the four-roomed house at 7 Walkers Place, their neighbours being a tailor's presser, woollen weavers and spinners. Riley also worked in the cotton industry as a card room worker at the age of 20 in 1901, at that time still living at the same address as his mother, a sister and his aunt although his father had now died.

Cotton Spinners in Rochdale circa 1900 (The Local History Centre, Touchstones)

Riley Duckworth was another of the tutorial class to be active as a member at Clover Street Unitarian Church and in 1902 was elected as Secretary of the Young Men's Social Union and then, recorded in the Monthly Messenger (the Unitarian magazine) the church representative on the town's Housing Reform Council.

Riley is mentioned briefly in a letter from Mansbridge to Tawney although there is no context either positive or negative, Mansbridge claiming 'not to be aware' of this student.

By 1911, his mother and aunt had died and Riley was living at 4 Leftkiln Street off Spotland Road. He was still in the cotton industry, now working as a cotton spinner/corder. There are records of his brief continuation as part of the Rochdale Education Guild in 1911 but this association faded in the following years.

Amy Fozard

Being a woman in the tutorial class was not as straightforward as it might be today. Amy Fozard was one of four such women who generally were expected to be in the home as supportive wives or family members, not learning about the economics and politics of the world ! Amy was a member of the Clover Street Unitarian Church and a Sunday School teacher there for many years (always referred to as 'Miss Fozard' even in her mid 30's). Her father was also active in the church, presenting a lecture in November 1903 (Monthly Messenger 1903) on 'Sanitation and Sanitary Reform,' indicating the bridge between social and faith issues at that church, but also applying knowledge from his own trade.

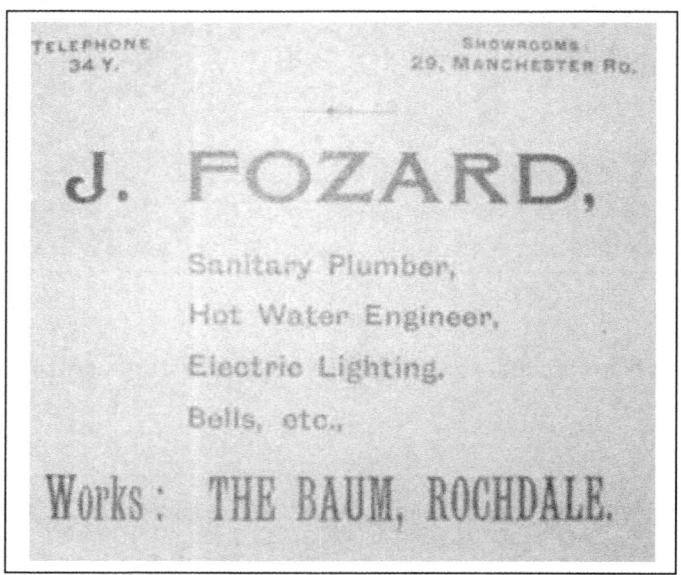

Advertisement from Rochdale Education Guild handbook 1909 (The Local History Centre, Touchstones)

Born in Southport in March 1882, she was the daughter of a plumber, living at 63 Molyneaux Street, a grocer and a cotton operative living on either side of them. The Fozard family lived in this four-roomed house, Amy sharing it with mother, father, three sisters and three brothers (one named Merlin !) all the boys following their father into the plumbing business. By 1901 the family had moved to 316 Entwistle Road with neighbours working as cotton waste dealers and another plumber. The Fozard family lived next door but one to Fred Hall (see below) and Amy was employed but at home, working as a dressmaker - an occupational descriptor for so many women at that time which hides more than it reveals in the arduousness of the task, women often working 14-hour days in taking-in seamstress work. By 1911 the Fozards had moved to the six-roomed 27 Manchester Road where Amy remained as housekeeper for her aging mother and father.

Amy did quite well educationally, receiving a scholarship in 1908-09 from the wife of the Secretary, Mrs L V Gill, and being selected to go on the German tour with the WEA group. She played a part in the WEA in other ways by acting as Rochdale distributor for The Highway, the Association magazine. A Unitarian all her life, by 1935 she was living at 20 Sheriff Street.

Amy died in December 1965 aged 83.

Frederick Greenwood

Another Clover Street Unitarian, Fred Greenwood was born in 1870 and throughout the early years of the 20th century was living, with wife and young daughter at his father-in-law's house – his father in law being a retired clogger - at Watch Hall Cottages, a 5 roomed house in Smallbridge. Before that he grew up with his parents at 34 Sheriff Street next door to a housekeeper and a dealer in cotton waste.

In 1909 Fred was sponsored for one of 8 travelling studentships by the Guild Society to go on the Rochdale Educational Guild's trip to Germany. Following the WEA tutorial class, Frederick remained active in the adult education of the town, presenting lantern slides on fine art subjects such as his Winter lecture on 'Turner' and on 'Oliver Cromwell' at St John's School Smallbridge in 1909. By 1910 he was lecturing again with lantern slides on 'Turner and his Pictures' for the Milnrow Education Guild.

Occupationally, by 1911, Frederick diversified slightly throughout his life, being a picture/art dealer and later a maker of picture frames. At that time he was living at 5 St Mary's Gate, his business at the same address under 'Greenwood and Co.'

Shops on St Mary's Gate 1920 (The Local History Centre, Touchstones)

George Edward Greenwood

Not a great deal in known about George Edward Greenwood except that, born in 1890, he lived at 12 Moss Street, on either side of the family house were workers in the cotton industry. From the 1901 census returns, it seems that George's father was working as a machine fitter in an iron works and the family had 4 sons and a daughter.

George was married in 1915 and died, at the early age of 43 in 1933.

George Greenwood's house on Moss Street in 2015

Fred Hall

If anyone encapsulates the link between religion, Co-operation and education it was Fred Hall. Born in 1879, the son of a foreman iron moulder who was also a noted co-operator, Fred lived for the first twenty years of his life at 31 Sheriff Street, his next door neighbours being an unemployed widow living with her dressmaking daughters on one side and a greengrocer on the other. Fred lived at this address with his mother, father and paternal grandmother but later was joined by a sister who took in dressmaking work at home.

Falinge Park Opening Parade in Sheriff Street 1906 (The Local History Centre, Touchstones)
(Fred Hall lived in the distant terraced row)

At the age of 13 in 1892 Fred was working as an office boy in the mill of John Bright and Brothers which suggests that he left school after the elementary phase, and thereafter was employed as a clerk in the same office. Fred seems to have been uncertain as to his career in the early years as he changed job regularly, working at Watergrove Raising and Printing Co of Wardle where he was Assistant manager and then as a secretary/traveller and subsequently manager for North British Eyelet Company. He also worked for a time as a tourist agency clerk. Quite early on, however, he was involved in adult educational provision, the second meeting of the Rochdale Education Guild (May 25th 1905) recording that a 'Mr F Hall was present'.

Fred Hall (1879-1938) (Workers Educational Association)

In 1907 not only was Fred married to another Clover Street member – Miss Ada Novello Briggs, a grand-daughter of one of the original Rochdale Pioneers, James Manock - but he was attending University Extension lectures initially in Littleborough and then in Rochdale. At the same time, now a qualified teacher having secured a teachers Diploma from the London Chamber of Commerce, he taught book-keeping and business methods at Rochdale Technical School whilst contributing in the evenings to the Rochdale Education Guild with talks on 'The Church and Social Questions,' 'The Sunday School and Social Reform,' 'Education and Social Reform' and 'Robert Owen.'

By 1908, the year of the tutorial class, Fred won the Shuttleworth Prize from Manchester University as part of his B.Com degree course. At the time he was still living in Rochdale, writing to Albert Mansbridge from 72 Park Road Heybrook and 3 years later living at 312 Entwistle Road. In addition to his academic achievements, Fred Hall was exceptionally active at Clover Street Unitarian Church, not only being a Sunday School teacher there and then Superintendent, but also lecturing at the church on amongst other things 'Cornwall as a Holiday District' (admission 3d) in 1907 and lead lecturer for the town's Ruskin Hall programme. The following two years saw Fred Hall not only as a student with the WEA but also lecturing for working men and women in Norden on 'Charles Kingsley' and in the same year for the Guild on his two favourite subjects, 'Economics' and 'Rochdale and Co-operation'.

Fred Hall was eager to add to his list of qualifications and after gaining a B. Com from Manchester University in 1908 he took and passed an MA (Hons) in Economics in 1910. In the same year, Fred bowed out of the Rochdale Education Guild's work in order to take a Principal Lecturer post at Belfast Municipal Technical Institute. The Guild's minutes at the time regretfully recorded that they would miss his help and guidance with the Summer classes and, similarly, the Clover Street Monthly Messenger suggested that 'no-one at any time has taken a keener interest in the Church and the

School' (Monthly Messenger April 1910). He was, however, still invited to make a contribution to the organisation of the Guild because in April he was minuted in a disagreement with Charlie Pearce (see below) about the fees that they should be charging for University Extension classes, Fred feeling that the cost to the working man should be reduced. Although not taking as active a part in lecturing for the Guild, he was in 1910 nominated for the Guild Council and continued to act, with T H Butterworth, as auditor for Rochdale's WEA classes.

By 1912 Fred Hall had been 'raised to Professorial rank' (Monthly Messenger 1912) and in the same year had written 'A Handbook for Commercial Teachers.' He later became an Advisor of Studies to the Co-operative Union but the high point of Fred Hall's career came with his appointment as Principal of Holyoake College – the Co-operative College – in the centre of Manchester. Fred Hall's great passion was Co-operation and not only did he prove himself a great leader and manager of education for the Co-operative movement but also wrote books such as 'Co-operation' (1937) with A P Watkins in which he mapped the social and economic history of the Co-operative Society as well as its roots in Christian Socialism. Nor did he lose touch with his old church, returning in June 1915 to declare the Clover Street Unitarian carnival open and in October of the same year acting as Honorary President of the Church Football Club, although given his roles in the Co-operative movement he could hardly have been closely associated with it.

As head of the Co-operative College, Fred Hall not only achieved great distinction in office but also a degree of wealth that enabled him to purchase, in 1931, Bamford Hall in Rochdale on the death of its then owner, Alderman David Healey. Fred Hall occupied the Hall, which, during the Second World War, was used as a military hospital. Sadly, the building has since been demolished.

Bamford Hall (The Local History Centre, Touchstones)

Fred Hall died at his Bamford Hall home in 1938 after a short illness and on returning from lecturing in Exeter. He was mentioned as 'Professor Fred Hall' with affection at Tawney's reunion in the town in 1939 and is buried at Rochdale cemetery.

James Henighan

From very poor beginnings, James Henighan certainly made a mark on the town – and, it seems on Tawney and Mansbridge too. Born in 1883, James spent the earliest years of his life up to 1891 in a lodging house at 44 Lord Street Rochdale which he shared with 16 others – most of them older people - plumbers, weavers and labourers, James being the nephew of Mary Barman, the lodging-house keeper. By 1901 he had moved to 29 Brunswick Street, his neighbours being carpenters and weavers, where his brother in law (a clogger) was the head of household. Nine people lived at the address at that time, the census records showing that James was not in paid employment. Some years later in 1908, and according to letters written by Henighan to Mansbridge, he was then living at 23 Norreys Street, having married.

Back gardens on Brunswick St circa 1920 (The Local History Centre, Touchstones)

James appears to have been particularly active in the Rochdale Education Guild in the years between 1907 and 1910 not to mention catholic in his interests. In 1907 for example he was presenting Guild lectures on 'Thomas Hardy,' 'Vanity Fair' and 'Papers on Socialism' and in 1908 (the year of his studies with the WEA) he gave a talk on 'Balzac and the French Novel.' In 1910 the Guild minutes record that he was lecturing at Heywood on 'A Critical View of Socialism,' and in Rochdale on 'The King's Speech,' 'Oscar Wilde' and again in the Summer on 'Adam Smith.'

Henighan was persuaded by Mansbridge to write an article for a journal edited by Tawney and his name appears in Justice (September 1908) referring to him as 'comrade' Henighan, also having a letter (with W M Humphreys) published in the same periodical although the editors of the journal mis-spelled his name as 'J Henighar.' This was followed by a further letter in the next month's edition of October 1908. A report on Henighan's talk in Rochdale entitled 'Constructive Socialism' was reported in this journal having drawn 120 members of an audience. So, as with a number of the first tutorial class, there seems to have been a fine dividing line (or none at all) between being a man lecturing to working people and the same man as student. Not only was he presenting talks to large groups in the town on a range of subjects, but he was also passing Horsburgh's examination in 'Political and Social Problems' in 1907 with the tutor's comments 'Good and organised ideas'. In 1908 he received a distinction for his work on 'English Novelists' and a Pass in the course on 'Imperial Rome.' He presented two lectures during the Winter season of 1907-08 and earned scholarships in the same year (awarded by Gordon Harvey MP), a Guild scholarship to the German tour in 1908-09, and was nominated for the Guild Council in April 1910.

James Henighan died at the age of 52 on 17th June 1935 having lived the last years of his life at 61 Belfield Mill Lane. There were no column inches given over to a specific obituary at the time of his death as was common in the Rochdale Observer for those having had lives of some social stature. Instead, there was simply a note in the 'Acknowledgements' column to the effect that he had died.

Henighan's cottage on Bellfield Mill Lane in 2015

Charles Hewitt

Although making little impact in the tutorial class – he gained no scholarships, nor did he draw any comment from Tawney about his work – Charles Hewitt's local mark was made eight years later during the Great War. Hewitt was born in 1882 and lived in Shawclough Road (initially at number 417 and then at 379) in an artisan neighbourhood in which shoemakers, textile machine makers and weavers were neighbours. Charles was the son of an office clerk and lived in their Healey home with his two sisters and an older brother, sharing four rooms. His older brother was a cotton weft carrier bringing home an average wage of 17/- per week. By 1901 times were hard with the mother having died, the father and Charles without work. By 1911 however, Charles Hewitt was married, living at 2 Healey Dell in Rochdale and working as a warehouseman.

Charles Hewitt's cottage on Shawclough Road in 2015

A nonconformist chapel-goer, he believed passionately that his faith stood in the way of active service in the Great War and he felt principled enough about the issue to be elected as President, in 1916, of Rochdale's Branch of the No-Conscription Fellowship from which platform he was charged with being absent from service, in other words deserting under the Military Service Act, and was arrested, saying to the police who came to his door 'I was expecting you.' The No-Conscription Fellowship, founded in November 1914 by Clifford Allen and Fenner Brockway, stood as 'an organisation of men likely to be called upon to undertake military service in the event of conscription, who will refuse from conscientious motives to bear arms, because they consider human life to be sacred' (Kramer 2015 p30) and it seemed that the North West of England was an important centre for No-Conscription, with branches in most Lancashire towns.

Hewitt's objection was reported in the Rochdale Observer on 22nd July 1916 following his Tribunal hearing held on 21st July. Aged 34, Hewitt was described as a 'warehouseman on finished cotton goods' and President of the Rochdale branch of Fellowship of Reconciliation and the article goes on to say that he put his argument to the Tribunal that in reflecting upon his own conscience he refused to obey a military dictat, did not believe in militarism at all and that he would not have his killing done by proxy, thereby rejecting a Pelham Committee adjudication to find work for him 'of importance' to the war effort. Hewitt, at all hearings did not deny his 'absenteeism' and was therefore admitting, through his arguments, to his moral and political objection to conscription.

Lowerfield Methodist Church (The Local History Centre, Touchstones)

Under questioning, he informed the court that he had had to resign from Castlemere and Lowerfold United Methodist Churches because of their attitude to the war, Castlemere Methodists having supported the war from the beginning, their Reverend C.B. Johnson calling for calm and urging his congregation to 'trust the government'. This, Charles Hewitt would not do, both on religious and political grounds. His appeal was dismissed and so went to County Court where it was dismissed again. In September of the same year he was arrested for a second time, tried in Rochdale and fined forty shillings but later court martialled and sentenced to 28 days hard labour at Wormwood Scrubs prison after which, in November 1916 he was taken to Wakefield Work Centre under the Home Office Scheme of the Brace Committee where he would be 'exceptionally employed' usually working on power looms in a converted, disused prison.

Conscientious Objectors from Huddersfield at Wakefield Prison 1918

To give an idea of his standing in the community, he claimed at his appeal to be a member of the ILP, the UDC (the Union of Democratic Control, concerned about the lack of democratic accountability in the making of British foreign policy), the No-Conscription Fellowship and the Independent Order of Rechabites (the temperance movement). From these platforms he claimed absolute exemption, saying that he would 'rather be in prison with single boys suffering for conscience' than fighting, and went on to proclaim that 'we have no quarrel with working Germans and I could not take their lives.' Charles said that he was sorry to oppose his fellow townspeople but that his was an act of conscience.

Charles Hewitt's was not an unusual case and police harassment was often targeted at ILP cardholders and members of other organisations who distributed leaflets against the war and conscription.

Charles Herbert Hilton

Charles Hilton, often referred to as Herbert Hilton, was born in Halifax in 1877 and lived for some years a fleeting life, moving from place to place with his father who was originally from Rochdale and a carpet weaver. In 1891 Charles was living at 64 Habberley Road in Kidderminster with two brothers and a sister, working for some time as a shop assistant which suggests that his education had been curtailed at the end of the elementary phase. By 1901 he was part of his father's carpet weaving business and the family back in Rochdale at 11 Millford Street with neighbours who were weavers and pawnbrokers. Charles' sister was a music teacher and they took in a boarder at that address which was now housing seven people. In 1911, the father was still head of the carpet weaving business (along with Charles and James, see below) but the mother had died in October 1905 and they now lived with a nephew at a new address : 6 Great Lee, a four-roomed house in Thrum Hall Lane, Shawclough.

Educationally Charles did well, passing University Extension examinations in 'English Novelists' in 1908 and earning a scholarship (from an anonymous donor) in the same year to the Oxford Summer School. As with so many of these students, he was also active in lecturing and was recorded as presenting a session on 'Hamlet' to an audience in Milnrow in 1909.

Charles Hilton was a member of the Clover Street Unitarian church and was Committee member and then Joint Secretary of the Young Men's Social Union in 1904 as well as a Sunday School teacher from around 1907. Charles (Herbert) Hilton was enlisted in the Great War in the Royal Garrison Artillery and attended the tutorial class reunion in 1939.

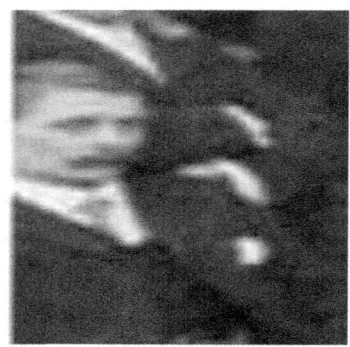

James Edmund Hilton

The brother of Charles (above), James was born in Rochdale in 1879 and experienced the same changes of address, moving from 64 Habberley Rd in Kidderminster in 1891 to 11 Millford Street Rochdale in 1901. It seems that the Hilton family expected their sons to follow their father (originally from Rochdale) in the carpet weaving business and when old enough, certainly by 1901, James had joined the business as a weaver in his own right. As was the case with the rest of the family, he was a member of the Clover Street Unitarian Church and served there as Joint Secretary (with his brother Charles) for the Young Men's Social Union in 1904. James was also on the Committee of the Rochdale Educational Guild from 1906.

James married on May 23rd 1907 at the Blackwater Street Unitarian Chapel but there are no records as to where he subsequently moved in order to set up his own family. He did, however, travel as one of the WEA students to Germany in 1909 and in October of that year shared his experiences with the Shawclough Institute with an 'Impressions of Germany' presentation for the Education Guild. He was also a regular at the Ruskin Hall lecture class for many years.

Ethel Kershaw

Born in 1883 in Rochdale, Ethel was the sister of Harold Kershaw (see below) and lived with her brother through their early years at 41 Free Trade Street and then at 30 Stanley Street, within walking distance of the town centre, where they were neighbours to a book-keeper and a glass cutter. Ethel's father was an iron turner and the family was large with six children (three boys and three girls). By the beginning of the 20th century, the family had moved to 7 Boundary Street, a five-roomed house where they lived for at least another ten years although by 1935 Ethel was living at 3 Falinge Road.

Ethel worked first as an elementary school teacher perhaps attending one of the teacher training classes 'preparatory for the Queens Scholarship and teachers Certificate examination' which were available in Rochdale (Rochdale Spectator 1880) and must have impressed in her chosen profession as by 1911 she was appointed to a Head Teacher post in Heywood, her father by that time working as a brass engraver. Ethel was still single and living at home.

As to her own education, Ethel was active and successful, gaining a Pass in Powys' course on 'English Novelists' in 1908 and being awarded a scholarship to travel with the Rochdale Education Guild group to Germany in 1909. By 1910 she was working within the Guild, being nominated for the Guild Council.

(Workers Educational Association)

Harold Kershaw

Born in 1887, Harold was recorded in the 1891 census as living at 41 Free Trade Street, closest neighbours at that time being gardeners and cotton dyers. Eight of the family lived in this four roomed house, two of the children already working in the cotton industry, the father, an iron turner. By 1901 they were living at 7 Boundary Street, Ethel (see above) now a teacher and one of his brothers a clerk, Harold was apprenticed to a firm of joiners. This suggests that he left school at the conclusion of the elementary stage. By 1911 his father was working as a brass engraver, sister Ethel by now a Head Teacher in Heywood and another sister a librarian. The suggestion here is of a family in which knowledge, learning and career aspirations were of some importance. By 1915 Harold was no longer at the home address.

Harold, it would seem, whilst being a talented woodworker, was an excellent student of politics and economics and following the tutorial class in 1909, Albert Mansbridge arranged for him to receive a residential scholarship for Ruskin College, Oxford – the first of the Rochdale tutorial group to achieve this (Brooks 2000 p72). Furthermore Harold was one of the Ruskin strikers of 1909 and, on his return

Ruskin College strikers 1909 (Workers Educational Association)
(Harold Kershaw centre carrying the chest)

from Oxford in the same year, was personally responsible for setting up a branch of the Central Labour College (the CLC) in Rochdale as a Marxist alternative to the WEA. Craik (1964 p92) writes that Harold's rejection of the WEA was the result of 'arguments some of us had with him in his early weeks at Ruskin.' By 1909, Harold was writing pieces for The Plebs magazine, the organ of The Central Labour College which taught and campaigned for direct action and whilst taking its general philosophy from Marx, took its voice from such activists as Noah Ablett (1912) who felt that 'the working class should enter the educational world to work out its own problems for itself' and advocated and agitated for the inevitability of class conflict.

The Central Labour College study class was, it seems, thriving in Rochdale under Harold and was able to draw into the town such radical educators as Charlie Gibbons (1881-1967) to lecture with him on Industrial History, Economics and Philosophy. In 1911 at the second national meeting of The Plebs, Harold reported (*Plebs Magazine,* 3, 1911) that one hundred and fifty students were attending classes in Rochdale, that classes were held seven times a week from October to April and a course of twenty one study lectures with the Labour College cost five shillings. It is clear from this article that Harold Kershaw and his local associates were successful in disseminating their Marxist-inspired message as classes, following the ones in Rochdale, were soon set up in Bury, Waterfoot and Oldham. The group became known as the Rochdale and District Classes which suggests that Harold was at the centre of the management of a number of thriving districts.

Harold was married to Eliza Anne Schofield in 1911 and by 1917, with wife and daughter Annie, then five years old, living at Springfield Cottage, 147 Belfield Road. At that address an attempt was made to enrol him into the armed services but he stood vehemently against it. It appears to have been a highly politicised household, as his wife was a member of the suffragette organisation, the Women's Social and Political Union, and the Rochdale branch often had meetings (and tea) at their house. Harold was 30 years old at the time of conscription and working as a joiner for Parker and Calvert's furniture makers. At a Tribunal held in Heywood, the company appealed, on his behalf, against his call-up on occupational grounds. The session was empowered to grant conditional individual exemptions but Kershaw went further and appealed on 'personal' conscientious grounds as well and these were refused although he was given leave to appeal against their decision.

Describing himself as non-sectarian and a Socialist, Harold's appeal was heard at the Police Court in Rochdale on 21st March of 1917 but before that, the authorities had issued a final notice of conscription to him on the 8th of the same month. His next court appearance was in April where he is reported by the Rochdale Observer to have said that 'to slaughter his fellow man was revolting to his feelings,' and 'it pays people to have war, so they have war.' He was sorry for those being killed and he was 'not prepared to share their fate, but I am opposed to those that cause it.' When asked who the responsible parties were, Kershaw replied 'Those people who control affairs.'

He was found guilty of 'disobeying a lawful command given by his superior officer' and sentenced to 6 months imprisonment with hard labour at Wormwood Scrubs. Thereafter he received a court martial at Hull for 'disobedience and going AWOL' and under the Home Office scheme was sent to Dartmoor Prison in July 1917.

Conscientious Objectors at Dartmoor Prison 1917 (The Peace Pledge Union)

Within eight months, Harold had escaped from Dartmoor but was re-arrested by the civil police in Rochdale in March 1918. Thereafter Harold was committed to employment 'of national importance' for conscientious objectors under the Bruce Committee until his discharge on demobilisation in March of 1920.

Albert Mansbridge, in his published statements, mentions Harold Kershaw as a particular loss to the WEA and recognised him as a 'good student and socialist' but regretted him setting up a more radical alternative to the educational classes offered by the WEA.

Harold attended the reunion of the tutorial group in 1939.

Eugene Kiernan

Born in Rochdale in 1886 Eugene's father was a printer's compositor. Initially living at 1 Crown Street – a two-roomed back-to-back cottage near to the town centre – the family moved by 1901, to 274 Dover Street, a four roomed house, by that time the household consisting of parents, brother and three sisters. Their neighbours included a shop manager, a grocer and the next three consecutive houses cotton spinners each one of them earning around 30 shillings per week. The fact that in that year the mother was now head of household suggests his father's early death. The mother is recorded as having no occupation outside of the household and so Eugene's fate was to go into the cotton mill at an early age as a machine minder.

Kiernan's house on Dover Street in 2015

By 1908, the time of the tutorial class, Eugene was married and had a young daughter. Eugene's wife, Bertha Kiernan was a member of the Rochdale branch of the Women's Social and Political Union and was involved in the mass demonstration for women's vote in London in 1909 (Working Class Movement Library, Salford). Throughout his life Eugene remained a worker in the cotton industry, for some time as a cop packer, a low-paid job in the mill.

There are no records of his achievements in the class, nor is there evidence of his continuation – in an official capacity – with the Rochdale Education Guild. In 1935, Eugene was living at 31 Bellshill Crescent between Smallbridge and Firgrove.

Livsey Lees

One of the physical attributes of Livsey Lees – mentioned by Tawney at the 1939 Rochdale reunion of the class – was his size, being over six feet tall which was unusual for men in the early 20th century. Born the son of a ginger beer merchant in 1878, Livsey lived with his parents and two sisters at numbers 29 and then number 11 Ipswich Street with neighbours including a machinist and a cotton overlooker whose wife, a Mrs Nuttall, was a staunch and committed suffragette and a member of the Rochdale Women's Social and Political Union.

Ipswich Street in 1968 (Dr Geoffrey Walker Collection, Link4Life)

The Lees family lived at this address in Rochdale up until 1891, at some point later moving to 6 St Luke Street, a three roomed house near to the town centre. By then, Livsey's father had died and his mother, working as a woollen weaver, was head of a household which had an extra step-daughter and a lodger living with them, no doubt so that they could make ends meet.

Towards the end of the 19th century, Livsey was employed as a cotton warper, a job bringing home about 15/- to 18/- per week (Wood 1910) and one of his sisters was a dressmaker. A decade later in 1911, the family – including Livsey – was still at St Luke's Street but by that time he had risen to become manager of a Labour Exchange, a post he had taken up in the January of that year. Previously he had been a registration clerk in the Rochdale office but then became manager of

Heywood Labour Exchange sub-office where he was their first manager in October 1910. The Rochdale Observer celebrated his taking on the same role in Rochdale (Rochdale Observer 11th January 1911) and suggested that Livsey was an exceptionally energetic worker in that he had doubled the size of Heywood Labour Exchange and made good connections with local employers and trades unions. (Ernest Thornton, the Labour MP for Farnworth in the 1950's, suggested to me by letter that 'several of the original WEA students were appointed to manage new Labour Exchanges which had recently been set up').

A Labour Exchange met a much-needed role in the town as there had been short time working in the cotton industry from as early as 1902. In 1904 the local Board of Guardians in Rochdale opened a Labour Bureau in Baillie Street to help those without work and there was increasing pressure on policy makers to make this a national support system. Interestingly, Tawney presented a lecture in Rochdale in March of 1908 with the title 'Labour Exchanges or Bureaus ?' which suggested that change was in the air, albeit contested. However it was not until 1910 that Labour Exchanges were opened under the Insurance Acts and Livsey Lees must have been one of the first managers to take up a post in such an institution in the exchange on Moore Street. The Rochdale Observer article (ibid) described him as a manager who did not simply register the unemployed but was active in finding them work, a role commonplace now but clearly seen as noteworthy and perhaps liberal in 1911.

Educationally, there is no record of Livsey's academic achievements although he must have impressed enough to secure the post that he did. A staunch trades unionist all his life, Livsey was at the Tawney reunion in 1939 at which their old tutor remembered that he used to cross swords in the tutorial class with Livsey Lees about half-time working, Lees claiming that he'd grown to 6 feet in spite of it ! Whilst there was much laughter from the old boys at this, it did suggest that Livsey Lees, along with others in the group, had been subjected to child labour in this way.

Benjamin Lord

Born in Bury in the year 1864, Benjamin Lord was probably one of the oldest of the students in the class. 1871 finds him living at 50 Buckley Walk in Bury, his father being a mechanical engineer and a niece living in the family home. By 1881 the family home was at 32 Manchester Old Road in Bury, the niece no longer with them and Benjamin a pupil teacher. His mother at that time was a shopkeeper.

Benjamin was affiliate representative from 1905 to the Rochdale Educational Guild on behalf of the Lowerfold, Shawclough and Healey Institute which was a literary and scientific education group. He made contributions to the Rochdale Education Guild's diary of lectures, in 1907 presenting sessions on 'Good Literature', 'Relics of Paganism' 'Shakespeare,' 'Laissez faire' and 'Primitive Man.' Benjamin was also part of a Guild deputation to St Edward's Men's Class to look at that church's proposals for new adult classes and as such, must have been entrusted to make effective decisions on behalf of the Guild.

Benjamin married Sarah Stevenson, a woman from Rochdale in 1888 and they moved to Dellar Street, Spotland for a short time before moving again to Grantham Place in Halifax from where he worked as a teacher at the Grammar School in Warley near to Sowerby Bridge in Yorkshire. At that address, it seemed that Benjamin had a career change because in 1901, now with a wife, three sons and three daughters, he is recorded in the census as being a chartered accountant. The six children were also recorded in the next census of 1911 but not his wife. He had, in the year previously, returned to education, securing a headmaster's post at Oxenhope Horkinstone Council School, a small village school of roughly 85 children in what is now West Yorkshire, Benjamin taking 30 children in the 1st and 2nd classes, Standards IV to VII, which represented the higher standards at this level. He was at this time living at Syke House and then at Rock Lea, a spacious nine-roomed house very close to the school.

Horkinstone School, Yorkshire in 2015

Benjamin continued as headmaster at the school until 1919 but temporarily broke away from this role in October 1915 to report to Skipton for military service in the Great War although by that time he was 51 years of age and therefore over the age for conscription. No doubt after being given some brief role in war service, he resumed his teaching duties on May 1st 1916.

As far as Benjamin's educational achievements were concerned, it is recorded in the minutes of the Rochdale Education Guild that he achieved a Certificate of Satisfaction for the lecture programme on 'Imperial Rome' in 1908, one of Hudson Shaw's lecture programmes. On his departure from Rochdale in 1909 the Guild's minutes recorded that he had done a great deal for the Guild and particularly for the Shawclough Institute where he had organised and presented a number of Winter talks, one in the 1909 series on 'The Yellow Peril'. The Guild wished him well in taking charge of the school near Oxenhope.

Benjamin Lord died in the town of his birth, Bury in 1934 aged 70.

Joseph Nuttall

When interviewed in 1986 about the WEA tutorial class, Ernest Thornton, a former Labour MP and Mayor of Rochdale, was quick to point out the diminutive figure of Joseph Nuttall in the photograph, claiming that Joe had known Tawney very well, although he had never been one of the star students in the class.

Born in Littleborough in 1872, Joe's father was a cotton weaver on a wage of 15/- per week and brought up his son as an only child in their four-roomed house at 364 Oldham Road which remained Joe's home for many years. From an early age Joe found work in the mills, suggesting that his schooling had been curtailed at the earliest possible date due to either his abilities or his family needs. He worked in the cotton mill but as a joiner, making shuttles, benches and cabinets and there became a strong advocate of trade unionism amongst the workforce. His father had died by 1901 and though Joe was now married, he, his wife and a two year old daughter remained, with his mother, at the family house on Oldham Road. By 1911 Joe and his wife were childless, their infant daughter having died in 1903.

Ernest Thornton, the former Labour MP for Farnworth, was a close friend of Joe and recounts a visit with him to London where they had a meal with Tawney at Mecklenburgh Square, the eminent economist greeting him at the door with 'My dear Joey !' and warmly embracing him. Although confined to her bed due to sickness Mrs Tawney expressed a wish to see Joe on that occasion, which suggests, yet again, the close relationships which must have existed between students and tutor.

Joe continued to work as a joiner throughout his life but at some point after 1911 he and his wife moved to 127 Summit in Littleborough and then on to 64 Mitchell Street near to the town centre. He died in his 80's but no records exist of his academic achievements.

Mitchell Street 1905 (top of photograph) (The Local History Centre, Touchstones)

Charles Herbert Pearce

Bertha Radcliffe, whose family had been close to the WEA, sent a letter to me in the 1980's with details of her father and mother's political allegiances, pointing out that in the early years of the 20th century they had both been socialists and frequently held SDF meetings at their house off Spotland Road. Charlie Pearce, she said, was always there.

Charlie was born in 1877 in Withington and from an early age lived at 11 Heron Street, Manchester. His father was a carter and he lived at that address with his parents, sister and aunt at least until 1891 although ten years later he had moved to Rochdale and was head of his own household at 3 Brearley Street where he lived with his wife and cousin. His neighbours at that time were velvet weavers and engineers. By 1908, they had moved further down the street to number 11, a four-roomed house where they stayed for the remainder of their time whilst in the town. In those years, Charlie worked as a machine packer in an ironworks and was something of a promising amateur footballer although he gave it up when the chance came to attend the tutorial class.

Pearce did well educationally in the WEA and other classes, and this must have been recognised by the organisers because in 1908 he was elected to the Guild's Executive Committee and in 1908-09 he was receiving a grant as a Guild Executive to go to Germany on a fact-finding educational tour. He continued this prominence in Guild meetings - in April 23rd 1910 suggesting that University Extension lectures were costing too much for the worker student. Thereafter Charlie Pearce was active with 1909 Winter lectures at the Castleton 'Lit and Sci' on the subject of 'Germany and Municipal Government' and in the same year at Milnrow Parish Church Debating Society with 'Some Aspects of German Social Life.' By 1911 he had become an executive member of the Rochdale Education Guild.

Later in the same year, Charlie had made enough of an impact with the Guild and with the national Association to secure the post of Manchester District Organising Secretary of the WEA, moving to a four-roomed house at 72 Broom Avenue, Levenshulme just outside Manchester to manage tutorial groups and lecture events for that area. At the time, his wife was working as a cotton ring-spinner which was a low-paid job in the mill, fetching approximately 12/- per week (Wood 1910). They had one child, another having died.

Pearce's time as a WEA organiser was not without issue. In a letter of reply to Tawney on December 22nd 1913 he made political complaint against matters that had arisen within the Association, something being a 'rotten business' to do with a claim for money as he writes 'I remember when I had to survive on £1 a week ! Phew what a struggle it was !' Further aspects of the letter suggest that this concerned a strike that was taking place nationally and a dispute over scab labour. Pearce claimed that he had been engaged in a long talk with Hookway (the successor to Gill as Rochdale Education Guild Secretary) and writes 'were it not for having the WEA at heart nothing would unseal my lips. Since August, Hookway has done ten times more in the same direction than Gill did in his natural life and Gill was asked to resign by Albert Mansbridge.' Speculatively this is a criticism of Hookway's views on this industrial dispute, perhaps because of his sympathies with scab labour, and Charlie took exception to it.

A second letter to Tawney on 18th April 1913 suggested that he had felt a personal slight at not being invited to a 'Mansbridge dinner' in London and wrote that, for some reason, this flew in the face of WEA principles, Charlie complaining that the (invited) speakers had done nothing to contribute to the WEA (unlike himself) – and these included Philip Snowdon who was invited ! Charlie writes that others saw him as 'a regrettable necessity to the WEA' and he felt strongly enough to comment that he 'should have left the Association' when he had the chance. 'I'm not going to be snubbed and sat on quietly,' he continued, and 'if Mansbridge desires the WEA to be a middle class institution then I am against it and have done with it forever !' The suggestion here is that the 'Mansbridge dinner' was by invitation only to acceptable (middle class) types – unlike Pearce, or so he thought. Charlie clearly had strong opinions but also, it appears, something of a victim complex when it came to the WEA hierarchy. On the other hand, he might have been right ! And yet contrary to this minor spat, he appeared to be close to Tawney and his family, in one of his letters confessing ill-health to his former tutor but then adding 'Don't mention it to Annie' who was Tawney's wife Jeanette, familiarity in using such a name suggestive of close personal terms.

By 1935 Charlie Pearce was back in Rochdale, living at 455 Manchester Road and attended the Tawney reunion in 1939. He died in Littleborough in March 1950.

Leonard Plant

Very little was recorded about Leonard Plant. With a father who was a retired iron monger, Leonard appears to have followed a similar career path by becoming a blacksmith and living near to the town centre at 66 Entwistle Road as one of the boarders in that house, later moving to 103 Rugby Road.

Alley behind Entwistle Road (The Local History Centre, Touchstones)

Leonard was involved with the Education Guild for some time following the tutorial class, presenting, in December of 1910, lectures about the humanist, political scientist and Bloomsbury Group member 'G. Lowes Dickinson.' Plant was also one of the three Honorary Secretaries of the Education Guild.

Either he must have been close to Tawney or had sufficient room in his house at the time because in 1919, when Tawney stood for election as the town's MP, he stayed at Leonard Plant's house the night before the announcement of the results of the ballot. This memory was mentioned at the reunion in 1939 at which Leonard was present along with Tawney and members of the original class.

T W Price

As one the historians of the WEA, Thomas W Price had been close to both the organisation and the experience of worker education in Rochdale from its earliest days. Not only was he a founder member of the tutorial class but he was also a student in a number of others, passing the examination in 'Political and Social Problems' with Horsburgh in 1907 and in the same year gaining a distinction in 'Shakespeare's Historical Plays' with J C Powys. Price also a scholarship winner from the Oxford University Extension programme and attended the Summer School in the same year, an account of his experiences then being printed as a leaflet and distributed at Guild meetings (Rochdale Education Guild minutes 26th September 1907). In 1908 he passed the examination on 'English Novelists' as well as 'Imperial Rome' with Hudson Shaw and once again received a WEA grant to go to the Summer School at Oxford, this time along with his wife, who received a 'Pioneers Scholarship' in order to attend. As with so many of these students, he was lecturing in the town and in 1908 could be found delivering one of the Winter Talks on 'The Future of Religion' for the Guild and there were also memories recorded by Mansbridge himself of Tom Price teaching Sociology and Economics in various venues across Rochdale.

In terms of his wider career in education, he was no less ambitious, resigning from the Rochdale Education Guild in October 1908 in order to become District Manager of the WEA for the Midlands and some years later – in 1913 - becoming General Secretary of the Association in Albert Mansbridge's absence. Following what was described as stalwart work alongside Mansbridge at WEA headquarters he went on to become Warden at Holybrook House in Reading, the place, of course, where the WEA had its first District.

Born in 1887, Thomas Price moved to Rochdale in his teens and lived for many years at a four-roomed terraced house at 20 Leyton Street in Rochdale his paid work being as a warehouseman in a bleaching and dyeing company.

Price's house on Leyton Street in 2015

Price was an archetypal and involved student with the WEA, being both a member of the SDF in the town as well as running the Reading Circle at Clover Street Unitarian Church, on its General Purposes Committee and Secretary to its Sunday School Committee. Price was delivering lectures at the Unitarian church as early as 1902 on 'Sociology', 'Psychology' and 'The Story of the Earth' but his Clover Street activities were not limited to academic matters, for example he was responsible for scenery and lighting for the 1901 church pantomime, Robinson Crusoe. By 1905 he was an Executive Member of the Rochdale Education Guild, a post which he held until he moved away from the town.

T W Price (Workers Educational Association)

Apart from his studentship and his management responsibilities with the WEA, Tom was also key to policy change in the Association, writing many influential pieces for The Highway in February, April and July of 1909 and then again in February 1910.

Following his rise within the WEA, it fell to T W Price to write in 1924, what Goldman (in Roberts 2003 p46) considers to be the best of the histories of the WEA.

T W Price was mentioned but not present at the reunion in 1939.

Eleanor Redshaw

One of the four women in the tutorial class, Eleanor Redshaw was born in 1883 and christened at St Chad's Anglican Church in Rochdale in May of that year. She lived in a three-roomed house at 68 Durham Street and in 1901 had neighbours whose head of household was a boiler inspector and a music teacher. Eleanor stayed at this address for two decades. Her father was a mechanic/spinner in the cotton mills and by the age of eight she was living with four brothers and two sisters the eldest of whom was already employed in a nearby factory. By 1901 however, the father's name is not to be found on the census, the mother now being head of household and the eighteen year old Eleanor in employment as a cotton weaver, which suggests her leaving school at the earliest age possible in order to earn a living to support the family. Depending on the number of looms the operator ran, this could be quite a well paid job, bringing home for a woman 26/- per week (Wood 1910).

By 1911 the family may have been struggling to make ends meet as the mother (now 70 years old) was still going out to work as a furniture dealer. However, over the years Eleanor must have attended vocational courses in the evenings as she had secured a post as a book-keeper in a textile engineer's company. Single, in 1911 she was still living at home with her mother, an aunt and a 'visitor.'

Eleanor died in Littleborough in 1970.

The Redshaw family in the 1890's with Eleanor (front left) and older sister Annie (top right) who married Joseph Wormald (see below)

Arthur Shore

The son of a stone mason, Arthur Shore was born in 1876 and was brought up in a four-roomed house at 2 Market Street, Healey. Arthur's immediate neighbours at that time were a flannel manufacturer and a family of cotton weavers. In 1881 the household consisted of mother and father plus two sons and two daughters but by 1891 an aunt had moved in with them. Later, the family was to have six children, most of them working in the textile industry although one of them was a pupil teacher. Arthur – still only 15 years of age - was a cotton weaver earning up to 26/- per week although that depended on him operating multiple looms. At some point towards the end of the century, the family moved to 94 Todmorden Road in Littleborough but by 1912 Arthur was living back in town at 288 Yorkshire Street.

Arthur was another student who took advantage of the University Extension courses, receiving a Pass (satisfactory) in 'Imperial Rome' with Hudson Shaw but thereafter in the Winter Talks of 1909 could be found lecturing to a group in Rochdale on 'The English Reformation' and 'Martin Luther' at the Bagslate Wesley Guild, at the Shawclough Institute on 'St Francis of Assissi,' but then on 'The American Revolution' at the Trinity Wesleyan Brotherhood in 1911.

An Anglican and an active member of St Mary's Men's Club in 1908 through to 1910, he was also an ILP member and presided over the branch in Littleborough. It was minuted in the records of the Rochdale Education Guild that he had been nominated for Guild Council along with James Henighan, James Hilton and Ethel Kershaw.

St Mary's Church, Balderstone (The Local History Centre, Touchstones)

Walter Ernest Stopford

There were a small number of silk processing mills in Rochdale in the early years of the 20th century and Walter Stopford's father worked in one of them as a silk dresser, preparing the raw material for weaving. Born in 1879, Walter was baptised at St Albans (Anglican) Church in Rochdale in June of the same year, the family living at 6 Napier Street Castleton with neighbours who were both in textiles, to one side a cotton machinery mechanic and to the other, another family of silk dressers and weavers. Soon the family moved to 311 Manchester Road between Castleton and Rochdale, by then the family having five children, Walter being the youngest.

1891 saw Walter following his father into the silk processing industry as a silk doffer, basically replacing bobbins in the weaving process, and was possibly employed at the Castleton Silk Mill which would have been conveniently close to their home. By now, in the same year, the family had seven children and most of them worked in silk although the 1901 census records that the mother was then head of household which suggests the death of the father. By 1901 Walter had left textile manufacturing as had other children from the family who were working in allied industries such as calico weaving. Walter took up a post as a case-maker in an iron works but his career path was to change radically soon after.

Walter was married at St Albans Church in Rochdale in July 1906 to Ethel Schofield Oldham but the marriage was short-lived as Ethel, at the age of 34, died in Milnrow in 1913. He re-married in the 1920's and the Stopfords had one son.

After the Great War, Walter trained as an Anglican priest and is first recorded as such at St John's Church in Bigrigg, Cumberland (now Cumbria) where he appears to have deputised for the ailing vicar of the new church there in 1923. The local newspaper has him presiding over a large congregation and being congratulated for his 'untiring energy and splendid powers of organisation' in making a success of their recent 'sale of work'. Reverend Stopford acknowledged the compliment and said that he too was surprised at the results of their endeavours, interestingly commenting about the church organ that 'he hoped he would be able to return to Bigrigg to see and hear it in the near future' confirming that his ministerial role there was a temporary one.

His own more permanent ministry, however, was at Cundall with Norton-le-Clay in the Diocese of Ripon, North Yorkshire which he held from 1931 to 1936. Thereafter, he was the vicar at All Saints Church, Pickhill again in North Yorkshire, a rural village where most of his parishioners were farm hands, farm labourers and minor gentry, there being no aristocracy in the immediate area. Walter was at Pickhill until 1944 and according to local archives made his first entry in the church log book in June 9th 1936. At the same time as his ministry at Pickhill, he was supervising the work of the senior class at the local school which had 62 pupils, the eldest being 14 years old. From January 1937 Walter seems to have been involved in the life of both the church and the school, supervising the General Examinations and County Scholarship Examinations throughout his time as vicar and regularly taking the whole school until 9.30am for their religious service and then 'signing off' the attendance registers. His wife also deputised for absent staff at the school. At Easter, Christmas, the Flower Service and 'Education Sunday' the whole school attended church for morning service and evensong with Reverend Stopford officiating. It is recorded that the vicar was also in the chair for the annual Christmas prize giving, followed by the school play 'in front of a large and appreciative audience'.

All Saints Church at Pickhill in 2015

Walter appears to have been in demand as records in the parish show that on 23rd March 1939 Walter congratulated the teachers and scholars for their 'brilliant performance' in the Swaledale singing tournament. In the same year a group of visitors, mostly from St Aidan's Church and one of whom was his sister Mary, travelled from Rochdale to see Walter at his church at Pickhill.
During the Second World War, over 100 evacuee children came to stay at the village from Sunderland and Gateshead and Walter was involved in their safe accommodation. On a more mundane note, the state of the church and school drains from the urinals and yard was a constant

worry throughout Walter's time and he was active in the supervision of their re-design, rodding and eventual replacement.

Records suggest that Reverend Stopford was involved in a disagreement about 'The Pickhill 24' which was a group of local gentry who had inherited, from as far back as the 16th century, a trust of money, land and property in the area. Evidently the incumbents in the 1930's had not been keeping transparent records of affairs and Stopford raised this contentious local issue, eventually stepping in to re-define the rules and set himself, as vicar, in the chair in perpetuity of the Pickhill 24. Stopford also revised the running of this group, making it more accountable and democratic.

Reverend W E Stopford, was at the reunion with Tawney in 1939 at which he said that his old tutor's breadth of outlook had helped him enormously in his clerical career.

He died aged 88 in December 1967 in Scarborough but is buried in Pickhill All Saints churchyard.

Fanny Taylor

Given the place of women in society in the early years of the 20th century it is no surprise that there is little recorded about Fanny Taylor and she is described by Price, not purposely but rather dismissively to modern sensibilities, as a 'working man's wife.' She did, however present lectures in the town usually on literary subjects. One such was a presentation for Ben Lord on 'Mrs Gaskell' at the Shawclough Institute in 1909 and a year later at Bagslate Wesley Guild she gave talks on '18th and 19th century Poets.'

Fanny Taylor (Workers Educational Association)

In the previous year she had been offered a scholarship from the WEA itself and went on the tour of German towns as a consequence. In 1912 Fanny was living at 200 Milkstone Road but in 1935 was at 10 Redcar Street.

Bagslate Wesleyan Church circa 1906 (The Local History Centre, Touchstones)

Frederick Turner

The son of a postman, Fred Turner was born in Rochdale and lived throughout his childhood at 204 Ashfield Road, sharing the four-roomed house with mother, father, two brothers and two sisters. By 1901 Fred was in employment as a commercial clerk and the family moved to 34 Ventnor Street, the father by this time having died.

Ashfield Road 1914 (The Local History Centre, Touchstones)

Fred seems to have done reasonably well for himself, having married and had one child by 1907 and was working as a clerk and then a manager in the furniture trade. Eventually the family moved to a six-roomed house at 204 Broad Lane, Milnrow.

There is no record of Fred's academic achievements either at or following the tutorial class of which he was a member, nor did he continue to contribute to the work of the Rochdale Education Guild.

A P Wadsworth

Alfred Powell Wadsworth perhaps went on to have most illustrious career, alongside that of Fred Hall (see above), of all the students from the original tutorial class. Born on May 26th 1891 in the short row of houses on Heights Lane, Alfred was the son of a tailor's foreman and attended Cronkeyshaw Day School before winning a scholarship to the Higher Grade School in Rochdale at a time when they were awarded to fewer than five out of one hundred pupils (Maclure 1970 p85). Often pupils were entered as fee-payers, in Rochdale the fee being 6d per week.

His mother had been forced to leave school at the age of seven to go into the cotton mill but his paternal grandfather was a successful tailor, a profession followed by Alfred's father who made both Sunday suits for foremen and riding coats for the Rochdale Hunt (John Rylands Library : Ref 147/3/2a). By 1901 his father had risen to the rank of master tailor with a shop at 58 Whitworth Road and was an employer in his own right, the family seeming to be set to meet all of its aspirations. However, the father's heavy drinking financially restricted his children's chances of going

Wadsworth's house on Heights Lane in 2015

to university, so instead his family hoped that Alfred would go into the Congregational Church, coming as they did from nonconformist and radical stock (ibid).

By the turn of the 20th century the family – now with two sons – was living at 55 Syke Road with immediate neighbours whose head of household was a post office clerk and a paper merchant and it would have been at that time that he became interested both in journalism (he submitted his first literary articles to the Rochdale Observer when he was 15 years old) and in the next year – 1907 – in education, gaining an examination distinction for 'Shakespeare's Historical Plays' and another distinction in Horsburgh's course on 'Political and Social Problems'.

A year later, Wadsworth gained a Pass in the course on 'English Novelists' with J C Powys and at the same time – a familiar story by now – he was acting not simply as a student, but also contributing to the Rochdale Education Guild's lecture programme with a Winter Talk in 1908 on 'Lancashire Folklore.' Wadsworth's first attendance at a meeting of the Rochdale Education Guild was on December 30th 1907 but thereafter he took an increasingly active part in their proceedings. In 1909 Wadsworth received one of eight travelling studentships to Germany under the auspices of the Guild, for whom he was now chair of the Committee for 'Societies for Popular Education' and Joint Secretary overall. By 1910 he was lecturing on the Guild's Saturday Evening Papers Programme on the subject of 'Robert Blatchford,' the contemporary Socialist.

By 1911 the family had increased in size and had moved to the larger, six-roomed house at 54 Syke Road. His career in journalism then began as a trainee with the Rochdale Observer under the

Wadsworth's house at 54 Syke Road in 2015

editorship of W H Hadley (a friend of the family) for which newspaper he wrote and edited 'Notes and Queries,' focusing on local history and folklore and then increasingly contributing pieces concerning the industrial history of the town. Following his time at the Observer, he joined the staff at the Manchester Guardian in 1917, being asked initially to submit a piece on Edwin Waugh the Rochdale dialect poet, but soon after that he was hired permanently. He worked there through the 1920's as foreign correspondent and – most notably – their Labour correspondent, covering the hard times of labour unrest in the 1920's.

In 1922 A P Wadsworth was married to Alice Ormerod at Union Street Wesleyan Methodist Church and nine years later they had a daughter, Janet.

On the death of W P Crozier in 1944, Wadsworth took over the editorship of the Manchester Guardian although in a letter from 'EJ' it was noted that he 'never a thruster' but had 'a brain like a needle' (from John Rylands Library : Ref 147/3/13a). All agreed, however, that he turned out to be a great Guardian editor, sometimes writing nearly all of the leaders himself, it being a post he held until 1956. Furthermore he was a modernising and reforming editor (the front page given over to news rather than classified advertisements) whilst maintaining the liberal principles of C P Scott, and he was a successful one too with circulation doubling during his time in post.

**A P Wadsworth by Low (Manchester Libraries,
Information and Archives, Manchester City Council)**

On his retirement in 1956 some praised him as being one of the 'Great men of the North' and having 'wisdom without dogmatism, awareness without arrogance and tolerance without sentimentalism' (Manchester Guardian 31/10/56). A J P Taylor wrote affectionately about him as a family man (he met him one day pushing his pram around Manchester whilst loudly pontificating about the international scene) and on a political note Pendeninis from The Observer wrote that he kept the Labour Party on the rails through the critical post-war years (ibid). Hugh Gaitskell recalled Wadsworth's former links with Tawney and the WEA, claiming that as an industrial correspondent and an editor he had a clear understanding of the labour movement due to the WEA experiences of his early years.

Wadsworth also contributed to the history of the region, writing (with J de Lacy Mann) 'The Cotton Trade and Industrial Lancashire' in 1932, and (with R S Fitton) posthumously publishing 'The Strutts and the Arkwrights 1758-1830' in 1958.

A year before his retirement, Manchester University conferred an Honorary LLD on him for his services to politics, history and literature. Wadsworth suffered a short, what he called a 'confounded illness' during which time he wrote to Donald Tyerman of the economist (John Rylands Library : Ref 149/T19/4) that he could not 'keep up my attempt to carry on the paper from my bed,' and a month later died on the 4th November 1956. At the time he had been living at 30 Old Broadway, Withington in Manchester.

It was clear from the outpouring of public and professional affection that he was well-loved and there were many tributes paid to him in the Manchester Guardian and other publications. R H Tawney spoke at a memorial service at St Dunstan-in-the-West Church on Fleet Street, remembering that in 1908 they had called him Alfie, the youngest of the WEA tutorial class. Tawney recalled :

> 'a precocious youth of 17 in the original tutorial class.... with impish sallies backed by batteries of recondite information which ensured that at the Saturday gatherings, everyone stayed awake !' (John Rylands Library : Ref 149/T19/4)

And Tawney in referring to Wadsworth, might also have been characterising the tutorial class as a whole and their Rochdale spirit with :

> 'they had their source not in the classroom but in …. an enlightened pig-headedness absorbed from the complex of prejudices, habits, mental attitudes, style of life, work and thought native to the region in which their early years had passed.' (ibid)

He concluded that Wadsworth had a 'blend of kindliness, remorseless realism and sardonic humour' that made him such a great man and a great journalist.

Wadsworth's daughter went on to work as an Education Officer for Granada Television and a commemorative sundial hangs on the south wall of St Anne's church in the village of Over Haddon in remembrance of a community involvement which would have delighted her father. In his will, Wadsworth left almost £1000 between his daughter Janet and The Manchester Guardian.

Alfred Wilkinson

In a letter to Tawney, Albert Mansbridge wrote that he was anxious to support Alfred Wilkinson's standing in an election to become a Labour councillor for the town, pointing out that 'he is actually a workman student.' And indeed Alfred did become a Labour Councillor for Rochdale from 1908 during which time he served on the Art Gallery and Museum Committee, the Paving Sewering and Scavenging Committee and the Tramways Committee. During his period in office, he was vociferous in his defence of Corporation employee pay.

Not much can be gleaned from the educational records on Alfred however, apart from the fact that he was present at Guild meetings from July 1906 onwards and was a scholarship winner in 1907-08. His occupational choices took him along the same lines as Livsey Lees and in fact, after some years as a registration clerk at Heywood Labour Exchange, took over from Lees as the manager there when Lees went on to manage the office in Rochdale.

Rochdale Town Hall square circa 1908 (The Local History Centre, Touchstones)

Albert E Wilson

Born in 1879, Albert Wilson lived throughout his early years at 37 Isabella Street, by 1881 having two brothers and a sister. In 1901 they were at the same address and had a carpet weaver and a cotton carder as his neighbours, Albert's father working as an iron moulder.

Iron Moulders and Pattern Makers circa 1910 (St Joseph's Church, Bonnybridge)

In the same year, the census records suggest that the family – father still iron moulding – had moved to 108 Joy Street in Rochdale but by now they had increased in number more than somewhat – to twelve children !

Albert, followed his father's trade and was, himself, an iron moulder from such an early age as to suggest him having left school at the end of elementary education. The family had moved on by 1911, Albert Wilson by then having married and living with wife and one daughter in a four-roomed house at 3 Bentley Street, where he remained until at least 1915.

Albert Wilson's house on Bentley Street in 2015

There are no records of Albert's academic achievement, nor of his continued work with the Rochdale Education Guild.

Joseph Wormald

The son of an iron turner, Joseph Wormald was born in 1879 and lived at Hare Street, Rochdale his nearest neighbours being a labourer, another iron turner and a blacksmith. Joseph lived there with his parents, three brothers and two sisters. A decade later, however, the family were at 4 Bedford Street, a cotton operative and a blacksmith as neighbours in their terraced street. His father was still an iron turner but by now Joseph only had one brother in the house, one sister and a live-in cousin.

In 1909 Joseph married Annie Redshaw, the sister of Eleanor Redshaw (see above) and in 1911 they lived in a four roomed house in Castleton at 54 Alexander Street, an address at which they remained at least until 1935. Joseph, like his father, became an iron turner or machinist but was employed as such in the textile industry.

In the affiliation records for the Rochdale Education Guild in 1908 Joseph's name is recorded under the Providence Congregational Young men's Class, being an important member of that chapel for many years.

Joseph died in September 1935.

Providence Congregational Church 1910 (The Local History Centre, Touchstones)

As organisers of the Rochdale Education Guild, L V Gill and A E Carter were key to making and sustaining links with the universities and with the WEA itself, and because of the importance of their involvement, sketches of each of them are presented here alongside those of the students.

Lawrence Vincent Gill

Lawrence Gill was not much older than many of the students in the tutorial class and younger than some. Born in Sheffield in 1875, he came to Rochdale in his late teens and by 1891 was living at 42 Charlotte Street with one neighbour who was an ornamental engraver and another, a house painter. They lived as a family of five, Lawrence having a brother and a sister. Gill's father was the manager/cutler of a spring/knife works, no doubt a profession he carried over from his years in Sheffield. Lawrence, however, had settled upon a career in education and in 1891 (aged 16) was a student teacher at a local Board School. Four years later the family had moved to a five-roomed house at 68 Syke Road where the Gills would live for many years.

Gill's house on Syke Road in 2015

1901 saw Lawrence as an assistant schoolmaster but by then with a wife and young child of his own. Gill resigned his teaching post in January 1909 in order to devote his time to the organisation of the Rochdale WEA District as the Education Guild. Alongside his management responsibilities, Lawrence Gill also lectured, 1907 seeing him giving various talks on 'Education and Life', 'Keats, 'Thackeray', 'Tennyson' 'The Mercantile System' and 'Robert Owen.' Of particular interest is the fact that in 1909 Gill also presented lectures for St Mary's Men's Class on 'The Worker's Educational Ideal' and for the Castleton Literary and Scientific Society, perhaps a publicity event, on 'The Work of the Education Guild.'

It was generally felt by Mansbridge, Tawney and Temple that Gill had been personally responsible for many of the advances with both the tutorial class and with the University Extension lecture programme as he seems to have been an excellent organiser and publicist. He also recruited associates effectively within the Guild and was joined in his role as manager and administrator in 1910 by Charlie Pearce (see above). Administration was not, however, Gill's only strength. He submitted numerous articles and letters to The Highway, the house magazine for the WEA, one of which, in January 1910, included a poem by Thomas Hardy :

> As pensive I have paced with loitering feet
> And gazed on Oxford's glorious grey and green,
> One presence I have felt in every scene,
> One shadowy figure have I seemed to meet
> In every ivied court or ancient street
> Wearing a worker's garments soiled and mean.
> And though his form obscure has never been
> Here in the flesh, yet have I felt the beat,
> Attuned to mine, of his torn heart, the fret
> And fever of the lifelong, hopeless strife
> 'twixt sense and soul, the yearning of the mind
> Unsatisfied, vain flutterings in the net
> Woven round his steps by Fate, relentless, blind ;
> This, too, I felt – to struggle, that was Life.

The effect of this poem on a working class student can be imagined - similarly struggling, sometimes wondering about the despair of his or her condition, but at the same time moving forward in hopes for self and for society. And no doubt Gill's experience in Rochdale and with his WEA colleagues was a catalyst for such a sentiment.

Gill's family continued to live in the house on Syke Road up to at least 1911 and by that year Gill – and from about 1906 – was not only the Organising Secretary for the WEA in the town but was the first North West District Joint Secretary along with H O Meredith. 1911 found him still in Rochdale with wife, two daughters and a live-in servant but soon after, according to Jennings (2002 p92), he moved to London to take up a post as Central Organising Secretary for the WEA with a salary of £250 per annum. Tom Price notes (1924 p44) that Gill's health had impelled him to leave Lancashire for London, Hookway taking his place as Organiser/Secretary for the North West District. However, in 1913 Gill resigned from the WEA to 'take up another post' (unspecified by Price : ibid).

Gill was not present at Tawney's reunion in 1939 but wrote affectionately to the gathering from his home in the Isle of Man.

Alec Every Carter

Born 1877, Alec Carter's father was a Unitarian minister in Rochdale, an important organiser of adult education in the town and Assistant Secretary for Elementary Education in Lancashire. They were a family of five sons and one daughter with two servants living in the town at 117 Hartley Street in 1881. Ten years later Alec was a pupil teacher, living with his family at 9 Summer Castle, his father now having retired from the ministry. Alec had three brothers and two sisters although in 1901 his home was at 'Cloverdale' where he lived with his one brother, two sisters, a cook and a housemaid. By then, all the remaining sons and daughters were working in education.

Alec himself taught first in an elementary school and then in a Higher Grade School in Rochdale. He continued to teach throughout his life in schools but also in adult education, taking his turn as lecturer on the Rochdale 'circuit', for example at St John's School in 1909 on the subject of 'Queen Elizabeth I.'

In 1911 he was still single, living at the two-roomed bungalow in Littleborough from where he enlisted into the Royal Army Medical Corps in November 1915.

He died in Lewes in April 1963.

Occupations and social class

Whilst focusing on the occupations of the tutorial class students it might be useful to consider to what extent these students were, in fact, workers. An early cohort profile provides a purely descriptive account in the Reports on Tutorial Classes (WEA 1909 p108) and suggests that the Rochdale class consisted of three groups : skilled artisans, unskilled labour and white collar professionals such as teachers, journalists, salesmen or public sector managers.

But it is as a class member himself that Tom Price (1908) is, perhaps, the most reliable guide as to what the members of the first cohort did occupationally, and he offered some supplementary detail in that respect, claiming that the youngest was 17 (A P Wadsworth), the oldest 57 years of age, and that 70% of them were between 21 and 35. This would have meant that many of them were amongst the first generation to benefit from the Education Act of 1870 and – if they had the opportunities provided by family support, the availability of resources, and the ability - they could have progressed from elementary education to Higher Grade school and potentially entered one of the middle class professions. As has been seen within the student sketches however, not all families were financially in a position to do this and the majority left school before Standard VI or at the end of the elementary phase, limiting their occupational horizons.

Accounting for their working status, Price writes that of those enrolled in the class (although this number is disputed and has ranged from 35 to 43), 12 were iron workers (8 skilled, 4 unskilled) and 3 were joiners. He (1924) goes on to say that :

> 'all the chief branches of the cotton industry were represented : spinning, bleaching, weaving and finishing. There were 2 carpet-weavers, a wool-sorter, a spindle-maker, a shuttle-maker, a printer, a house painter, a picture-framer, an accountant's clerk, a cashier, a teacher, 2 journalists and an insurance agent. Of the ladies, there was one clerk, one dressmaker, one a school mistress and one a working man's wife' (ibid p5).

With the benefit of census and other records we are in a position to put some names to these occupational groups. In the class were 12 iron workers, 8 skilled amongst whom were McLean, Leonard Plant and Albert Wilson, and 4 unskilled including Pearce and Stopford, 3 joiners who would have been Harold Kershaw, Joe Nuttall and Joseph Cryer. Price records the presence of cotton workers, amongst whom were spinners, weavers, bleachers and finishers and those would have included Price himself, Arthur Shore, Riley Duckworth, Charles Hewitt, Eugene Kiernan and Joe Binns. The 2 carpet weavers would have been Charles and James Hilton, the housepainter Arthur Collinge, the picture-framer Frederick Greenwood, the accountant's clerk Harold Briggs, the cashier -

either Frederick Turner or Alfred Wilkinson, the teacher - Benjamin Lord, the 2 journalists – these would have been Stanley Dawson and Alfred Wadsworth and the 'insurance agent', possibly Livsey Lees. Of the lady students, one was a clerk – Eleanor Redshaw, Amy Fozard was a dressmaker, one was a schoolmistress - Ethel Kershaw, and the fourth, a working man's wife' would have been Fanny Taylor.

A glance at the second tutorial cohort in Rochdale (1909-10) shows that it constituted a similar occupational spread and serves to confirm the 'worker' credentials of both groups. This second cohort which assembled on April 12th 1909, consisted of 8 shop assistants, 9 clerks, 9 textile workers, 5 metal workers, 1 each of farm workers, painters, medical botanists, leather workers and a labourer. According to the Oxford University Delegacy (1910 p24) the shop assistants who were present seem to have sacrificed their one free evening to attend the second programme and – as with the first class - many were committed to voluntary activities with churches, chapels, trades unions, Trades Council and the Co-operative Movement. This second tutorial class included the Secretary of the Cotton Spinning Mutual Improvement Society, the Secretary and Treasurer of the Field Naturalists Society, 8 Trades Union officials and a number of Sunday School workers. The majority of the cohort was young and there were no women. Gott (1990 p4) suggests that 75% of the first two tutorial classes in the town were made up of what he terms working men and women.

Further light, by comparison, can be shed on the Rochdale class by looking at the occupational make-up of the first cohort from Longton in Staffordshire which was meeting at the same time. Lawrence Goldman (in Roberts 2003 p46) writing about that particular Potteries group, maintains that they had both middle and working class students within their number and therefore perhaps represented more proportionately the spread of students which would characterise the WEA of the future. A Report on the Tutorial Classes (1909 p105) suggested that the Longton class consisted of 40 students amongst whom was a gardener, plumber, potter's thrower, basket-maker, miner, mechanic, baker, several clerks, librarian, grocer, miller's agent, railway agent, clothier, insurance collectors and elementary school teachers.

A separate but affirming impression of the working status of the 1908 class in Rochdale came from the inspectorate. The Report on Tutorial Classes for the Board of Education submitted by HMI Headlam and Professor Hobhouse in 1909, concluded that the members of the classes were largely working men 'with a sprinkling of teachers, clerks and commercial travellers' and that 'the women were, in the main, teachers' which was inaccurate and somewhat dismissively labelling. Similarly in 1910, the President of the Board of Education, Mr Pease, described the Rochdale students from that particular cohort as 'progressive working men' the first adjective here suggesting again a section of the working population in a position to be aspirational as opposed to groups of more socially compliant working men and women.

Whilst it would seem that the first Rochdale class was indeed comprised primarily of skilled artisans, unskilled labour and aspirant white collar workers, social class identification is problematical in a sense recognised in the Board of Education's 'Reports of Lecturers' (1908) in that some lower middle class 'professionals' who attended classes such as clerks, in actuality earned less than many of the artisans and therefore may have lived in the poorest circumstances in the town. A similar point is made by Mansbridge and Temple in the First Report of the Tutorial Classes Committee in 1909 when they write that there was a high concentration of manual workers in addition to which there were clerks and teachers, but whilst the clerks and shop assistants enrolled and were not 'usually classified as workpeople,' the majority of them still 'belonged to working class families.' They did, however, have certain advantages, Mansbridge suggesting (1913 p101) that office workers were in a better position than many in being able to get away from work and being paid a week or sometimes a fortnight's holiday money. This enabled them to prepare for sessions, write essays and attend Summer schools without the demands of piece-work, officious clocking-in or the pressures of physically exhausting work.

Rochdale had a view on stratification however, which came to light in an interesting minute following a Guild meeting of March 1910 in which it was recorded that although scholarships were available for class members to go to the Oxford Summer School that year, these awards were restricted to artisan applicants only, teachers being ineligible. The Guild's direction of travel is clear from this in terms of their notion of 'worker' affiliation but would have been somewhat in conflict with the national (WEA) directive for open entry to a tutorial class or for a scholarship which represented a more socially liberal and inclusive position. Others still however, would have seen the WEA's directive as conciliation towards middle class students and applauded the Rochdale stance.

Analyses of the WEA student body by social class have been carried out on a number of occasions over the years since the first tutorial group. Constable notes that by 1914 of 3035 students, 21% were clerks, 10% teachers, 5% shop assistants, 8% women working at home and 42% employed in skilled manual labour (in Parry 1920 p188). This suggests a healthy proportion of bona fide working class students. However by 1924 their proportion of the whole was judged to have declined nationally and an occupational breakdown of West Midlands WEA students which took place two decades after the first tutorial class in 1928 recorded that 30% of them had been teachers, 10% fitters and turners, 18% clerks, 19% postal and telegraph workers and 21% housewives. Styler (1953) captures this continuing shift in worker participation nationally by recording that their numbers declined from 32% in 1938-9 to 25% in 1944-5, to 20% in 1947-8 although he suggests that this not only included regional variation but differences in the engagement of manual workers from town to town. Generally though, the picture is clear and by the 1950's only 10% of WEA students were classified as workers, their earlier high numbers being replaced by those from white collar occupations, much to Tawney's critical regret (Doyle 2003 p47).

It could be claimed therefore that the earliest classes, both in Rochdale and Longton and, one would presume in other industrial towns, was primarily working class and it is fitting to note that Tawney affectionately called the original Rochdale class his 'weavers' (Pedley 1974) which was slightly erroneous but once more suggestive of the class students' approximate place in the occupational spectrum. A distinction must be made, however, between the skilled and semi-skilled artisans represented here in some numbers and the manual labourers who were less in evidence. Perhaps these were the 'real' workers. Fred Hall, responding to Mansbridge's request for feedback on their early tutorial classes makes interesting reading in this regard with his comment that members of the 'manual labouring classes' had joined them (interesting and indicative also that he uses the word 'them'), and that they were the ones that had often been most reluctant to engage with education, yet were in the greatest need of it. This comment implies a degree of involvement from workers other than the 'genteel' working class, and that the opportunity was being grasped by those whose cultural life was not normally attuned to learning.

Taking issue with this, Foster (1977) claims that organisations such as the WEA had, indeed, been the preserve of the 'labour aristocracy' and set this sub-class apart from those he dismissively sees as participating in 'the public house culture.' Whilst it is dangerous to make too definitive a cultural distinction, to some extent this is confirmed with the Rochdale WEA students through their wider cultural interests, where they lived and particularly in their active connection to the chapel. Rusoff (in Roberts 2003 p61) bearing this out, writes that in comparison with the poorer strata of society, the worker students in Rochdale who attended the tutorial classes were of a status akin to those artisans that Thompson (1991) felt constituted the backbone of 19th century reform and whom Garrard notes as the ones developing the abilities to organise trade associations (1983 p132).

The artisans' occupational skill-set and their strategic position in local decision-making afforded them a prestige and leverage denied to those of the working class whose interests lay elsewhere or were too exhausted by physical labour to be 'citizen participants.' The point which Thompson makes is apposite here in that there was a tendency for self- and mutual-improvement groups to arise from a particular sub-section of the working population, one which might be described as artisan or 'genteel' and which repeatedly took advantage of their occupational prestige. Projecting this onto the tutorial class, a historical connection shines out when one looks at the occupations of the first group of Co-operators in Toad Lane Rochdale, the original Pioneers of 1844, and the WEA tutorial group with its same artisanal cotton operatives, skilled joiners and iron workers.

Styler (1953) develops a different theory, suggesting that success in the educational recruitment of those from within the manual working classes may have depended to some extent on the size of the settlement, maintaining that more students from lower status social groups were recruited in smaller (under 10,000) as opposed to larger towns. A similar point is made by Thompson regarding the prevalence of radicalism in smaller settlements and this may have been a function of the ease of communication across tight and well-managed networks that could be found in tight geographical areas which made it possible to publicise widely and to target students effectively, thereby to control recruitment. This certainly characterises the efficient management and organisation of Gill and Carter at the Education Guild in Rochdale. Furthermore, ease of communication through chapel meetings and newsletters would have further maintained the homogeneity of student groups.

Values and beliefs

Jennings' overview (in Roberts 2003 p21) of WEA tutorial classes, including the one in Rochdale, maintains that each cohort would have had its own distinct character and make-up in terms of social class, political belief and religious faith and he writes of the Rochdale class of 1908 that it had an inclusive nature, taking an all-party rather than a non-party stance, although it becomes evident on close reading of the records and reports that, in terms of party membership, the class consisted mostly of committed socialists from the ILP and the SDF to the exclusion of those outwardly affiliating to the Conservative or Liberal parties. Given the tenor of the time it seems clear that these student allegiances were representative of political grassroots feeling and reflected the crest of a left-leaning, reformist wave. A local article quoting Tawney bears this out when he claims that over half of the class belonged to socialist organisations, the others being trades unionists (Rochdale Times March 1908).
M. Riboud a French visitor to the class in 1910, similarly found most of the Rochdale students to be socialist and revealingly adds the comment that 'the contrary could only be surprising,' once more suggesting the prevalence of this political sentiment. Certainly, given open recruitment and the existing mood of political change, the tutorial class in Rochdale or Longton would have been attractive to political radicals or reformers. This is interesting not least because one of the tenets of the WEA, and certainly one that Mansbridge held particularly dear within his Christian Socialist

liberalism, was that the Association should maintain its political neutrality. A non-partisan stipulation on access did not, however, signify non-partisan entrants and the innovative and participatory nature of this experiment would have appealed to those seeing it as challenging the established orthodoxies of, for example, University Extension. Its form may not have been socialist but its principles were communitarian and open.

Riboud adds a twist to this however, that whilst 'there had not been modifications of political ideas' due to class attendance, the students had, through the course of study with Tawney, come to realise a naivety inherent in their own opinions. The implication here is that strong, broad-brush political positions which had been held initially by the students were tested if not weakened over the course of the programme :

> 'All those with whom I spoke expressed regret that they formerly allowed themselves to form opinions too hastily and to make speeches too readily. They have acquitted precise knowledge, they have grasped the importance of fundamental facts, they have accustomed themselves to discuss theories and they have realised, as one of them said, that there are two sides to every question, even the fiscal question.' (ibid)

This critical reflection on preconceived ideas may have been the result of Tawney's skills as a teacher in having them consider alternatives, getting them, during discussion, to posit negative theoretical positions to ones already held, playing devil's advocate or even, as critics such as Craik (1964) or Millar (1979) maintained, challenging them with his own representations of establishment and quasi-socialist views. What is clear is that the political perspectives held by the class on coming onto the programme initially adhered to the political left and although the complexion of the talks and lectures around the town came from lecturers holding a range of beliefs (Horsburgh to one side Hudson Shaw to the other), the presiding spirit was socialist.

However, it is important to ask not only what sort of socialism was taken into the class but what, if socialism at all, was taken away from it. The fact that such large numbers came from the nonconformist churches suggests a predilection for reform but one set within boundaries marked by socially-acceptable constraint. Not for the Clover Street Unitarians Marx or the syndicalism that was rising in some parts of the country and in Europe at the time. Instead, fighting the good fight with the emphasis in more ways than one on 'good,' meant countering the inadequacies rather than the iniquities of capitalism, of reforming it rather than overturning it. This would have been the acceptable position not only of Mansbridge and Tawney but also of Fred Hall, Tom Price, A P Wadsworth and Benjamin Lord, men who emerged from the tutorial class with reformist ideals intact to be pressed into legitimised service within social norms, be they the ones of journalism, teaching or the church. The sole renegade voice – and one suspects the one which offered Tawney the greatest challenge in the class - was Harold Kershaw who later turned reformist zeal into Marxian fervour by setting up the Central Labour College in Rochdale with the express intention of overthrowing capitalism.

In contrast, and supportive of the view that each district and each cohort was different, Roberts (2003) writes that the Reading Branch of the WEA was politically more concerned with class struggle against capitalism and whilst also containing many members of the SDF, he compares it to Rochdale as representing a more extreme wing of socialism. These differences may have been due to individuals signing up for the class (Kershaw seems to have been rather solitary in his extreme political views in Rochdale) or the fact that many of those in the Rochdale class were drawn from the church or chapel and thereby had dual moral affiliations as did Mansbridge, Temple and Gore. Kershaw proclaimed himself non-sectarian at his conscription tribunal and appears to have had a less encumbered, some might say less compromised, vision of social injustice.

ILP Mural (courtesy of The Independent Labour Party)

As has been seen, if there were two abiding but connected characteristics held largely in common across many in the Rochdale tutorial class of 1908 these would be sympathy with a reformist co-operative socialism and a tendency towards religious nonconformity which projected, from the chapel, a communitarian fellowship. And it is clear from the student profiles that nonconformity – and in particular a Unitarian and Congregational nonconformity – was the moral and spiritual anchor for many in the group, so although Price (1908) maintained that he had seen all shades of religious affiliation, recruitment into the class from Clover Street Unitarian Church must have been particularly effective as so many had come forward from that ministry, Price himself included !

Nor was this only a case of effective recruitment. As has been suggested, the Unitarians amongst all the chapels and churches, promoted through their teaching and principles critical social thought, democratic decision-making in their own organisation and a strong sense of social morality which blended self and societal improvement. These qualities met many of the WEA's early ideals. The unambiguously principled lives of Fred Hall, Stanley Dawson, and Alfred Wadsworth describe a taut line stretching from faith to social policy with the moral basis of their professional lives rooted in nonconformist socialism. Similarly Joseph Binns, Harold Briggs and Amy Fozard in the Unitarians, Arthur Collinge in the Society of Friends, Arthur Shore and Walter Stopford in the Church of England were all active within the various denominations upon which their politics was founded, continuing to be so, long after their experience in the tutorial class.

Women and the tutorial class

Expectations of women at this time, and these were mainly male expectations, were low. Notwithstanding the advances made by the Education Act of 1870, girls and women still found their progress through the education sectors and into higher education largely blocked. Carol Dyhouse (2012 p3) writes that 'from early childhood girls were encouraged to suppress (or conceal) ambition, intellectual courage or initiative – any desire for power or independence' and she points to the way in which a woman's personal aspirations in Edwardian England was constantly contested by pressures to maintain a socially constructed 'feminine identity.' This would affect all aspects of a woman's life but particularly education which held out the promise of providing one of the few routes to personal agency, power and influence.

These obstructions were certainly institutional but were also cultural, sometimes reaching into language itself. Those using the term 'bluestocking' to denote a female university student were doing so not in flattery in the Edwardian period but often out of sly discrimination and repression and it should be remembered that even by 1908 a woman's entry into a university was a novelty, the first students having been accepted only 40 years previously. Into the 20th century there remained a reluctance by the universities to allow women a place in these institutions and even when accepted they were sometimes required to request permission to attend classes, particularly biology or anatomy lectures, which were thought likely to upset a feminine sensibility ! Nor was entry onto a graduate programme a guarantee of eventual professional progress as women were often restrained from using a university award, an example being Christabel Pankhurst who, although achieving a law degree from Manchester University in 1907 was prevented from practicing as a barrister due to her sex.

And even informal classes outside of the university sector set up cultural barriers to women, Rose (2010 p73) claiming that 'women were mostly excluded from mutual improvement societies before the late 19th century' and 'this accounted for the scarcity of female proletarian intellectuals and autobiographers' (ibid p76). Rose goes on to suggest that only through the emergent Labour Party, the Co-operative movement and the trades unions were working women eventually and gradually to find a voice in any number.

Women attending a University Summer School 1909 (Workers Educational Association)

Fanny Taylor (top left)

The 1909 Report on WEA Tutorial Classes echoes this restraint on women's education when it notes that 'it will be easily understood that for working women to attend classes and write essays is no easy matter' although the Report goes on to show that those women who did attend, did so consistently, with 85% of the possible attendances met by the four women in the Rochdale class. Not only in Rochdale either, for this was the case across most of the classes in WEA districts with statistics from 1911 suggesting that the numbers held up throughout as did standards : 'the records of work and the attendance of women students compare favourably with those of the men' (WEA 1911 p11-12). Tawney's Tutor Report in 1910 affirms this with the additional comment about the

Rochdale class that there had been 'promising work done by two women in particular, both employed in the mill for long hours during the day'.

However, numbers were small in comparison with male students and women in the class were usually younger than the men. Davies (in Parry 1920 p140) suggests that over the next five years numbers increased, possibly as a result of the Great War, with the proportion of women in classes rising from 16% in 1912-13 to 39% in 1917-18. This number was not to be continued however, and Williams and Heath (1936 p264) show that of their 1930's respondent Ruskin Hall students, only 9% were women, interestingly a similar proportion (10%) of those attending lectures with the early Mechanics Institutes a century before (Chadwick 1857).

Nor were barriers simply systemic. Domestic approbation might just as easily deter women from attending classes, particularly if the subject was one normally associated with men. Attendance at a tutorial such as Rochdale's first one, concerned as it was with history and economics, might raise suspicion and perhaps hostility :

> 'Alice Foley recalled that her sister Cissy – a suffragette, Labour Church member and textile worker union officer – found a circle of girlfriends in Bolton who met to discuss 'politics, men, votes for women and culture'. Together they took an Oxford Extension course on Robert Browning, and talked of William Morris and Karl Marx. Their mother dismissed them as 'fusspots' indulging in 'long-curtain talk' which was a sign of moving up in the social scale' (Rose 2010 p77).

So instead of making strides into the wider world through education and self-improvement, girls and young women were expected to hold back any aspirations that they might have had and either find a place in the factory or, if from a middle class family, go into the teaching profession which was considered woman's work in the late 19th century. The other option, if financially viable for a family, was to stay at home and prepare for the duties of a housewife. The very idea of women discussing the affairs of men, because that was what the economic and political world was at that time, would have been anathema to many, even within more liberal households. It took a strong woman to take a seat in this class.

And some of these women were strong, strong enough to stand and be counted against the central social problem of the day for women, which was the extension of political franchise. The suffragette movement at the time had roots in the North West of England with the Pankhursts, Annie Kenney and Flora Drummond **in Manchester** and a lively branch of the Women's Social and Political Union in Rochdale, although this organisation was thought by some to have middle class exclusivity in its limited franchising objectives, especially the ones voiced by Christabel Pankhurst. None of the four women from the class belonged to this group but some of the male students had wives and daughters who were active in its cause such as Mary Collinge and Eliza Kershaw.

Women in the suffragette movement (The Local History Centre, Touchstones)

Notwithstanding the emergence of women's policy agenda, joining a tutorial class which focused upon political or economic theories was still difficult for many women. Munby writes (2003 p21) that 'should any girl show a tendency to politics, or to ideas of her own, she is looked upon by the majority of women as a person who neglects doorsteps and home matters, and is therefore not fit to associate with their respectable daughters and sisters.'

One woman who wore here political colours proudly and had a broader understanding than most of the WEA and its place for women was Maude Royden, later to become the wife of Hudson Shaw. Maude was invited to a meeting of the Rochdale Education Guild in 1909 and her speech was reported in full in the Rochdale Observer of April 17th 1909.

She moved 'that this meeting welcomes the efforts of the Workers Educational Association and the Guild to promote the education of women equally with that of men.' She complimented the WEA for its gender inclusivity, saying that :

'What women like about the WEA is that from the start it put them on the same level as

Maude Royden (courtesy of Mike Royden, see websites p230 below)

men. In the political world women have yet to establish their right to be regarded as human beings and as grown up (laughter and applause). There are still a number of men ….. who are secretly convinced that they really know what is best for their women folk to study (laughter). It is said that women had special power to cook and sew. The majority have. Some have more considerable power to understand political economy (laughter)'

and

'What women object to is to have limitations laid down as to what they can or cannot understand. If women have defects as compared with men, education is the thing to correct them'.

The four women students who attended the tutorial class were all roughly the same age - 25 or 26 - and represented, it has to be said, a rather narrow occupational range with two in lower middle class occupations (Eleanor Redshaw working as a clerk and Ethel Kershaw a school mistress) and two at home - Amy Fozard working from there as a dressmaker and Fanny Taylor 'a working man's wife.' What is noticeable and perhaps surprising is that there were no women from the factory floor in the class although later cohorts did include them in small numbers. Perhaps their absence might be explained by the pressures of exhausting physical employment and the long hours as well as the additional domestic responsibilities after work which precluded women with labouring jobs from attending. Davies (in Parry 1920 p139) is more specific and points to the difficulties that women had, not so much with attending the class but in having the time to complete the reading and writing required to continue in it.

One account from a female student within the WEA (TUC Library : Ref 3/6/7) captures such difficulties graphically. This unnamed student writes of working life being difficult with a 'bullying boss' who would 'scold you if you put your shawl on before the engine stops' and expresses her frustration at the conditions in the mill especially if they increased the speed of the machinery. When she became angry at such things, her women friends in the factory would say 'Time and patience, time and patience,' and she often had to laugh to stop herself from crying. Some relief came from her attendance at the evening classes but she believed that studying Literature seemed trivial when she saw young children having to go to work at 5.00am. She goes on : 'Studying Shakespeare is all right for the chapel and for England's Glory but when one considers the conditions of the workers it is not right to study such a thing.' Nor was the situation easier at home with a husband who became ill and then died 'due to poverty' (ibid).

The WEA soon became aware of the problems of women in adult education and set up a Working Party to study this issue as early as 1907. By 1910 a Women's Officer had been appointed by the Association but it was not until a decade later that there were women coming into study on anything like equal numbers to men. Credit should be given to the women's groups and the suffragette movement in particular, not simply for its pressure to change the franchise but for raising women's profile to greater prominence in health, education and social affairs. This can be seen in a local history group in Rochdale (Living History Group 1975) recalling that in 1908 'Mrs Taylor joined the Clarion Club and became one of the dedicated band that helped lay the foundations for modern left wing politics in Britain' and how the 'Clarion Club members sang the Red Flag at her wedding.' She remembers that

> 'the main aim of the group was political education, there was constant discussion and argument, the passage of Bills through Parliament was eagerly followed and discussed. They had meetings with first class speakers – Blatchford, Hyndman, Berisford, Macdonald, Snowden and Bruce Glasier. They held meetings at the Town Hall square on Sundays and organised public lectures on economics and a man called Sutcliffe for example lectured to them on 'Money' (ibid).

Whilst it might have been extraordinary (if not unnatural) to the many men and women who wanted to preserve the status quo, courageous women were nonetheless making headway into male domains be they political, social or educational. Amy Fozard, Fanny Taylor, Ethel Kershaw and Eleanor Redshaw were indeed pioneers for franchise, for equality and for the rights of men and women.

Student homes and houses

In the year of the tutorial class, 1908, the Borough of Rochdale was divided into eleven wards, each ward having not only its own boundaries and community but also its own challenges which the insufficiencies of infrastructure, transport and communication would have accentuated, characterising the space within these boundaries with a sense of place in miniature, a place of personal and communal identity. These were times as much for the district as for the town or the county, and across the borough, wards would have been known for their specific qualities - posh or dangerous, infamous or benign, places to visit or neighbourhoods to avoid. Families would have been committed to their small geographical co-ordinate, often working in the same area, sharing a sense of place with others, pooling resources and mingling in the same chapels, street corners, pubs and parks. Nowhere would there have been the mobility that we now take for granted, especially for the working class. Nor was there much opportunity to travel very far away unless you took an uncomfortable bus or train journey or caught one of the electric trams which were replacing steam vehicles and from 1902 were spreading out to the outskirts of the town.

Rochdale tram in 1908 (The Local History Centre, Touchstones)

And this communal fixity can be seen in the minimal migration made by most of the students in the tutorial class – often when they did move house, they 'flitted' down the street or just round the corner, possibly to remain close to a workplace or to stay near to supportive families. The Castleton students Alfred Wilkinson, Joseph Wormald, John McLean and the younger Walter Stopford for example, stayed Castleton people as if their movement was restricted by impermeable boundaries.

Similarly the very existence of district Societies (in all senses of the word) such as those at Shawclough, Milnrow, Hamer and many others, suggests a local identifier which determined the area's activities and meant that students born in particular areas tended to stay, work and play in those areas. Only in cases of notable and extraordinary social mobility would an individual move into a better, or a poorer, district.

It is difficult though for us, in an era of information technologies and instant communication, to imagine how circumscribed these rather close areas were, so that each ward - and sometimes each district within a ward - was separate and different, with conditions and social patterns emerging over time. However this seemed to be so, the differences being palpable in Rochdale, particularly the further one travelled from the town centre. Those living in the Castleton Moor ward for example, although only eight miles away from the town hall square, enjoyed by far the best social and housing environment.

So where did the students live and what were their living conditions ?

Fortunately we have answers to these questions from a study conducted by Dr Anderson the Borough Medical Officer in 1911 who undertook a ward-by-ward survey of the housing conditions in the town and the implications of them for the health of inhabitants. Thanks to the detail in this study it is possible to map the home addresses of the original WEA students onto Anderson's Report and draw from it tentative conclusions as to what the students' houses were like in relation to the rest of the town and, if possible, make a national comparison. In doing this we might better understand the links between their place in the social mix and their educational impulse, perhaps to escape from it, perhaps to change it.

Table 3 (overleaf) indicates, ward by ward, where the students lived and where each of these wards was positioned by Anderson in terms of rent price, overcrowding, general living conditions and implications for health and longevity.

A point to make preliminary to any discussion about this Table is that not only were there differences in conditions between wards but according to the Housing Reform Council there were also differences within wards, so whilst it is useful to scrutinise these statistics, it remains a 'broad brush' analysis at best as there would have been many exceptions to generalised statements. This within-ward difference would certainly account for the mixed messages in the statistics, for example that some of the areas with high rents had poor housing conditions, for example in Castleton West which had houses of variable quality close to each other.

As has been suggested, although most of the students experienced more than a single house movement, many stayed in close proximity to family and friends and so remained in the same ward for many years. Charles Hewitt, Ethel Kershaw, Livsey Lees, John McLean and Albert Wilson all lived within the district of their birth at least until middle age and many others moved to adjacent wards at most. The census and obituary reports that can be found are a good and reliable guide concerning family moves and therefore account for the numbers of houses experienced by the students in Table 3.

Ward	Number of houses of the WEA students	Rent prices 1-11 Low to high	Overcrowding (2 roomed house) 1-7 High to low	Overcrowding (4 roomed house) 1-7 High to low	Housing Conditions 1-7 poor to good	Death Rate 1-10 High to low
Wardleworth East	9	2	5	5	4	2
Castleton North	2	3	4	4	1	1
Wardleworth West	4	1	7	7	3	2
Wardleworth South	6	5	5	7	5	4
Spotland East	16	4	5	7	5	5
Spotland West	0	7	4	5	4	8
Wuerdle	4	6	6	6	2	6
Castleton South	16	9	1	2	4	7
Castleton East	6	8	2	1	5	3
Castleton West	1	10	3	4	7	10
Castleton Moor	8	11	3	3	6	9

Table 3 Student houses, living conditions and death rate (Rochdale Housing Reform Council 1911)

The first point to make is that a substantial number of the houses occupied by the worker-students over the years up to 1911 – exactly half of the total - were to be found in just two of the wards - Spotland East and Castleton South – although there were further concentrations of individuals in the Castleton Moor, Wardleworth East and South, and Castleton East wards. What must be noted initially is that both of these popular wards were within half a mile of the town centre, the others no more than three. The Living History Group in Rochdale (1975 p7) recalled the conditions prevailing close to these wards at the time as constituting an urban press towards the centre of the town with :

> 'The Mount, The Paddock, Wardleworth and the area along the river banks …… crowded with housing, back to back and often lacking basic amenities. Most had only one cold water tap, some had no piped water at all and most shared a pail closet with several families.'

The most notorious corners of Rochdale stood within Spotland West, a ward in which, significantly perhaps, none of the students in this WEA cohort lived. However, they didn't live far away and in fact the WEA students had addresses in two of the wards with some of the poorest housing conditions in the borough although, again, this would have differed from street to street, house to house. For example the back-to-back 2-roomed dwellings in Spotland East were found in the Report to be overcrowded but not so the 4-roomed 'through-housing' in the same ward, with only 1 in 37 of them overcrowded, (1 in 16 in Castleton South), and these tended to be the type of housing – 'through terraced' rather than back-to-back cottages - in which the students lived.

Rent was relatively inexpensive in both of these 'worker-student areas' and this is reflected in some nearby housing conditions being amongst the most depressed in the town. Both of these popular wards were located in old parts of Rochdale, especially the areas on either side of Oldham Road in Castleton South where dwellings were subject to damp as a result of poor building and maintenance. Furthermore, houses in the two wards were huddled together, the worst around Milkstone Road

Milkstone Road (The Local History Centre, Touchstones)

many of which were 'hardly fit for human habitation' (Rochdale Housing Reform Council 1911 p58) and this is where some students and their families had addresses : on Oldham Road lived Joe Nuttall, on Boundary Street the Kershaws, on Milkstone Road was Fanny Taylor, and on Ventnor Street in Deeplish was Frederick Turner.

Albert Collinge and Eleanor Redshaw both lived on Durham Street and on Ashfield Street was Frederick Turner. These students would have experienced some of the harshest living and housing conditions in Rochdale at the time, Anderson's Report noting that many inhabitants in these wards being 'careless and thriftless with neglected and dirty homes and ill-cared for children' (ibid p58). Other parts of this ward were, on the other hand, commodious 'with baths' (ibid). Indicating the diversity in each ward, the Report continues that some parts of Castleton South were 'populated by respectable working-class people in fairly good circumstances' even though these people were living adjacent to overcrowded slum areas.

Spotland East, which was the other ward in which many of the students lived, had 80% of housing that was in good or passable condition (ibid p37) although the worst of the houses stood between Bury Road and St Mary's Gate where Harold Briggs and Frederick Greenwood lived. This was another old part of town, 'irremediably damp,' 'merely shelters at night rather than homes … (for) persons who follow no regular employment and have little knowledge of real home life and family rearing' (ibid p41). Although crowded and congested they were within a stone's throw, in the same ward, of good 'through' 4-roomed housing such as those on Sheriff St where Fred Hall and Amy Fozard were brought up, in an area which was paved, clean, with wide streets and spacious communal yards.

One critical aspect affecting the lived experience in both of these wards, was the number of people to be found in each household, domestic housing being considered overcrowded where there were more than two persons to a room throughout a dwelling place. Anderson reports (ibid p41) that the Spotland East ward around St Mary's Gate was the most overcrowded with 'rents as low as possible irrespective as to the separation of sexes or domestic convenience.' At least six students from the tutorial class experienced overcrowding, Eugene Kiernan living in a 2-roomed back-to-back cottage along with a family of seven, John McLean in a 4-roomed house with ten altogether, Arthur Shore in a 4-roomed dwelling of eight inhabitants, Albert Wilson severely overcrowded in a 4-roomed house at 108 Joy Street with fourteen people and Joseph Wormald in a family of eight living in a 4-roomed house.

As the statistics from the 1911 study indicate, there was a strong correlation between overcrowding and a relatively high death rate, so this was a serious matter particularly where the internal and external conditions of housing were also poor. However, given that the majority of the students tended not to live in overcrowded accommodation, that their housing conditions were on the whole passable-to-adequate and that the death rate and infant mortality in their wards (Rochdale Housing Reform Council 1911) relatively low in comparison to other wards and sub-districts, again suggests that individuals from the tutorial class were drawn in the main from that section of the working population which was industrious and looked after both its own property, its family and its future well-being. The better conditions sought by these families would have alleviated some of the more severe social challenges undergone by many others in the town, the ones for example on the brink of pauperism, those living in grossly damp conditions in overcrowded rooms, with a high infant mortality rate and the prospect of an early death.

Raspberry Place circa 1905 : 'An area of poverty and ill-health'. (The Local History Centre, Touchstones)

One or two from the tutorial class did, however, live in the harshest environments. The Collinge family lived at least until 1911 in a poor part of Castleton East, and the Hilton boys again stayed in Wardleworth West until 1911, a district which, in housing and social amenities, was severely deprived. The majority of the students though, lived in those areas suggestive of a 'respectable' working class, 'industrious and clean' as Anderson puts it (ibid p50). Foster's (1977) claim that organisations such as the WEA were the preserve of the 'labour aristocracy' holds up again here and this community of self-respect 'sets them apart' from other sections of the working population. In the life-portraits of the individuals in the tutorial class this is confirmed in their occupational status, where they lived, their projection from the chapel towards 'good works and improvement' and their commitment to education.

The question as to whether they undertook the tutorial class to leave behind their streets and places of habitation in order to enjoy social mobility may be partially answered by the addresses they subsequently kept. Some examples certainly did suggest this – A P Wadsworth, Stanley Dawson, Walter Stopford, Ben Lord and Fred Hall all moved on to other towns and cities, to grander houses and more salubrious lifestyles linked to their new-found positions of authority and responsibility. Others, it must be surmised, also found upward mobility through education but their move was less pronounced in geographical and social terms. Livsey Lees, Ethel Kershaw, Harold Briggs, Eugene Kiernan and Eleanor Redshaw entered the professional lower middle class through vocational qualifications and went to less crowded, 'better' parts of the town. Some – Lawrence Gill, Tom Price, Joseph Cryer and Charlie Pearce - stayed with the WEA and achieved similar status. Others yet, the majority, stayed in textiles, in the iron works or continued in their jobs, and thereby, the streets of their childhood. Harold Kershaw, Thomas Bailey, Joseph Binns, Albert Collinge, Joe Nuttall, Riley Duckworth, James Henighan, the Hilton brothers, and Thomas Bailey and the women who were tied to their family through restricted gender mobility such as Amy Fozard or Fanny Taylor, stayed in the town, remained with their occupational life style and often the district of their birth. The WEA rarely pretended to be an association set up to provide social mobility for working people and this position is confirmed by the few from this class who moved from the area and from their communities of birth.

A final point on housing. The particular wards in which the students lived are near to the centre, in 2015, of a much larger town – now part of Greater Manchester - than they were in 1908. However, over the intervening years they have lost none of the stains of yesteryear. These areas – Spotland East and Castleton South – remain deprived areas for many, far from any prospect of gentrification and with low house prices and rents, poor living conditions and high population density. The development of these wards has been stymied by under-investment and the white working class and Bangladeshi communities that have settled in them continue to suffer from multiple deprivation indices which include those concerning income, employment, health and disability, education, skills and training, barriers to housing, living environment and crime (www.odpm.gov.uk/indices, 2004). The square mile inclusive of the Spotland East ward, a place close by those houses popular with the tutorial class students, was, for three consecutive years until 2013, thought to be the most deprived area in England with 'a housing estate where three out of four people are on benefits and four out of five children grow up in poverty….The latest figures also show 72 per cent of people living on the Falinge estate in Rochdale, Greater Manchester, are unemployed' (Gore 2013). Times have changed, it seems, very little, with living conditions and prospects for the worst off no better than they were in 1908.

Reflections on the Tutorial Class

The Curriculum

Following the shortcomings of the University Extension programme, there was a consensus that the new tutorial curriculum should be built around a topic which Rochdale people identified as beneficial for themselves and that was small enough for effective tutor-student contact. Given the institutional contestation of the space between the universities and the WEA, this was not, however, plain sailing, and a short time before the beginning of the tutorial class a dispute arose about the first of these, the subject to be studied. It seemed, as a letter suggests from Gill to Tawney as late as December 10th 1907 (6 weeks before the start of the class), that the Rochdale group had not, by then, heard that their request for a series of tutorial sessions on 'Social and Economic History' had been acceded to by the university. The Rochdale Education Guild Secretary wrote with restrained pique that 'I should like, however, to hear from you that we are to have the subject we asked for,' whilst reassuring Tawney that 'you will have a class almost, if not entirely, made up of 'workmen' in the strictest sense of the term.'

But the university, and Marriott as its contact, was delaying things with its own protocols so that by the 3rd December they were still wrangling with Tawney over the details of his syllabus, insisting that he submit them by 10th January. This was cutting it perilously close, as that date was two weeks before the start of the course. Rochdale must have felt that its title and subject requirements were being ignored, having completed its practical arrangements early in securing a room, students, publicity and enthusiasm. Gill writes to Tawney from Rochdale on 10th December that :

> 'I see on the formal notice that the subject put down is 'Social and Economic History in the 17th century' (that is for the first 12 classes). What we asked for was 'The Social, Economic and Industrial History of England with special attention to the 17th 18th and 19th centuries'

and then added 'I hope they made this clear to you.'

It would seem that the university was determined to promote its own title, perhaps in tune with its existing courses, perhaps in line with what Tawney himself felt comfortable in teaching. Gill continues forcefully to Tawney that 'I should like... to hear from you that we are to have the subject we asked for.'

In the end, Tawney's programme for the tutorial class was entitled 'The Industrial History of England focusing on the 16th and 17th centuries' and so was not what Rochdale requested, but rested within

Tawney's comfort zone. Speculation might have it that the reason the Rochdale people wanted the programme's scope to reach into the 19th century was that it brought it up to date relatively speaking but also connected it to their own socio-geographical area, particularly as it would have included regional repercussions of the industrial revolution. Henighan, giving an insight into how the eventual curriculum was developed in practice, writes that 'their tutor went into the psychology of history and the part that people play in it, comparing the 17th century to the 20th and then discussed industry before the Industrial Revolution.' Similarly Fred Hall comments that in the class there was debate enough to connect the past to the present, so it appears that Tawney – meeting the Guild's initial request - attempted in the second hour's discussion period to bring together his students' experiences with historical precedence.

However, the University's published syllabus did little to suggest this interaction, focusing as it did on population issues and the rise of early manufacturing, the growth of Mercantilism and the problems of industrialisation (Poor Law etc), then going on to questions resulting from the enclosure movement and the position of tenant farmers. The social and political fallout from corn taxation and the growth of the wool trade was covered as was government intervention and protectionism, colonial expansion with the New World. The breadth to these questions and issues skirted the development of the industries with which the students were all too familiar and with which they were engaged on a daily basis and at first sight must have been something of a disappointment to them. And yet, as suggested above, this would be to take the syllabus at face value. It was a wide sweep certainly, but only by looking at the student essays does one sense that depth was not sacrificed to breadth even though later industrialism and its social repercussions were not covered in detail in the lectures *per se*. No doubt though, that the students would have made Tawney aware of the connections and specific, local labour issues would have been brought up in questioning as these were of interest to the students, particularly the effects of industrialisation and the early indications of a labour movement through trade guilds.

Apart from mere content, there was great deal to be learned from the sessions' 'hidden curriculum' in the tutorial class, with critical thinking, presentational skills and with the making of connections between one era of history to their own no matter how dissociated that might have initially seemed. Furthermore the skills developed in self-expression, questioning and argumentation were as important to the students, if not more so, than the substantive knowledge itself. Wadsworth may well have developed a degree of critical thought here that stood him in good stead as editor of the Manchester Guardian. Price, Cryer, Pearce and Hall may have understood first-hand the critical depths to which worker students could study and took this with them to other WEA districts or to the Co-operative College. Stopford and Dawson may have seen links between New Testament teaching and policy which they carried into their future lives in the church. The intense questioning of German authorities on their tour of 1909 by Ethel Kershaw, James Henighan, Charlie Pearce and James Hilton may have owed something to the liveliness of debate and interrogation that they had experienced in the tutorial class.

Teaching and Learning

The second charge against an ineffective University Extension series of programmes concerned the 'delivery' of syllabus materials and the poor interaction that had been noted between some tutors and their student groups. This was addressed within the structure of the new tutorial class, the proposal being that the sessions should run across a two-hour block, the first hour being a lecture followed by a one hour discussion which theoretically allowed free rein with student questions and debate. There was, in this, a sense that students should not so much be pupils but rather be 'co-operators with the tutor,' part of a teaching style developed by James Stuart and practiced by him in Rochdale in the 1870's (Twigg 1924 p19). This mode of teaching – perhaps very different to the didacticism of previous lectures (even the ones by Hudson Shaw and Powys) - meant a palpable relaxation of the relationship between the academic and the student in a way deemed appropriate to worker-learners unaccustomed to cap and gown protocols of the lecture theatre. And it was also a classroom situation, at least in terms of the student body, which Tawney had long desired, writing to Beveridge three years before the class that 'teaching economics in an industrial town is just what I ultimately wanted to do' (William Beveridge Papers 1905) although whether he was anticipating at that time as close a teaching relationship as he found in Rochdale, is not known.

Two years after that thought however, and with the imminent prospect of teaching in Rochdale, Mansbridge is writing to Tawney advising him on an appropriate teaching style to employ in order to engage worker students, one letter from Mansbridge (December 3rd 1907) being particularly interesting in that respect. It seems that Tawney, having been appointed as tutor, was becoming increasingly anxious about pressure being placed upon him by John Marriott, then Secretary of the Oxford University Extension Delegacy, to teach particular topics in a particular way. A letter from Marriott (December 3rd 1907) had been undisguised in its prescription that to include 'dates' within a study of economic history was less critical than would be the case with political history. This judgement may have been on subject grounds but could also have been because Marriott was anticipating lower abilities in the student group. Other letters with a similar determinist tone must have been sent to Tawney, certainly, one triggering a response from Mansbridge : 'what can you do with a man like Marriott ?' and urging the young tutor not to worry about Rochdale : 'You do your best, it will be quite good enough.' He goes on to write to him that 'it does not so much matter at the outset as to what you might call the scientific presentation of the subject, but it does matter that you make common cause with the class' and 'Do not unduly (*word entered in pen afterwards*) exaggerate the academic side' (TUC Library Ref : WEA CENTRAL/3/12/07).

However, Tawney was somewhat uncomfortable, 6 weeks before the first session, about both his own abilities and his preferred teaching style in view of the task in hand and how it might be received by worker students. Mansbridge's guidance clearly takes more account of the learner and his/her needs than the subject or the teacher, and this advice would stand Tawney in good stead in the Rochdale sessions. The message from Mansbridge was to get to know the students and their needs and the rest would fall into place. Strategically, this shows Mansbridge to be in a position to pull strings regardless of Marriott's concerns or predilections.

In his evaluation of the tutorial class, Price (1908) reflects on their classroom experience, recording that it ran from 2.30-4.30pm but that 'the tutor is rarely liberated before 5.00,' the second hour lively with discussion and questions, the discussion section of the class being, it seems, particularly impassioned and effective. The obituary of Tawney (TUC Library : Ref RHT) suggested that the class were indeed lucky to get someone with the empathy and temperament of him as a tutor, someone '…. of such human stuff as Tawney was made of, in an age when patronizing pomposity or academic frigidity might easily have been the fare offered to the first worker-students.'

Tawney's own reflections on the learning that took place are interesting in that he found quite the opposite of passivity in the student-tutor discussions, commenting to Price that the students had not simply 'taken him by the hand' in their exchanges, but that 'a certain section seemed to want to take him by the neck !' This suggestion of political dissent from sections of the cohort would fit with the make-up of the class, mostly socialist, some like Harold Kershaw closet Marxists. Price notes in his feedback to Mansbridge that whilst there had been 'wholehearted sympathy between students and tutor' that 'when 39 students of varying political and religious views sit down you must expect things !' This was the inevitable 'collision of mind with mind' that Mansbridge (1913 p53) had not only anticipated but encouraged with adult workers wrestling over alternative and conflicting points of view.

So the classes, it seems, were characterised by an intense and lively seriousness, with everyone - student and tutor alike - in earnest. Price goes further :

> 'I sometimes wonder whether the men at Oxford or Cambridge who acquire their culture in pleasant places can ever realise quite what it means for working men and women to pledge

their scanty leisure for two years to study, and what a monument of serious human purpose this Tutorial class is' (1908).

No doubt Tawney contributed enormously to this outcome with his personal teaching style, demonstrating in practice that simply to read lectures to a class like this would not only be ineffective but demeaning to the individuals involved. It would also have been more akin to the lectures of University Extension than the classroom closeness of the tutorial. Instead, he engaged in an exchange of views with them, a reciprocation of theory with experience, a running debate following a lecture. Reflecting upon this mutual engagement many years later, Tawney himself writes that 'I can never be sufficiently grateful for the lessons learned from the adult students whom I was supposed to teach, but who, in fact, taught me' (Tawney 1953).

He also remembered that the questions posed to him by the worker-students were both disconcerting and surprising with their genesis in an experiential curiosity rarely seen in traditional university settings, questions 'alive in the working class', coming as they did from a different point of view to those of secure middle class minds. And it may well have been this practical experience of the student workers that provided the spark which was so combustible to the educational proceedings, invigorating their tutor to use such experiences in the development of his own later thinking, policy pronouncements and research. It was this grounding by the students which coloured their mutual development. Reading the essays submitted by members of the class suggests their tangible knowledge of specific working environments, something that Tawney himself acknowledged as a lesson to himself :

> 'Asked where I received the best part of my own education, I should reply, not at school or college, but in the days when, as a young, inexperienced and conceited teacher of tutorial classes, I underwent, week by week, a series of friendly, but effective, deflations at the hands of the students composing them' (Tawney in Hinden (ed) 1964).

One example of experience being brought to theory, although coming from a student in the Longton group, can be seen in part of an essay (which received an A- from Tawney) entitled 'Unemployment in Coal Mines.' The points made by that student are replete with specific knowledge as well as asides about the changes in the mining industry and are telling with such phrases as 'even in my lifetime experience' and using such technical terms as 'following the crop cut,' knowledge of practice such as 'workings are limited to 30 or 40 yards at the limit' and that 'workings were not carried very far because of little knowledge of roofing and gasses,' must have appealed to Tawney, accustomed as he was to a more theoretical knowledge within the vacuum of university life. This was the real stuff !

Similarly one essay from Stanley Dawson in the first Rochdale class which received an 'A' and 'Good' from Tawney addressed the question 'What are the Main Causes of Unemployment in the Cotton Industry ?' and drew a vivid picture of short time operations in cotton mills including practical matters such as the increased availability of spindles or the artificial scarcity of raw materials. At the same time though, it dealt with the more theoretical matters of price inflation by speculators, captured in a knowledgeable and local voice : 'Well now, with raw cotton at fancy prices and the demand falling off for cotton products, the local economy became increasingly stressed'.

Experience was not everything though, and Mansbridge, reflecting on the student work from the first tutorial classes (1913 p78) felt that the challenge to experience by theory or new critical thinking changed student presuppositions which were often based on the flimsiest of empirical evidence. The coming together of theory and practice, like the coming together of Tawney and the workers, created a powerful and productive alchemy for new knowledge but the right balance had to be struck.

Albert Mansbridge (Workers Educational Association)

Price (1924 p34), in his early feedback to Mansbridge, comments that perhaps because there existed all shades of political and religious belief in the class, this made for lively and interesting discussions which tended to go on so long that 'the caretaker became restless,' the debate having to be continued in the street or in a house of one of the students. As a result of such enthusiasm, Tawney frequently arranged :

> 'to have tea and spend the evening at the home of one of the students and on these occasions other members of the class would crowd into the house to the limits of the accommodation – and even beyond – and the discussion would often go on until the early hours of the morning' (ibid).

Mansbridge himself in later years (1913 p127), describes the tutorial class as being akin to a 'fireside discussion' and Tawney (1914 pp74-5) writing of the interactive groups, explained that

> 'thanks to the fact that they are small, tutor and students can meet as friends, discover each other's idiosyncrasies and break down that unintentional system of mutual deception which seems inseparable from any education which relies, principally on the formal lecture. It is often before the classes begin and after they end, in discussions around the student's fire, or in a walk to and from his home that the root of the matter is reached both by student and tutor.' (Ibid)

And a flavour of these informal meetings has been caught by a Longton student, E S Cartwright (1929) recalling that when the formal session finished, tea and biscuits would be taken and the talk would range free and wide, Tawney on one occasion reading Walt Whitman's 'When Lilacs last in the Dooryard Bloom'd' to the assembled group. Some of the verses must have hit home to worker students, especially the idea of raising voices from bleeding throats :

> In the swamp in secluded recesses,
> A shy and hidden bird is warbling a song.
> Solitary the thrush,
> The hermit withdrawn to himself, avoiding the settlements,
> Sings by himself a song.
> Song of the bleeding throat,
> Death's outlet song of life, (for well dear brother I know,
> If thou wast not granted to sing thou would'st surely die.)
>
> And the charm of the carol rapt me,
> As I held as if by their hands my comrades in the night,
> And the voice of my spirit tallied the song of the bird.

> (Whitman 1855)

And if Tawney wasn't tackling the Rochdale students after the class or in the street, he could be found in the Education Guild Club on Lord Street, treating the place like a College Common Room in the centre of town (TUC Library : letter from James Henighan 2/2/08) and gathering groups of excitable worker students around him.

Often essays from the tutorial group revealed another, more critical aspect of their engagement with higher education and that was the need to comply with academic standards and protocols. This point was made clear in the tutor's annotations on their essays, in particular the omission of useful references and the occasional example of poor grammar and spelling. Tawney, in the first of his Reports on the group (Rochdale Education Guild 1909 p21) confirms this when he writes that 'some….. found considerable difficulty in expressing themselves on paper' and that students were 'hampered by the mechanical difficulties of correct composition' (ibid). In some ways this was to be expected with so many of the students having left school by the age of 14 to begin employment, Goldman (in Roberts 2003 p47) quoting the Board of Education's Inspector's sympathy with the worker student in this regard :

> 'There are several of the newer members who find the subject very stiff owing chiefly to their defective preliminary education …. One thing this has brought home to me, personally – how very difficult and distasteful the mere physical act of writing is to a miner or a potter. I can see that this is a very big obstacle to surmount.'

Price (1908) also notes that students in the class were not naturally inclined 'to be book-worms' and whilst some were dedicated more to sport than to study, others fought to maintain concentration levels, it being no light sacrifice to do so after a hard day's work or at weekends. Many had to work overtime and most had to give up their only free day, Sunday, to struggle with language and fresh concepts, not to mention the presentational demands in submitting essays once a fortnight.

However, the completed essays were generally good and seen to be so by the Inspectors. Price's essay for example (TUC Library : Ref 3/6/2) on 'The changes in the economic position of England brought about by the discovery of the New World' covered a great deal of advanced ground concerning economic theory although, as Tawney points out, it misses the opportunity to cite supportive references. The essay, however, did manage to merge theoretical thinking with practice and experience – for example the effect that increasing overseas trade had on domestic prices and wages – and this was recognised by Tawney in his comments in the margin.

One educational and extra-curricular aspect of the workers' experience of the class was a visit to Germany on May 28th 1909. Following applications from Guild members, eight full travelling scholarships were allocated to students by a selection committee. Individual applicants were asked to include a statement as to what features of German life they wished to study and 'what they have done to make themselves acquainted with similar English institutions' (TUC Library : Ref 4/1/2/1). The students who travelled from the class included Arthur Collinge representing the Union of Co-operative Employees, James Hilton and J W Lees from the Ruskin Hall Class, Charlie Pearce (Guild Executive), Ethel Kershaw (studentship), Frederick Greenwood (Guild Secretary) and A P Wadsworth (Guild Executive). The trip was organised and paid for through public subscription to cover travelling expenses, board and lodging and loss of wages (ibid). Conditions of travel were that each participant should, on their return, give a full Report of the trip and 'pledge themselves to five essays descriptive of their tour to affiliated and other Societies, if desired by the Guild' (ibid), Charlie Pearce and James Hilton doing so. The group, which was complemented by members of the Spinning Mutual Improvement Society, visited German factories, schools, a Labour Exchange in Dusseldorf as well as being treated to a number of talks on social and economic topics. As part of their educational tour, they met Trades Union officials and went to look at living conditions in Dusseldorf. The Highway (August 1909) magazine records, befitting the inquisitive nature of these students, that they had inexhaustible questions for their hosts.

German Trip photo 1909 (Workers Educational Association)

The Teaching Role of Tawney

Lawrence Gill felt it necessary to write, when faced with the prospect of losing him as a tutor two years after the first tutorial session, that 'R H Tawney has established for himself a position in the town and his withdrawal from Rochdale would be looked upon as a calamity by a far larger circle than the members of the class' (Pedley 1974). Gill is, no doubt referring to the impact this would have on the continuing experiment with tutorial classes, and this is emphasised by Brooks (2000). A key question following the success of the tutorials, therefore, was to what extent it depended on the teaching style, the personality and beliefs of Tawney ?

Although it would seem that he was unsure of his approach to the class before engaging with them and needed Mansbridge's reassurance that he would be fine as long as he was less academic than personable, Tawney's style in his teaching won over the students from the start, to the extent that he felt (perhaps more in retrospect than at the time) that he was becoming a student through the experience as well as a teacher. More than any considerations of his own skills as an educator, he respected the basic instinct of all men and women to be curious – particularly about their own position, their own inherited social place – and the fact that, given the right environment, they were hungry to learn. Regardless of their starting point educationally, he knew that they brought with them knowledge which, with the appropriate teasing out – with each other, with him – could be elevated to anything experienced in the university. This Socratic view of teaching and learning gave him access to their knowledge as well as their trust.

Sometimes though, this position set Tawney against the university authorities as they tended to take a less inclusive, a more 'establishment' view of the potential of <u>all</u> men and women. An example of this comes through with his anger ('sulphuric acid' Mansbridge called it) at the university's interference immediately prior to the start of the class and largely from the pen of Marriott, head of the Oxford University Delegacy, in wanting to direct his teaching towards a more didactic style. Mansbridge's response points to the two-way reciprocal learning that he felt that Tawney would find, and did find, in Rochdale.

Certainly the effect of his tutoring and his charismatic persona on the class seems to have been electrifying, a letter from Gill to Mansbridge of the 2nd February 1908 claiming that 'he made a magnificent start. Tawney captured them right away. He is splendid,' and that it was 'love at first sight on both sides.' Gill goes on to say that 'his lessons are brilliant and inspiring – somewhere between a lesson and a lecture…. lectures for an hour and then an hour's sustained and unflagging questions and discussion.' Contrary to the letters from Tawney to Mansbridge about his workload and fee, Gill writes that 'he is perfectly happy here – a most winning patience….. I may seem extravagant – but ask Henighan !'

Nor was Tawney simply active in tutoring classes in Rochdale and Longton during this period, he was also eager to spread the word about the WEA, visiting the Littleborough group (WEA 6th Annual Report 1909 p32) and giving talks at the time to the Milnrow and Newhey Education Guilds.

Tawney said on many occasions that he gained much from his work in tutoring these students and regarded his experience with them as a 'fellowship of learning.' He noted too the spark from the students and that 'the friendly smitings of weavers, potters, miners and engineers have taught me much about the problems of political and economic science which cannot easily be learned from books' (Jackson no date). And it was this person to person dialogue which distinguished them as 'classes' rather than lectures, depending as they did for their success on the informality set up by the tutor.

Attendance, attainment and difficulties

In the course of the programme, of the initial 43 students enrolled to the class, only three had to withdraw before it concluded and attendance at the sessions, apart from those with ill health, was 100%, several of them going on to attend the Summer School in Cambridge.

In terms of the level of study, the class members, although keen to learn under a tutor as eminent as Tawney and certainly (at least for a number of them) accustomed to attending lectures and writing essays, were now being asked to apply themselves to a more trying intellectual test. Not all of them could cope, and for a number of reasons. Some found difficulties with the requirements of regular reading and writing at home and the challenges for the working person of doing this were clear : lack of books, a crowded home, exhaustion, fear of unemployment, overtime, duties outside of work and home such as trades union activity, Co-operation and political involvement. Related to this last point Tawney recalls his surprise (Oxford University Delegacy 1910 p13) that the General Election of 1910 had not interfered with attendance as much as might have been expected, although he felt that it probably accounted for them being a little behind in their essays, the suggestion being that many were politically active and their tutor aware of this.

Restrictive circumstances in the home and at work drew great sympathy from Tawney (TUC Library : Ref 3/6/1) and he writes that 'the tutorial classes are university education carried out under extreme difficulties' the difference between the two being that a traditional student studies 'at a year's leisure' and with a number of tutors, compared with worker-students employed throughout the day, studying in the evening and then seeing one tutor on their day off.

Other inconveniences concerning tutorial study were recorded in the WEA 5th Annual Report (1908 pp13-14) in particular the pressures of overtime, shift-work, curricula suitability, evening attendance and fees. Tawney, similarly, highlighted the fact that overtime was detrimental to sustained study and attendance, drawing the attention 'of sympathetic observers in all classes to the grave dangers involved in allowing human intelligence to be sacrificed to the immediate exigencies of production' (TUC Library : Ref 3/6/1).

If conditions at work were unfavourable to study, home life was little better. Helen Gill (1986 p63) records tutors saying that 'we have known students to regularly sit up, completing an essay till 1.00 at night and enter the mill next day at 6.30 or to attend classes on Saturday afternoon after a week containing 12 hours of overtime over and above the standard 53 hours.' The Highway (August 1909) similarly records student problems, noting that they were often too exhausted to concentrate, that home life was difficult, being cramped and poorly resourced, that children were sometimes 'knocking over the candle' and on a physiological level noting that the miners' fingers (in the Longton class) were too stiff and not used to holding a pen, which meant that writing was physically awkward. The fact that coursework on the programme was assessed in essay form made this particularly penalizing for many for whom extended writing was alien.

Some faced the pressing problems of ill-health and the hardships of inadequate housing and most suffered from the demands of work in being tired at the end of a long working week. Members of one class in Littleborough in 1910 were recorded in the Tutorial Class Annual Report as having minds that were 'never freed from worry and depressing thoughts of the morrow' due to the unpredictability of employment (TUC Library : Ref 3/6/3). Others again, to take a specific example from Roberts (2003 p295), could barely stay awake through the lectures, having to rise at 3.30am, work until 2.00pm on a Saturday and then attend lectures in the afternoon before returning home to write essays and then get up again at 3.30 am for a Sunday shift. This could hardly be said to be a timetable conducive to reflection or to considered academic work, but these were the conditions faced by many in these classes.

An inspector's Report of the Littleborough WEA in 1910 by a Mr J Walkden, claimed that 6 out of 24 had had to resign from one class due to 'industrial conditions' and there not being the time for reading to support their essay work. This inspector adds that there was an inadequate supply of books to go round even though Mr Tawney 'had leant books of his own to help out'.

Whenever a student was absent from classes, this was recorded. A few of them missed a session or two due to political commitments around election time, one of the students, for example, having to leave because of 'urgent business' – he was secretary of a political party in the town and was called upon to distribute leaflets. Three or four were missing on Shrove Tuesday which the Rochdale class, by a substantial majority, decided NOT to take as a holiday although many schools (for example Benjamin Lord's school in Oxenhope) did take off as a festive break. As a summary, Albert Mansbridge gathered the WEA's statistics for the year 1911-12 and showed that the main reasons for absences from the two Rochdale classes running at that time had been illness 22%, overtime 60% and Trade Union or other Public Business 18% (Mansbridge 1913 pp184-185).

In his evaluative piece for the WEA in the early days of the Rochdale class, Price writes that the organisers of the tutorials and the tutors themselves should recognise the difficulties that men and women who have been working all day face in coming to the classes, and that the programme should be made as easy for them as possible whilst maintaining standards.

Essays and Assessment

One of the initial conditions set by the universities prior to the running of the tutorial class was that there would be essays submitted every fortnight. Tawney himself set the essays, offering a choice of one of five titles and the tutor giving, wherever possible, individual attention to each submission (Joint Committee of University and Working Class Representatives 1909 p60). Certainly the essays were rigorously marked by the tutor although Mansbridge himself reflected some years later in 1913 (p154) that feedback comments had sometimes been scanty due to pressures on the tutor's time, and whilst the Joint Committee (1909 p64) suggested that essay criticism should be followed by feedback interviews with each of the students, no record exists that this, in actual fact, took place. However, there was a consistency of tutor annotation in the margins and at the end of the essay dealing with content understanding and critical awareness whilst also making points about grammar, punctuation and expression.

Evidence from the 'Reports on Tutorial Classes' (WEA 1909 p105) makes it clear that most students submitted papers to the tutor and the same source (p107) points out that the essays written were 'of great excellence.' However, as has been suggested earlier, writing essays must have been the most demanding aspect of the programme given many students' living conditions, working lives and academic abilities. In a monthly section of The Highway magazine which celebrated the student voice in a humorous but (sometimes) enlightening way (1909 p16), one student is saying to another 'I'm writing nobbut English in t'next essay,' which suggests that they found – as many students today find – academic language to be different to their own as a means of expressing thoughts and experiences.

During an interview in Rochdale with Bertha Radcliffe in 1986, the daughter of a Tawney-tutored second-cohort WEA student in 1909, she remembers her father having to concentrate hard on his essays, saying that her mother 'used to help him with this on a Monday evening after washing the clothes.' Following his three years of study with the WEA, Bertha's father attended the Summer School at Oxford University. At the time, he was a carter and a collector for the Carter's Union and worked for Ormroyd's Leather works in Rochdale, the company generously paying his wages to the family whilst he was away at the university.

Mansbridge writes in 1913 that due to the difficulties under which the students worked 'some of the earliest essays were of a very elementary character' and then adds encouragingly 'but it is precisely here that we find the greatest improvement' and 'the more important powers of arrangement, lucidity and fullness of expression developed on the whole in a satisfactory manner' (p148).

Given the spread of occupational groups in these early tutorial classes, it is unsurprising that students approached their academic tasks in different ways and from individual points of readiness. Williams and Heath note the same (1936 p201) when they record a tutor's comment that :

> 'I think the biggest drawback is the varying standards at which the students start...... manual workers have not often experience in essay writing and debate, while to other members of the class (say, of the teaching or professional classes) these things come much easier.'

Resources

To compound the difficulties faced by worker-students engaging in high-level study, there was the problem of lack of resources to support it, even though the universities promised that they would do what they could to provide books. Commenting upon this prior to the start of the classes, Gill wrote (December 10th 1907) to Tawney about the set books for the programme and particularly the use of Townsend Warner's 'Social and Economic History of the 17th Century.' It appears that this was not the book that the Rochdale students had requested in the weeks prior to the class and Gill supported their position to the tutor, writing that 'they wanted a bit more expansive reach, but of course you know best,' again perhaps voicing a concern that limiting the study programme to that century would restrict the experiential interest of the worker students. A compromise seems to have been reached as Price later writes that Townsend Warner's book 'Landmarks in English

Industrial History' which took a wider and more modern sweep, would be the one for the class and could be purchased for the discounted price of 3/4d at a local bookseller, the usual retail price being 5/-.

Whenever possible, each member of the class bought texts for themselves but that was never easy as one wrote : 'A man who is supporting a family on 24/- a week cannot afford to buy more than 1 or 2 expensive textbooks' (TUC Library : Ref WEA CENTRAL/3/6/1-12). Aware of this problem and in order to boost their stock of available texts, Mr A E Zimmern, a Fellow of New College Oxford, in 1910 donated over a hundred books from Oxford University to the Rochdale Education Guild Club library and Price notes at about the same time the important role played by the Oxford Travelling Library, the volumes from the Fabian Box and a 'number of volumes leant by local sympathisers.'

Officials at the Public Library in the town played their part too by providing the students with a list of available titles from their shelves on Economic History and whilst the course was running a selection of them was housed at the Technical School where the classes were taking place. Typical of the support for each other in this class, in the summer months a Reading Circle was formed at the Guild Club on Lord Street by one of their number, although it was made clear that this was not exclusive to members of the tutorial group - so the local Ruskin Hall Class arranged to study the same subject in order to participate in the discussion groups. The group which assembled to discuss these issues was therefore much bigger than the 43 studying under Tawney on the Saturday and in that way they could share resources, co-operate over course material understanding and act as their own mutual resource.

Tutorial Class Evaluations

From an early date there were calls for evaluations of the tutorial class which ranged from feedback about the academic standards of students and tutor, local facilities and the management of study. These were not confined to formal inspections carried out by HMI for the Board of Education but also included Reports commissioned by the Rochdale Education Guild, student reflections on their experiences, a visitor's account of the class and a considered opinion (at the time and in later years) from Tawney himself.

Evaluation from Inspectors

As part of regulatory evaluation of adult education at a national level which included the tutorial class, formal Inspections were required to be carried out, J W Headlam (HMI) and Prof L T Hobhouse being appointed to undertake one of the early visits, and they produced a thorough but cautious report in 1910, concluding that with few exceptions, the quality of teaching and learning conformed to 'the best standards of University work.' One other inspector, a Mr A L Smith, similarly reported but he recorded that only 25% of the essays matched the standard of work submitted to the Honours School of Modern History at Oxford (from Price 1924 p35), suggesting, as above, the difficulties that the students found in essay writing.

Evaluations from students in the class

As well as receiving reports from formal inspections of the tutorial class, those at the organisational centre of the WEA, Mansbridge and Tawney in particular, wanted to know, first-hand, what the students felt about their experience and so, within weeks, they requested feedback from them. The following is a synopsis of individual student reflections :

T W Price : letter of response to Mansbridge : 2nd February 1908

Price began his assessment humbly but cautiously, wondering what use his opinion would be at such an early stage in their progress. He continues, however, that :

'the session was an unqualified success – I went down to the class last week in a state of nervous anticipation .... Hope was struggling with fear ... I realised how much depended on the success of the class and I trembled, but after the class I went home as if I were walking on air. I was so exuberant my wife wanted to know what was the matter with me.'

Price points to two main reasons for this success :

'1. We have the right man – Tawney gained the entire confidence of the members in the first five minutes 2. We have the right kind of men and women in the class – they are in earnest even though many of them have no knowledge of the subject. There is a quiet determination of one and all, better than the wild enthusiasm that flares up and dies out. On the Saturday evening after the class, two students came to my house to talk of books on Industrial History and to borrow them, more came on Sunday on the same errand and I've had visits during the week.'

On the subject of resources and in particular textbooks, Price points out that there is 'need to mention the kindness of the Town Library Committee and the Pioneers Co-operative Society Education Dept. Both have prepared lists of books in their libraries on the subject for each student' but he reserves his greatest praise for teaching and learning. In this he was effusive in recognising a radical element to the class :

'None of us, now that we have become acquainted with Mr Tawney and his methods will be contented any longer with the ordinary University Extension lecture, we want lectures to stimulate us to work, not lectures that are half-popular entertainments. What I mean is when the WEA has gripped the working classes thoroughly we shall see a revolution in University Extension to the gratification, I think, of the Delegacy. The WEA has begun at the right end by responding to demand rather than going for what is popular, converting the class into some sort of corporate body of student feeling or atmosphere like that of a college, thus forming a kind of an outpost to the university.'

James Henighan : letter of response to Mansbridge : 2nd February 1908

Henighan was only too pleased to respond to Mansbridge's request for an evaluation of the class although, as with Price, he wondered whether it was too soon to be voicing a clear and considered opinion. However, he writes that there were 40 students meeting in the class including 3 ladies and that :

> 'an eager, expectant but communicative air was clearly visible on every face with some speculation before the class as to who and what the tutor might be. At nearly 2.30 Gill entered the room followed closely by a <u>young man</u> wearing a gown.'

An interesting side-note about L V Gill from Henighan records what happened at that moment and shows his admiration for their Secretary :

> 'A few words from Gill – it is always Gill – wherever there is any work, there you will find him. He certainly has missed his vocation – as an organiser he is worth a thousand a year whilst his heart is as big as the universe.'

Henighan goes on in reflective mood that he was 'surprised at his youth (ie Tawney) and the sweet affable charm of his presence.' Then, and tellingly, Henighan writes : 'I felt pain. Pain as the lecture clearly showed how backward my study of this particular subject had been'.

Regarding the demeanour of the group, Henighan writes :

> 'at question time an air of calm pervaded the class, most of the students seemed to be feeling their way. Suddenly a murmur arose as one daring student was firing a question. He was neatly answered and this was contagious as many more questions were asked and answered with a smiling face. Tawney then gave out questions to the class and, amidst universal regret the session was brought to an end.'

In a subsequent letter from Henighan (March 2nd1908) to Mansbridge, the student complained that there was 'not much time to talk about essays in the class itself,' no doubt the students seeking more feedback than Tawney was able to give to so large a group, although he confirmed that '[Tawney] is all that could be desired.'

James Henighan must have been invited to go to the Sumer School at Cambridge as he writes in the same feedback letter that regretfully 'on regards to Cambridge, that must for the present lie over. I am not sure that my wife would go even if she were able, which seems doubtful.'

It seems that this was not the only invitation to Henighan, as he also responds to a request about the publication of his views :

> 'And now about this article. I received your letter yesterday and will attend to your request as soon as possible. When do you want it ? I have seen Price tonight and he casually mentioned that the first number of the paper is due in August. I am not a very swift or effective writer'.

Henighan concludes by suggesting that 'your duty as Editor will no doubt be to burn it.'

A third letter from Henighan on the 14th May of the same year begins with an apology for having misplaced an 'enquiry' (was this a questionnaire ?) passed to him by A P Wadsworth. However, he answers this by claiming 'complete satisfaction with the course and with the tutor.' Henighan, interestingly records that within the class there were 'various levels of knowledge and literary proficiency' and then writes that this is 'a fact which in many ways obscures the results obtained,' suggesting the varying abilities and potential of class members. Again, writing about individual competences, Henighan notes that 'not all might talk, but all should be able to write' but then goes on to suggest a growth of confidence in the student body :

> 'Many students show a self-reliance and an independence of judgement which was hitherto foreign to them….. and in some cases one is almost afraid of their eagerness.'

He continues that 'close attention was paid to the list-book' by the tutor (this is probably the Reference and Reading List) and as a consequence work had been steadily progressing. However, he suggests that 'attention is also to be paid to essay writing' which sounds as if it had been identified in class by Tawney, as a problem.

Henighan then raises a point which would be familiar to anyone having taught at any level from primary school to Higher Education by noting that 'in the discussions the same persons invariably take part week by week. This is not as it should be' and offers a suggestion that 'smaller classes might help'.

On a personal note, Henighan exudes enthusiasm, writing that he has 'just commenced a summer class to continue the work and prepare for the next session' and then jovially perhaps, concludes with his signature and 'Au Revoir !'

Alfred W Wilkinson : a Rochdale workman on the Joint Committee (TUC Library : Ref 3/6/1-12)

Wilkinson was brief with his feedback but wrote that there was 'splendid attendance at the last session' and that 'those absent longed to be with their comrades in learning,' in point of fact this absentee was Wilkinson himself ! He recounts that later in the evening after the first session, Tawney gave an address at the Rochdale Education Guild Club in Lord Street and the discussion 'was so taken up that they had to extend time.' Commenting, as so many did on Tawney as their tutor, Wilkinson writes : 'If you can get a don like him we can turn England upside down in a few years…. We in Rochdale are fortunate with Gill and Tawney.'

Fred Hall : a letter of response to Mansbridge : 7th March 1908

Fred Hall began his response theoretically by identifying

> 'two extremes in the working class – those that denounce conditions and would erect an ideal commonwealth but have not got the knowledge of economic and social history to build wisely and would commit the errors of the past ; then there are the apathetic….. If there is anything that will rouse the apathetic it is surely something that deals with their own conditions.'

Hall comments on the exchanges within the class that 'we hear extreme statements in the discussion and find the past criticised in the light of the present day.' All told, however : 'I think that the class can be considered a splendid success. Today was the 7th class and there were no more than 3 away than (those who) started,' feeling that the 'class has gripped the interest of the members and it is most suitable as a working man's course.'

Hall then raises a number of issues about the written work required by the programme including the point that the 'essay writing was difficult at first but is a useful discipline,' although 'if the writing of the essays is too strictly enforced, I am afraid to say that it may cause some to drop off which would be a pity.' He was also critical of the class size, comparing it to other educational programmes in the town : 'our class is quite big enough. We can get more expressions of personal opinions and questions at our Ruskin class with only about half the number.' Specifically, he goes on :

> 'I am glad of the numbers of purely working men who come…. This afternoon I sat between a warper (*probably Arthur Collinge*) and a shuttle-maker (*almost certainly Joseph Cryer*) – whilst next but one was a moulder (*either Albert Wilson or John McLean*)'

Hall writes that

> 'we have in the class teachers (*either Ben Lord or Ethel Kershaw*), journalists (*probably A P Wadsworth*), accountants (*Harold Briggs*) etc and thus we are fulfilling our object in bringing various classes together.' (my italics).

Sensitively and with pleasure, Hall writes that the tutorial class was inclusive of the manual labouring classes and adds 'no offense. They are the class that are hardest to get hold of but in greatest need of help.' He writes that 'the professional classes can look after themselves' whilst noting that 'we are getting ….. working men who come to our classes generally lifted above their old level,' and portraying those attending but who do not normally come to such classes as finding 'wider and deeper interests in life than they ever conceived.' Given his strong Unitarian background Hall writes interestingly that 'each must become a missionary, spreading the light amongst his fellows..... Thanks, for this to Mr Tawney who excites such enthusiasm in the class.'

Suggesting a personal aspiration which was borne out by his subsequent academic successes, Fred Hall writes that 'Oxford have (sic) promised that if I pass the Co-op Union exam they will recognise our class and allow our members to sit for their examination.' Further to this, Mansbridge must have already offered Fred Hall the opportunity to go to the University Summer School : 'You ask if I'm coming to Cambridge' but then states that he is 'almost unemployed although hoping to be qualified for some educational work. I have had the desire for several years to attend the meetings (in Cambridge) but circumstances have been unfavourable so far.'

In terms of publicising the class, Fred Hall wonders if it were possible 'to have some open-air addresses on this subject ?' commenting that many educational questions were dealt with at open air lectures 'from the party standpoint,' no doubt referring to political and church rallies. He concludes by commenting that if, as he feels to be the case, 'from the teaching point of view and the seriousness of the students, our class compares favourably with real University work,' it 'should be talked about.'

Evaluations from visitors to the class

A letter from a Mr Charles Knott of Dinting near Glossop on March 25th 1908, an interested observer of the tutorial class and a Branch Secretary of the WEA Glossop District, recalls his visit to Rochdale and enthuses that 'I shall work on a similar class to this in Glossop. We must have one,' claiming that the visit to Rochdale had been an object lesson and that 'Tawney is the right kind of tutor. He has won the hearts of the students.' Particularly impressed by the lively interaction in the room, he writes : 'Question time brought a surprisingly large number of questions' and there was 'difficulty in stopping them from asking all their questions at once.' He goes on to say that 'some of those with views different to Tawney's were keenly critical, and their criticisms revealed a very clear understanding of the subject.'

Regarding student assessment, Knott felt that 'the fortnightly essay is a strong feature' and on a monitoring and quality note, he writes that

> 'whilst I was there two Government Inspectors looked in, and in the course of their investigations asked if they would be allowed to see one of the essays. Tawney handed one over and they, ignorant of the fact that he had purposely selected what he considered to be the poorest of the lot, remarked on the high standard of the work it represented.'

As others noted however, he considered the size of the group a problem, and thought that 'the class is too large though Gill tells me that Tawney would have it larger still.'

From France a M. Riboud visited the tutorial class (Riboud 1910) and found that the work was characterised by an enthusiastic and earnest spirit : 'The keenness of the pupils is shown by the fact that the average attendance was 95%' and 'a better proof still is that although the class finishes in April, the students have continued to meet during the whole of the summer to revise what they have learned.'

An evaluation by Tawney

Evaluating from the tutor's point of view, Tawney comments (1909) on the marked progress in the work of the students over time : 'Improvement is so great as to be astonishing' he writes, especially 'the excellence of the first five or six students' although Tawney goes on to write that some of the poorer students would benefit from continuation classes in writing and composition and pointedly suggests that 'stops are important', maintaining that 'confused writing is confused thinking' though even in this respect students had shown some improvement. On a practical note, the tutor again mentions his concerns about the imposition of overtime to the detriment of the students' learning and ends by thanking L V Gill for his 'indefatigable exertions in smoothing the way for both tutor and learner.'

From a separate source and referring to the second cohort (Oxford University Delegacy 1910), Tawney suggests that 'the work of the two classes in Rochdale and Longton has continued to be good but both of them have had particular difficulties to contend with,' Tawney reporting that three of the best students from Rochdale have been unable to attend regularly due to serious illness and one 'owing to a lock-out which compelled him to move to a village 12 miles distant, from which, however, he frequently comes on a bicycle.' Out of the class of students originally enrolling, he records that 66% were regular attendees and that some of the students were extremely promising.

It seems, interestingly, that the class that subsequently was set up in nearby Littleborough was not so satisfactory because Tawney felt that the group – 19 in total – was too small and the students were a 'little more backward' than in Rochdale. He did contend, however, that there was, in the Littleborough class, some promising work done by two 'persevering women', both textile workers who 'do very exhausting work during the day.'

Returning to the initial Rochdale class, Tawney records that they continued to make progress and that their 'interest and enthusiasm was as great as ever, the discussions even keener probably due to the nature of the subject – Economic Theory.' He later went on to write that members of this class (and the second cohort in Rochdale) had planned to attend the University Summer Class in Economic and Industrial History, a revision and self-help group, to be held in Rochdale's Guild Club and concludes by claiming that :

> 'a striking feature of both groups is that members are keen enthusiasts for education and have been the means of securing a great deal of support for the local branch of the WEA as well as taking a large part in its work, both educational and executive.'

Alfred Zimmern, then a Fellow at New College Oxford and on the WEA Executive Committee, confirmed this assessment of the student work, remarking (in Jennings 2002 p52) that the class was 'fit for university admission' !

As far as available resources were concerned, Tawney notes that the supply of library books had been 'on a more lavish scale' than previously, due to the generosity of the Joint Committee, there now being a Class Librarian in post - Mr T Lee - who had been most efficient.

Motives and motivation

The social and political conditions were right for change, the town was the one best prepared and equipped to carry it out, and – as has been seen - the students came forward and were prepared to engage seriously with their subject of choice. The 'experiment' of 1908, in years to come, was to turn into an international movement for the education of working people.

The interesting questions arising are theoretical ones individualised in practice. Serious students perhaps, but serious about what and what was it that motivated them ? Why did they bother when so many others preferred to stay away from study ? In what sense was their engagement a response to social or political conditions ? What did they go on to become in their lives and was this the result of their involvement with the WEA ? Were their motives for joining the class based on individual or collective need ? Was the reason so that they could get a better job, so familiar to our meritocratic sensibility, or was there an acceptance of their place in society, an implicit recognition that it would not change for them ? Was it for self-improvement or enculturation ?

Famously, Williams and Heath eighty years ago asked just such questions of a national sample of WEA tutorial classes and Ruskin Hall students. Whilst my concern is on the smaller scale of a case study, breadth in research is not the only difference. I feel that the previous work by Williams and Heath, as tireless as it might have been in recording the voices of worker students, fails to capture substantial themes from those voices and instead produces a polyphony of ardent opinion from different times and from different towns, creating a narrative which overwhelms and dizzies the reader. I wish to avoid that by focusing on individual students and their stories but set them against themes arising from the academic literature and evidence from minutes of the Rochdale Education Guild .

Of course there are no single or simple answers to the questions of motive, individuals responding to their own family needs, their own drivers from faith or from politics and their own educational standpoints in ways which make it likely that they had multiple, even conflicting reasons as to why they joined the class. One way to look at this (amongst many possibilities) which may open up this multiplicity of incentives as well as indicate their subsequent lives and careers, is to identify a number of constructs which, as idealised as they may be, help to structure the evidence available to us. The constructs chosen to do this, hinge around possible extrinsic and intrinsic motivation, though, again, it should be borne in mind that the students may have been influenced by a number of these factors.

Extrinsic motives : Attendance at lectures as normative practice

There can be no doubt that from the late 19th century, lectures and presentations for adults had become an important part of the intellectual life of the town, there being few other vehicles for the formal dissemination of knowledge outside of schools and the church. I would not wish this to be a claim as a special characteristic of Rochdale, as throughout the United Kingdom similar educational provision – both formal and informal – was available in small halls, outdoor meeting places, school rooms and lecture theatres. University Extension classes and Ruskin Hall correspondence courses from some far-off and rather forbidding 'centre' sat alongside something as informal as a church get-together. Often organised village by village, Literary and Scientific Societies popped up in any spare room that was big enough to offer talks on subjects from astronomy to biology, from Dickens to Plato. Rochdale, as other towns, was awash with attempts at diffusing knowledge. And within established institutions, especially the chapels and churches, secular talks had been held for many years, being frequent and well-attended.

An indication of how the tutorial group ran alongside other classes can be seen in the Rochdale Education Guild Handbook and Calendar for 1908-09 in which it was announced that at the same time as his WEA tutorial class, R H Tawney would be conducting lectures in the Examination Hall of the new Secondary School on the first Sunday of most months, that Smallbridge and Hamer districts were organising 6 lectures fortnightly on 'Political and Social Problems' (Thursdays at 8.15pm) and that Mr A Lewis, the 'Honorary Operator' would be presenting Guild Lantern Lectures (with cylinders, gas, sheet and lamp) throughout the town.

Such was their ubiquity and therefore the public familiarity with these educational activities, that there would have been little surprise when another lecture programme – perhaps one of a different nature - was announced in the press. Rochdale, being a small town replete with networks through which interested individuals would have found current information and with a good educational publicity machine manned by effective organisers, had the veins through which knowledge of (and perhaps excitement at) a new lecture series could flow.

Having said so much, this enthusiasm should be set in context. Out of a Rochdale population of 85,000 in 1908 a large proportion of which were working people, only a small number of them were participants in this or any other kind of educational activity. The pressures of family life, the poverty of living conditions, the very grind for daily survival in harsh and unhealthy housing must have been, in 1908 as in any other year, the grim priority for many. So, whilst 43 stepped forward to attend the first tutorial class, many more ignored the call or were not even in a position to hear it, a further example of the fractionalisation of the working class with the many unconnected to self or mutual improvement but a small minority eager to engage. It would be comforting to romanticise the working class and see them as pioneers all, but the reality of a plural culture which catered for every taste and need, was as alive in 1908 as it is today.

What draws one individual or family towards that section of the working class which has educational or aesthetic aspirations, what separates men and women from the same street or factory who need to study, to paint, to write poetry and others who want to follow different interests, is a question for social-psychology. I make no value claims here for the precedence of high or low culture but simply point to a divergence of human interests made manifest in many forms and in many places including the pub and the football ground, the library and the concert hall. My spotlight here though, is on those who felt strongly enough about a need to understand Economics and History to give up their precious spare hours, even if exhausted from manual work.

It can safely be claimed, therefore, that many of the tutorial students were not only aware of the WEA but were also attending other programmes at that time in the church or in the town. Attending lectures, for such individuals, was as common as going to a football match. Furthermore, in a pre-television, pre-technological age, individual enlightenment outside of the institutions of school and church was largely in the hands of the newspaper industry or publishing houses, so being informed was limited to far fewer outlets than we have today. The world for an individual was restricted and tightly bounded so that public lectures were one of the few ways to access new knowledge. Such opportunities would have been only too familiar to those in this tutorial class. Fred Hall, Ben Lord, James Henighan and Amy Fozard, for example, were involved in a number of educational groups across Rochdale, Charlie Pearce, Joe Cryer and Tom Price lectured for the Guild, the WEA and the Unitarian church, Hewitt and Kershaw were connected both to the WEA and addressed meetings of pacifist organisations in the town. These individuals were 'in the know' when it came to the possibilities for adult education in the town, and their familiarity with lecture programmes both as students and as lecturers lends further credibility to the normality of the new tutorial class.

Extrinsic motives : Social mobility

It would not be surprising if it could be shown that the students were attending the WEA in order to become more socially mobile as social mobility had become more realizable in the early 1900's than at any time previously. The establishment of elementary school education from 1870 and with it the narrow but visible gateway through to Higher Grade schooling and possibly beyond, provided an early indication of the potential for individual progress for many in the working population. Furthermore, in the wake of changes in the industrial base and an increase in trade and industry throughout the 19th century, new commercial and service enterprises were appearing and with them career and job opportunities.

This was particularly the case within a growing public sector as the increase in central government control over expanding agencies such as in education and health meant that posts in the civil service and in local administration became increasingly available. Furthermore, as many of these were semi-skilled positions they were accessible to sections of the working community previously consigned to mill-work or jobs involving physical or semi-skilled labour. Familiarity with new communications technologies such as wireless telegraphy, the greater ability to access print media and an improvement in local transport systems meant new networks had to be supervised and administered, calling for managers and white-collar workers who had sufficient skills, but not necessarily more, in literacy and numeracy. The ubiquity of lecture programmes, although not yet what could be called a knowledge revolution, supported occupational shift and pressed increasing numbers of individuals towards social aspiration.

These new (lower middle class) jobs were not, however, within the reach of everyone. What was required of applicants were personal attributes of persistence, punctuality, care and attention to detail alongside basic skills. In the absence of formal qualifications, these were essential specifications and such characteristics – providing the possibility of rising through education on the beginnings of a meritocratic wave - facilitated individual advancement and offered the opportunity for lower middle class entry. They were rooted in such individualist aspirational ideas as those promulgated by Samuel Smiles' 'Self Help' (1859 p4) in which he claimed that

> *'daily experience shows that it is energetic individualism which produces the most powerful effects upon the life and action of others, and really constitutes the best practical education ….. consisting in action, conduct, self-culture, self-control,—all that tends to discipline a man truly, and fit him for the proper performance of the duties and business of life.'*

And part of life's business was to succeed, to get on, and critically to get on *as an individual* rather than as a class or community, to look to your own needs, value-system and morality rather than depending for success or failure on the community in which you lived, or a centralised state, or the vagaries of the national economy. Individual aspiration had become a key late-Victorian concept even though it must have sounded discordant not simply against the rise in socialist thinking at the end of the 19th century but also to those whose morality was based, as with the nonconformist chapels, on fellowship and communities of collaborative improvement. Joining a self-help group was, as the name suggests, based on just such individualism and some individuals may have enrolled into the tutorial class expressly intending to rise as a consequence.

To take teaching as an example of the social mobility made possible at the time. The Education Act of 1870 had thrown a critical light on the drawbacks of the monitorial system and the inadequacies of the curriculum in a time of change, and this led to an urgent re-assessment of how children's minds might be developed in a more effective and sympathetic way and to elevate the skill levels of teachers in order to support necessary change. A revised national system sought the professionalization of teaching by calling for its certification, although such a meritocratic initiative was slow to catch on across the country, and for many years, due to the surge in demand for teachers under the new Act and the fact that School Boards wished them to be employed as cheaply as possible, large numbers of un-certificated teachers continued to find work in schools.

However, in 1906 the Board of Education increased the level of grants for teacher training, a result of which was that individuals from all social classes were drawn into teaching for a number of reasons : it raised their personal status, it was an occupation in high demand (especially elementary school teaching), and the introduction and implementation of regulations requiring *even more* formal qualifications was slow to come through into tertiary education. It also offered a reasonable salary – D H Lawrence was earning £100 a year in 1911, 40% more than most skilled workers in textiles. Many who entered teaching at this time were women from upper working class families, mostly employed in elementary schools as those seeking work in secondary schools required further and higher qualifications. It is interesting to note that the two teachers in the tutorial class, Benjamin Lord and Ethel Kershaw, both went on to become heads of their respective schools but entered the teaching profession at a mature age following their WEA experience in 1908-09.

Teaching was by no means the only career which promised a rise in social status, Livsey Lees and Alfred Wilkinson becoming managers of Labour Exchanges in Heywood and Rochdale, a good example of the growing opportunities for new managerialism in the public sector. Openings in journalism were clear too from the successes of Wadsworth and Dawson, neither of whom had university qualifications. The career progression of Fred Hall stands out from others in the class as he attended university quite soon after 1909 to gain a B.Com in Manchester and then a Masters in Economics although he first taught book-keeping in adult education. Some of the worker students sought employment through clerical and accountancy vacancies (Briggs, Redshaw, Turner) and they experienced upward mobility in that way, even though other members of their families remained working class by occupation and continued to live at the same address in the town.

Education for entry into the public sector was anticipated by the Education Guild (November 1909) at a meeting which had neutrality of the Association as the point at issue. They pledged that their educational provision 'will not make men into churchmen or nonconformists, into Conservatives, Liberals or Socialists, it nonetheless gives….. men and women trained for social service.' Rusoff (in Roberts 2003 p62) substantiates this, claiming that tutorial class education improved not just the lives of the individual students but the working class as a whole, primarily through student entry into public sector occupations. Education therefore, not to be better machine minders but to be better public servants, and Rusoff points to a multiplicity of aspirations for worker-students when he writes :

> 'The motivation of these students is not entirely different from those early WEA recruits who, as Rose has shown, did use access to liberal culture as a class stepping stone as well as a method of widening horizons and enriching the intellectual content of their everyday lives' (ibid p287).

Tom Price, himself a member of the tutorial class, reaffirms the aspirational motive behind the WEA but centres it upon the universities when he looks forward 'to the day when the great universities shall be National Universities, where in the place where the nation's leaders of yesterday were trained…. the working class shall be equipped for social service,' feeling that the tutorial class 'will bridge the gulf between elementary education (where the education of the working man usually ends) and the university' (Price 1908).

When he identifies *secondary* education as the great engine of social mobility, Stuart Maclure (1970 p90) confirms this Edwardian surge of educational opportunity, and whilst this might have been true, it is important to recall just how many of the tutorial class left school at the end of their elementary phase, usually at 14, and therefore how few went on to Higher Grade schooling. Furthermore one of Williams and Heath's correspondents (1936 p50) warns against any automatic correlation between education and 'getting on,' commenting that the genesis of the phrase comes from '19th century history and has done much mischief with the disillusionment of wider knowledge. All men have not the natural capacity to be scholars, but good workmen, yes.'

And it is certainly true that some saw social mobility through occupational change as marginal to their lives. Tawney's view for example, was clearly at variance to the position of educating for better-status work : 'we do not want education for the workers in order to make them better machines. We want it in order that they become better human beings, free men and free women' (1912). This was also a possible critical reference to the Owenite notion of philanthropy being a good foundation for industrial efficiency. Tawney's lifelong struggle was against an association that had come to pass between the assumption of the importance of work and status and a concomitant loss of freedom which was a possible outcome of the individual's experience of the capitalist-occupational nexus. Individual agency had all too often been traded for status. Education, he believed, was more than occupational aspiration.

And Mansbridge himself issued a warning about the objective of some working people becoming socially mobile through the universities. He asks 'To what will the education which we wish Oxford to offer working class people lead ? And what career will they follow after leaving University ?' (in Joint Committee of University and Working Class Representatives 1909 p82). Rather, he suggests that the appetite for university education should be channelled to 'fulfil with greater efficiency the duties which they owe to their own class and as members of their own class, to the whole nation' (ibid). George Orwell (1963), in the 1930's, dealt with similar issues in writing that there existed two types of working class intelligentsia (although this could have been a claim made two decades before). These were either the type that remained in the same social class 'who goes on working as a mechanic or a dock labourer.... and does not bother to change his working class accent or habits but who improves his mind in his spare time and works for the ILP or the Communist Party,' or the other type who climbs into the middle class. For Orwell, this latter type was not so admirable (ibid p143). Mansbridge envisaged the tutorial students to be primarily the first of these, inevitably returning to their own towns and their own trades but better equipped to do their jobs, to enjoy life and more able to be 'an influence for good' in the factory and the town. For Mansbridge this was enough.

Extrinsic motives : The Prospect of Graduation

Whilst the appeal of going to university may have been a dazzling dream for some who engaged with either a University Extension course or with the WEA tutorial class, it remained a too-distant horizon for most, as throughout the 19th century and up to end of the Great War university attendance was primarily the preserve of those from middle class families seeking entry into the established professions. And yet the prospect of a Diploma and a place at university was held tantalisingly before the tutorial students as a possibility at the conclusion of their programme (Joint Committee 1909 p67). Furthermore, both Tawney's charismatic academic presence in the town as well as the students' dalliance at a Cambridge or Oxford Summer School must have made the life of the university undergraduate seem tempting indeed compared to the hardships experienced in the mill. Moreover, the university was doing its part to widen access by being prepared to suspend some of its regulations such as 'at least one foreign language' as an entry requirement or blurring the necessity for 'a good general education' in order to open the university doors as wide as they could to worker students without compromising quality.

Quinney (1983 p65) writes that students who passed with distinction after two years of extension study with the WEA were allowed to come to the university 'as residents' and further scholarships were quickly set up to enable continuation for a full degree 'for exceptional students.' However, even this loosening of regulations did little to attract students from the first Rochdale cohort. Of the 43 students who took part, only Fred Hall went on to Manchester University and Harold Kershaw to Ruskin College within the first few years following the class, and even then Kershaw dropped-out following the Ruskin strike of 1909. A P Wadsworth may have been presented with an honorary Doctorate many years later as was Tom Price, but the transition from Rochdale to Oxford or Cambridge direct seems not to have happened, none of the class going on for the Diploma.

In fact, the Rochdale class took up a characteristically determined and communitarian position about this and rejected outright the idea of selective certification or 'testamur' for the successful completion of the programme (Beaton 1918), Goldman commenting that they baulked at the idea that 'some' of their number would qualify for scholarships and not others. If only three of their number were to go to Oxford in 1910 they said, they preferred to reject the idea outright ! The universities became sufficiently concerned about this unprecedented snub that they sent H H Turner, an Oxford Professor of Astronomy, to investigate the situation, but if he had come to talk them round, he was soon disappointed as he discovered the Rochdale class holding fast to their resistance to cherry-picking successes. Turner reported that he found the Rochdale students to be digging in with their opinion that they should not go 'in ones and twos' and they felt affronted that a year or two at Oxford had been 'dangled before us' when they hadn't had a fortnight's holiday in their lives. They concluded their rail against the University's proposal with a stamp of a Rochdale foot : 'Tell the Committee straight, we absolutely refuse this offer, thanking them for nothing' (Goldman in Roberts 2003 p52). The suggestion here is, as with Tawney's (above), that at the conclusion of university life they would more than likely, they felt, be returning to their trades, weaving sheds and benches and saw no point in extending study further when nothing would come of it. Social mobility through graduation they felt, was a mirage. Financing such a venture would also, of course, have been a consideration.

Nor was this the only denial from them about the prospects after possible graduation. One respondent to the research by Williams and Heath (1936 p225) is recorded as saying : 'The whole conception that a Tutorial class should aim at a University Honours standard should be avoided. It is just a fiction which is likely to damage the movement,' and Mansbridge himself recognised this : 'the real proof that the students give of their desire to study for self-development rather than for position, lies in the absence of desire for diplomas or certificates. They finish their course and ask for no record of it' (1913 p56). Eventually, finding that the students rejected the testamur, the university decided to withdraw it.

Some, with Mansbridge, were delighted at this. Tawney had never wanted the tutorial classes to be simply a route to universities which at times he declaimed as 'finishing schools,' the idea of which he wanted the tutorial classes 'to destroy' in the minds of the workers (TUC Library : Ref RHT). Rather, he hoped that the worker-students would maintain the dignity of their own class. Others, however, and Tom Price was amongst them, saw the university as the ultimate objective, writing that 'the Tutorial Class will set the worker on the very threshold of the University ready for the next step which shall take him inside' (TUC Library Ref : WEA Central 3/6/7). Notwithstanding Price's optimism, twelve years later it remained a distant dream, Constable (in Parry 1920 p203) a WEA student himself, writing in rather forlorn hope that 'whether the Tutorial Class will, in the future, serve as a channel for bringing work-people to a University as internal students, is difficult to say.' Simon (1965 p341) writes that it was not until scholarships from secondary schools began to come through in the 1920's and 1930's that university education began, but slowly, to be within the reach of a few from working class families.

Extrinsic motives : The raising of working class students to power and influence

The words of Tom Price, himself a member of the tutorial class and a guiding presence in Rochdale at the time and later, are indicative of some of the motivations of the students and the changes they hoped that study could make to their lives. He writes (1924 p81) that working class students rarely seek knowledge for its own sake, but are drawn to study by their interest in the working class movement – 'that is to say in the efforts that are being made so to modify and transform social and economic conditions as to afford opportunities for a fuller life for himself and his fellows.' He clarifies this by adding : 'At the back of his mind is the idea that the knowledge he gains will be of use to him in the movement' and 'it follows from this that the lines of study likely to be desired by working class students (and particularly in history, economics and political science) will differ from those pursued by students who are not concerned with the disturbance of the status quo'.

Incremental social change such as is being suggested here can be seen in many of the pamphlets and Reports from the WEA at the time and served – though they were tacit political statements – to fuel the frustration of many of those, for example in the Labour College, whose demands and expectations for radical change were more immediate and militant.

So what or who did study actually serve ? The records of the tutorial class suggest that many continued in their manual jobs after 1908 although some students such as Arthur Collinge in the ILP, Lees and Wilkinson in employment agencies, Stopford and Dawson in the church, exercised an influence for good in social life. Others such as Joseph Binns recognised the advantages to the general workforce of being 'officered' by men of education such as himself and on those grounds undertook leadership roles within the Trades Union movement. Some continued in one form or another in education and became teachers in schools, taught in tutorial classes themselves or became active in spreading the educational message through the WEA in neighbouring towns. James Henighan, for example (Rochdale Education Guild Minutes, January 1910) was lecturing in Heywood on 'A Critical View of Socialism' and 'Adam Smith,' and Fred Hall carried out a personal crusade on behalf of Co-operation although he was, at that point, about to take on a lecturing post in Belfast. By April of the same year, familiar names were being mentioned in the management of the Education Guild and maintaining its influence in the town, Charlie Pearce for example discussing the cost of University Extension classes, and James Henighan, James Hilton, Arthur Shore and Ethel Kershaw being nominated for the Guild Council. So it would seem that a number of students stayed in Rochdale, working to affect the conditions in their own trades or continuing with their cultural interests (most of the class who had been chapel-goers remained so) although some went on to positions of national importance such as Tom Price, Fred Hall and A P Wadsworth.

And this idea of education as civil duty was recognised by M. Riboud, whose visit to the tutorial class from France was reported in the Rochdale Observer (1910), Riboud commenting passionately but with a militaristic edge about the individuals he observed and their educational initiative and motivation :

> 'There is a new political personnel which as soon as possible ought to be educated ; then behind that front rank there are the rank and file of the army of workers. An attempt must be made to raise them little by little to the benefit of their destiny. It is on that educational work that the Workers Educational Association has been engaged with success for the last seven years.'

Riboud adds that this campaign (again militaristically referring to the tutorial class) 'will be one of the last phases of the struggle between feudalism and democracy for the government of England'

and goes on to suggest that Oxford and Cambridge should now train leaders for workers' organisations and administrators for great industrial communities, thereby raising the profile of the working class and once more suggesting the validity of incremental change as opposed to a more radical, if not revolutionary, alternative.

The speech by Sidney Ball at the 1907 Conference addressing the issue of 'What Oxford can do for Working People' suggested that the objectives of the WEA were not that individuals should raise themselves out of the working class, but that they should raise the working class as a whole. Given that this is a long-term and hardly observable objective, it is impossible to judge whether the tutorial class contributed to anything of this nature. However, development at an individual level certainly elevated working class concerns in public, and key members of the class who could lay claim to have done this were Wadsworth through his editorship of the reformist Manchester Guardian, Fred Hall as a driving force behind the Co-operative College, Alfred Wilkinson and Arthur Collinge's work with the Labour Party and trades union movement in Rochdale and Livsey Lees' and Alfred Wilkinson's work in the progressive development of Labour Exchanges.

Others, along with Fred Hall, continued to affect social awareness through education. Charlie Pearce and Tom Price trusted in the power of the WEA and maintained its non-sectarian and non-religious stance, believing that through broadening the mind, a working man would raise himself up. A different position was taken by Harold Kershaw though who, through his experiences with the strikers at Ruskin College and his subsequent organisation of the Central Labour College in Rochdale believed education to be part of class struggle and influenced many in that respect.

In another sense, the question as to whether the WEA class was one small step in changing social class attitudes and stratification within society may be asked in a different way - whether it enabled more working men and women to enter higher education. The answer to this is probably no as far as this group was concerned, turning away as they did from proffered certification and graduation (see above). Millar felt much the same but for different reasons, writing about Tawney's championing of the WEA : 'again and again in Tawney's writings and speeches, he showed how the education system helped to underpin the existing social system' suggesting that the universities had been as closed as they ever were to working people. At the level of institutional change the same might be claimed. Simon (1965 p311), although commenting that the tutorial classes had been popular amongst the groups targeted by the WEA, felt that their success did nothing to widen access to universities which maintained their elite guardianship for many years, protecting their interests in those social groups with power, whilst offering blandishments to others. Williams and Heath (1936 p173) nicely catch this when they write that what the universities at that time :

'cannot bear is the thought of educational changes which, by raising the whole level, will alter the relations between classes. They are willing to allow small gaps to be made in the walls of educational privilege, but they shudder at the thought of those walls being thrown down.'

Extrinsic motives : politics and the WEA

From its launch in 1903 the WEA maintained that it did not set out to propagandise but to inform, and for that reason it stood by its non-political, non-sectarian claims, ignoring the imputation that information of any sort must come from a necessary standpoint. Mansbridge was eager to maintain this neutrality as a key principle and set up the association in order to devolve power to the districts, to the members and to their affiliates rather than control it from a determinist centre, although Brooks (2000) amongst others, have challenged the veracity of this claim.

WEA impartiality was in sharp contrast to what Mansbridge maintained to be the partisan position of the Central Labour College (CLC) and the Plebs League. The WEA set out their transparent emphasis as something politically less extreme and more gradualist, believing that social change might come about through the cascade-effect of education rather than from class organisation and class conflict. Social differences, it was thought, would be equalised through knowledge, incremental faith in the dignity of labour and by the grace of God. In taking this stance, the WEA hoped to send students not to the barricades or the front line but to the universities for further study, to the Labour exchanges as managers, to the schools and to the WEA itself to lay further educational foundations for change. So, to what extent, if any, was political idealism a reason for joining the class ?

First it is important to identify terms. In contrast to the WEA, the political ideology of the Central Labour College (the CLC) and the Plebs League (basically the same organisation) was unambiguous as one respondent makes clear in Heath and Williams' (1936 p12) study when he states that adult education for the CLC is seen as 'a training in the strategy and tactics of class war...... to equip the working class with the knowledge and desire to defeat the capitalist class, and, having done that, to build up socialism.'

Such singular objectives were worlds away from those of Albert Mansbridge although his desire for working class political reflection and intellectual inquiry into the nature of economics and history may have had a similar effect in the long term. That, however, was cloaked in uncertainty. The idea of intellectual 'balance' as promulgated by Mansbridge does not preclude radical political outcomes even though the critics of the WEA maintained that such a 'balance' is achieved only by the restatement and reinforcement of the status quo and thereby of the already empowered.

Mansbridge's position, stated with calm clarity in a letter to The Blackburn Times (1909) was that he wished ALL points of view to be brought to the table and not just one, that the WEA provided a 'platform to state various theories, clearly and impartially, with due balance and without bias.' Mansbridge and Tawney – for the sake of adult education – asserted that they were prepared to suppress their own political instincts even though they might publicly approve of socialist-leaning figures such as Reuben George, 'a former soap box orator ('down with all that is up') or Alfred Williams a railway works blacksmith (Roberts 2003 p7). Their approval of the ideas of such men, however, was predicated on the priorities of education and learning, not on political theory.

However, as the early years of the 20th century passed, the strategies of the two camps – the CLC and the WEA – concerning the way forward for adult education, polarised and became entrenched so that a rift opened up across the left which separated those incrementalists of the WEA from those espousing the more Marxist ideas in the CLC. Simon (1965 p302) gives context to this by pointing out that Marxist ideas were making a serious impact upon some elements of the working class movement in the United Kingdom in the first years of the 20th century, providing a harder theoretical edge than fellowship socialists such as those in the Clarion movement and pointing to determinist links between power, privilege and social class. Maclean catches that Labour College mood by proclaiming that 'I am especially interested in such education as will make revolutionists' (Jennings in Roberts 2003 p106).

It takes only a small step therefore for some on the extreme left to see the central government funding that was being granted to the WEA as a clear indication of the preservation of power within and by the establishment. The question raged then as to whether the WEA was an ameliorating, paid puppet of central government (and therefore the capitalist class) or a vehicle for reform. Harrop (1987 p45) goes to the heart of the matter with :

> 'The WEA/tutorial class movement was welcomed by the establishment as a bulwark against revolutionism, a moderating influence and a form of social control. It helped to channel and reduce pressures and conflict, neutralise class antagonism and integrate the working class into British society – just like its 'partner' the Labour Party.'

A tendency for splits within movements around the approaches to reform was nothing new. Simon (1965 p33) and Cole (1948 pp96-7) both point to the division that occurred amongst the Chartists with Feargus O'Connor's insistence on the taking of immediate power through strikes and insurrection set against William Lovell's knowledge Chartists and 'moral force' men such as Joseph Sturge the Birmingham Quaker. Thompson (1991 pp818-819) saw the story of the Mechanics Institutes as bedevilled by ideological schism, with radical artisans and trades unionists on the one hand seeking financial independence and the right to change educational policy by combative debate, whilst on the other a middle class support for centralised financial and curriculum control in order to calm potential worker disaffection. Craik (1964 p81) shows his colours by claiming that the London Mechanics Institute covertly served the established social order instead of serving to help in disestablishing it. And a final example came to light at the same time as the WEA-CLC debate when those engaging in women's struggle to win the vote experienced a split between suffragists wishing to do so through lawful means and suffragettes willing to change things through direct action.

The institutional rift between the two camps of the WEA and the CLC often appeared in the same town and certainly this was the case in Rochdale. An article by Brooks (2000) provides a fascinating insight into the political divisions of that time and how Mansbridge, in seeing a threat from the CLC in the very town that was championing the WEA's tutorial experiment, decided to continue Tawney's important tenure in Rochdale in 1910 in order to stave off any Marxist competition. Brooks believes that this, however, was at the expense of the Wrexham WEA class which had also been promised Tawney as their tutor. The WEA felt that Rochdale was, politically and strategically, too important to lose its students to the CLC. Before Tawney's re-instatement in Rochdale, Mansbridge even considered drafting in extra tutors for the Rochdale class in the form of heavy hitters such as Eva Hubback, freshly graduating from Cambridge and soon to become director of economics at Newnham and Girton College (ibid p73). Politically the struggle seems to have been intense over Rochdale.

And the early struggle concerned the (partial) allocation of funds to the WEA from central government that had been promised by Robert Morant at the 1907 Oxford Conference, seen by some as a 'golden stream' of government largesse which stood in sharp contrast to the funding from student fees (6 shillings per course) plus trades unions and socialist party grants which went to the Central Labour College. This, the CLC felt, put the WEA in a compromising situation by placing them in the hands of the funders and therefore having to tow their line continually. In turn, this meant keeping the working classes in their place. Millar claimed the WEA to be 'an agency for giving gentlemanly dope to the working classes' (Daily Herald 1922) and Craik characterised their political objective as 'sand-papering' (1964 p58) the working people. The Plebs magazine weighed in and saw it as 'education from above' whilst others drew parallels between the WEA and the Christian gradualism of the Fabian Society (Cole 1948) intent, as Millar saw it, on bringing about social class 'reconciliation' through education. The Horrabins (1924) thought Mansbridge naïve in believing that he was accepting progressive educational philanthropy. Interestingly, at the same time, other forms of social recreation which were popular within the working class community were being targeted in the same way. Dave Russell (1997 p45) notes that Victorian and Edwardian socialists were critical of football and rugby for example, because they believed that these activities provided the opportunities to 'deflect the working classes away from their true political and economic interests,' and Waters (1990) offers similar points about the effects of the Music Hall as class distraction.

Price (1924 p82), amongst many, responded quickly to these claims by suggesting that if there was any bias at all in worker education, it came from those wishing to impose on students 'a certain set of social and economic doctrines,' and held fast to the belief that the WEA's internal and devolved structure safeguarded political neutrality and therefore educational validity. Furthermore he rejected the assumption that the working classes were passive in the face of political manipulation and asserted otherwise, suggesting active and independent minds at work which could counter top-down spin with attitudes and thoughts of their own.

But the divisions went further. Many years later, Millar (1979) pointed out that nearly all of the tutors for the CLC had been union men affiliated to the TUC whereas most of the WEA had come from elitist universities. Not only that, but there was the implication that these same university tutors were demonstrating bias (Justice magazine 9/1/09 p10) in their teaching, an example from the same journal being a letter from Mr A C Barrington claiming that Professor Kirkaldy from the University of Birmingham was propping up capitalism through his WEA Economics class, recommending ideas on 'how to combat socialism' and showing 'deep-seated prejudice if the students questioned him.' Tom Price, by that time managing the WEA in that region, responded to this attack on 'our branch at Coventry' and dismissed the idea that the professors were biased capitalists, writing that a) the university appointed the men and not the WEA, and b) the University of Birmingham acted out of political neutrality.

On an ideological level too, Millar saw divisions. Whereas he perceived the WEA to be fulfilling the wishes of established power and interests, the CLC represented a working class education 'aiming at meeting the specific needs of the workers as a class and undertaken by the workers themselves independently of, and even in opposition to, the ordinary existing channels' (Millar 1979 p60). Lyster-Jameson (1927) took the argument into a pedagogical field by suggesting that the subjects taught by the CLC were weapons to be used in a class war whereas the WEA subjects were supports for the status quo. Griffiths (1969 p25) substantiates this when he writes that :

> 'the curriculum was designed to equip us for the stern battle ahead – industrial history, economics, trade union law and practice, to which was added a course in philosophy as set out in the Positive Outcomes of Philosophy by a German Marxist, Joseph Dietzgen'.

As suggested above, in Rochdale the argument took an institutional form for a while, with Harold Kershaw – following his experiences as a striker at Ruskin College in 1909 where Craik recalled the arguments they had with him in his early weeks and that 'his experiences there, soon led him to think about the WEA and its education as <u>we</u> had come to think about them' – returning to the town to contest the prominence of adult education by setting up a branch of the Central Labour College in 1909-1910. Jennings (2002 p110) writes :

> 'With an impudence bordering on blasphemy the spiritual home of the tutorial class movement was invaded, and the Rochdale and District Labour College was formed. To rub salt into the wounds, the organiser was Harold Kershaw, who had been sent to Ruskin in January 1909 on a WEA scholarship.'

Kershaw, now branch Secretary, was joined for a time by W W Craik who was posted to Rochdale by the CLC to take seven classes. Organisationally things were run by Kershaw who was named in Plebs magazine 'Gamaliel from the worker ranks,' an odd choice of epithet as this suggests a doctor of Jewish law! Charlie Gibbons was another recruit to the teaching staff at Rochdale's CLC and this period is recalled affectionately in his memoir (1959), tutoring avid students and receiving small sums of money raised by class members and local committees.

Under Kershaw, by 1910 the Rochdale branch was overseeing five weekly classes in Rochdale, Bacup, Bury and Preston and Harold was kept busy by visiting trades unionists in the town 'pointing out a narrow way which leadeth to an understanding of social questions and inviting their members' assistance to start classes to propagate the good stuff !' (Plebs 1910). By 1914 there were 18 CLC centres (including Rochdale) across the United Kingdom receiving support from the trade union movement, in particular the railway workers and the miners.

By the winter of 1909 both the WEA and the CLC were competing for worker students across Rochdale with similar subjects of study – Economics, History and Logic – and similar study requirements, students being asked to write two essays per month (Kershaw 1910) in both classes. Exceptional students from the CLC were offered scholarships at the Central Labour College at Oxford (Plebs 1910) a point which would not have gone unobserved by Kershaw himself, a Ruskin renegade !

Whilst there was a great deal of tension and dispute between the two educational factions – the WEA and the CLC – there was much idealism in common. They had similar broad objectives in the extension of education to working adults and basic socialist ideals on each side were related, Tawney himself claiming that he was 'made a socialist by the Rochdale experience' (Brooks 2000 p70). Simon (1965 p304) suggests that both organisations rejected the idea of education as a means of 'getting on' and both 'held that the worker should not separate himself from his class' (ibid). The differences that pulled them apart were questions about where funding should come from to fulfil their aims, and also the end-objective, one working for a society of enlightened and free individuals, the other for a transformation towards a socialist society.

Furthermore, there was little or no difference between the students that attended classes in the CLC and those with the WEA. They came from the same streets and wards, they were employed in the same factories and some even attended the same churches in the town. Millar (1979 p194) confirms this in his depiction of CLC students : 'With few exceptions they were wage earners. A sprinkling of teachers and professional people apart, they were nearly all either manual workers, clerks or shop assistants' - the same social grouping, in fact, as the WEA tutorial class. Tawney's comment that over half his WEA class were members of socialist organisations, the others being trades unionists would also have chimed with the sorts of students drawn to Labour College sessions. Moreover the leaders of both groups would have found common ground theoretically with Mactavish, an avowed socialist, when he suggested that the WEA wished for 'social and industrial emancipation' for the working classes, although this comment raised dissent if not outright mockery from those in the CLC.

Although J P M Millar was a Labour College man, he too recognised the close affinity between it and the WEA, writing that when he went to speak at a new CLC centre he offered them a choice of the two and advised them that to make up their own minds as to which suited them best, the WEA or the Plebs/CLC. And Goldman (in Roberts 2003 p54), standing back historically, writes that the distinction between the WEA and the CLC produced a false antithesis between individual liberalism and class-based revolutionary socialism and refers to words by the WEA students themselves in seeing 'no contradiction between meeting the personal needs of individuals and the social needs of working people more generally' (ibid).

Notwithstanding Brooks' (2000) sense of outright enmity at what he felt was political manoeuvring by the WEA, many saw no reason why both bodies should not work in the same town (which they did) simultaneously holding their own either tacit or overt political and educational manifestos. As the WEA Executive Committee minutes (11th January 1909) suggest, 'there was common cause.'

Extrinsic motives : A community of learning

One aspect not to be overlooked in considering the motives for joining the tutorial class is the obvious appeal of group activity and the fellowship of joint endeavour. It is easy to imagine the discussions that might have taken place after the Clover Street Unitarian's Sunday service about the new tutorial opportunities offered in town and the sense in which companionship might have carried them through the programme's doors. Similarly, individuals from the same street, the same geographical community or workplace might agree to attend together rather than individually. Dobbs (in Parry 1920 p39) writes that small groups of individuals :

> 'had the advantage of a close connexion with some definite social unit – a compact neighbourhood, a factory or a circle of friends – of complete freedom, and of a sociable spirit aroused by the devotion of fellow-workers to a common task.'

A group from Castleton, for example, including Alf Wilkinson, Joseph Wormald and John Mclean joined the class and may have travelled together by tram into town. Gill lived a stones-throw from Price, Arthur Collinge a few doors from Eleanor Redshaw and, as has been seen, most of the class lived in two wards near to the centre of town. Similarly groups under a political banner, many of this class meeting regularly with the SDF or the ILP, or coming from committees within the Co-operative Society, would attend as a band of brothers, security in numbers.

And it is clear from its publications that the Rochdale Education Guild had been a force for bringing such communities together with its organisation of lectures and its development of district provision. Announcements through the Guild's Handbook and Calendar, disseminated to outlying areas in Milnrow or Norden for example or Shawclough or Newhey would have helped to draw what were at that time disparate local communities into a more homogenous whole, a convivial learning fellowship. Davies (in Parry 1920) writes of the importance of leafleting study groups or chapels from which friends might have been attracted, and a confirming footnote can be found in Williams and Heath's study (1936) where they reveal that when asked how individuals had been recruited to the tutorial classes, high on their list was 'personal recommendation.' Styler (1953 p80) reinforces this in his claim that most WEA recruitment took place through 'personal contact.' Perhaps most telling in terms of the close networking that must have been taking place across Rochdale is the promptness with which individuals were able to set up supplementary study groups <u>before</u> the programme started, as was the case with one of Horsburgh's courses. This suggests an effective and close interactive community, separated by short distances, brought together by common interests.

Intrinsic motives : The search for knowledge

Standing in contradistinction to suggestions of the extrinsic and material vocational or social reasons for individuals attending the tutorial class, are ones of personal curiosity or drive. Undertaking study simply to make oneself more rounded or to lead to a fuller and richer life was certainly the motivation behind the membership of many of the lectures and short programmes under the Rochdale Education Guild. And the Guild often claimed to provide no more than that, no sense of an end product in many of the presentations in the Literary and Scientific Societies, no certification in the lectures for the various church Men's and Women's Guilds. To use a cliché, self-improvement was in the journeying and not the arriving, an enrichment that offered an interior personal liberation. Some suggested that the mere prospect, for many working people, of glimpsing your own world through the lens of another was justification enough and that the disinterested search for truth was the most honourable form of education. Education, in this view was culturally enriching and spiritually ennobling (Millar 1979 p55).

Rose (in Roberts 2003 p286) concurs that the reason why students wanted to access the WEA was often a cultural one, wishing to partake in what some saw as 'the best that has been thought and written' and thereby give them 'access to the culture of the class where power lay.' Tawney saw this as an entirely honourable motive, especially as it put down the 'smiling illusion that culture is the prerequisite only of the wealthy' (1914 p72).

And there are many examples of this in the literature. Williams and Heath (1936 p49) record one of their tutorial class respondents saying that 'it may continue to be a hell of a life, but the inhabitant of Hell might find it less intolerable if he learns something about its history, its chemistry and its social customs,' the perplexities of living, illuminated and explained with further study so that the 'terrors and the pains and penalties are all relegated to their proper place. Life has more pleasure for me in a larger outlook,' says another respondent (ibid p85). And this confirms both the Rochdale student who revealed joyously that the world 'was bigger for him than it was before' and the Longton student who writes that 'the tutorial class has made for something more than mental training, it has made for the development of the human spirit; and for many of us opened the door to a wider and deeper life' (Goldman in Roberts 2003 p49). Speaking at the Rochdale class reunion in 1939 Tawney captured the same sentiment : 'If education means anything it means that a man escapes from the narrow world of his individual isolation into the greater universe of ideas and interests into which he can enter and which he can share with others.'

Rather than conceptualising this thirst for knowledge as an undifferentiated whole however, it may be useful to look within it, and distinguish a number of more discrete motives. For example, the passion for self-improvement may not simply be intellectual but may be aimed at attaining moral or political enlightenment. It may lead to spiritual development in a rejection of crude materialism or be witness to the refusal to accept commodified awards and certificates. It may be seen in the lack of concern that a programme of study does not necessarily lead to a better job. Mansbridge himself (1924 p135) enthusiastically saw this complete indifference to material 'outcome' as 'the law of his being,' underpinning a key principle of the 'old original faith' of the WEA.

Price (1924 p81) hints at a hidden curriculum within the tutorial class which relates to intrinsic worth when he writes about skills that were developed but went unpublicised in the syllabus :

> 'Beyond those thousands (of potential scholars) are the millions whose educational demands are of a more elementary kind : whose needs are for the knowledge of essential facts, and the development of powers of judgement and mental alertness that will make them proof against cant and shibboleths – the satisfaction of this demand is part of the claim made by the WEA on behalf of the working class of this country.'

The visitor to Rochdale from France – M. Riboud – recognised something of similar value in the tutorial class providing education, not simply to fit a man for a trade but for a life, suggesting that what the workers initially needed was 'education civique' or a citizens education, without which the political and economic power they held was only a danger to society and to themselves. In the same vein, Mary Stocks wrote that workers 'wanted to know something of the forces which had made them what they were' (1953 p46). In these ways, shifting and diaphanous though this may be, students in Rochdale as elsewhere in worker education were searching for their social and political roots in order to understand who they were and what their lives meant. This 'higher ideal, a higher mode of life, a nobler purpose' as recorded by a Longton student (Goldman in Roberts 2003 p50) or the fact that tutorial study opened the door to wider and deeper understanding, hints at an important existential motive for study.

Final Reflections

The questions I asked myself whilst browsing in the library at Lancaster University all those years ago have been answered partially although, as with most historical questions, with speculation borne of limited evidence, like lifting the curtain of time and squinting through its distorting glass. Records have been destroyed, photographs lost and memories fade, especially within families of those thought to have led uneventful lives. Whilst the details of the establishment of the WEA as an organisation are manifest in published documentation, the backgrounds to the students - like silhouettes cut out of dark paper – are there in outline though with little detail for most of their number. The others have had careers recorded and celebrated.

Some matters, however, have come to light as a result of my research into the tutorial class of 1908 which offer not only material for further discussion but also a demand for more questioning. These, I present here as final, reflective issues and by doing so, hope to remember those worker students whose activities have so far gone without note.

The differences between University Extension programmes and the Tutorial class

The charismatic presence of lecturers such as Hudson-Shaw, Powys and Horsburgh must have been mesmerising to worker students in the early years of the 20th century. Their cultural status wrapped up in professorial gowns, the mere fact that they had tenure at a world famous university, the wealth of knowledge and awards accumulated by these academic titans, would have held many audiences in thrall outwith their lectures on literature, history or politics.

But the key word here is 'audiences.' Captive enjoyment and information yes, but engagement less so, not until the tutorial 'class' with its individualised attention to students both in an interactive dialogue with a tutor and through the marking and assessment of submitted work. The limitation placed on the size of the tutorial group and its design as a continuing programme of lectures, one nesting into another rather than a one-off academic spectacular, ensured for the tutorials a distinctiveness that University Extension could never have achieved. In so doing, the experience of the classes would have been one centred upon something other than itself, having 'programme' objectives dependent upon student progress. So the tutorial was a 'class' almost in a schooling sense where individuals were, or should have been, valued as individual learners. James Hole identified a similar distinction in his critique of the Mechanics Institutes in 1852 when he wrote that 'the most valuable lectures are those which partake of the nature of class instruction' (Dobbs in Parry 1920 p50) and Canon Barnett's 1887 view in that 'students must have not only the directions of the professor, but the constant care of the tutor' (ibid).

Constant care ! This was only possible with a move away from didacticism, away from the lecturer as epistemological centre and towards in-class discussion and an individualised attention on not only student strengths but also their weaknesses. Only through personalisation would a sense of ownership pervade the programme.

A further difference between University Extension and the tutorial classes concerned the degree to which localism and voluntarism acted upon the design and the experience of study. The development of an effective recruitment base in the town, the identification of a subject close to the interests and lived experiences of local people and a dedicated place of their own – such as the Rochdale Education Guild Club – all contributed to a sense that personalised learning was being recognised and valued. This was important in that it held and nurtured individual commitment to what might have seemed to be a distant university and maintained attachment to a long and intensive programme.

Interactive teaching and learning also had an iterative effect with past (and present) students maintaining momentum in local tutorial education by contributing, themselves, to lecturing in the town. Students, as has been seen many times, turned tutor. Whilst this has some echoes of the discredited monitorial system, it was at least parsimonious with the best students being close enough geographically, psychologically and occupationally to new cohorts to know what they wanted from study and how to engage them in it. There was also something of the self-help principle in this akin to the interactivity of a close neighbourhood, individuals within communities helping each other out. Knowledge was not something to be privatised and cosseted but a resource to be shared. So, fellow congregants across the nonconformist scatterings in Rochdale chapels welcomed the opportunity to disseminate what they had learned in the tutorial class (Hall, Stopford, Dawson). Similarly, through political groups (Collinge, Hewitt, Shore) the cascade of information and debate would spread or a portal provided through the Co-operative Societies for discussion and new knowledge (Hall). The process at work here was one of enthusiasm for learning disseminated to others from this tutorial class and acting to 'leaven a whole town' with its influence (Joint Committee of University and Working Class Representatives 1909 p58).

Nor was this iteration of a programme simply a repetition of curriculum content, it also replicated a discursive style of teaching and learning that applies to the WEA today as much as it did when alumni from the first tutorial class themselves became tutors. This represented, of course, another step-change from University Extension with its closed curriculum boundaries and its separation of lecturers from worker-students. This iteration of learning which was made possible by students becoming tutors must also have consolidated a sense of community which was made actual with neighbourhood groups attending the Rochdale class, members of the same church congregation enrolling together or affiliates to political or trades union groups seeing a communal reason for joint attendance. Nor did such collective stirring end when the classes finished, but often it overflowed into the lives of those taking part. A. Cobham, an ex-WEA student writing in Parry (1920) recalls camaraderie in and out of the classroom with rambles organised by the students, tutorial group picnics at villages and parks, 'springs of mirth flooding the swamps of austerity and breaking down the fences of conventionalism' (ibid p221).

Church, chapel and the tutorial class

One fascinating aspect of the story of the tutorial class of 1908 was the extent to which its organisation was buttressed by Christian faith. We have seen how the central group of Mansbridge, Temple and Gore was informed and engendered by a committed Christian Socialist ethos and how this was institutionalised in an Anglicanism towards which Mansbridge moved throughout his life, having been drawn as a young man to cathedral services which, he suggested, gradually became his university (Mansbridge 1940). This transition was not unusual. T S Eliot, Gladstone, Charles Kingsley, and later, George Orwell amongst many others similarly gravitated towards a 'higher' denominational calling in the Church of England, perhaps, some might say, as their public status was elevated.

What is interesting, however, is that the Christian message, at least for the first Rochdale class of 1908, was most enthusiastically received within a *low-church* environment, one which was less contemplative than active, less ceremonial than socially determinist. Those nonconformist students who may have agreed with William Law about the Church of England that 'We live in the coldness and deadness of a formal, historical, hearsay religion,' may have done so out of recognising in it a lack of purchase on real life events. And yet the church which Law alluded to was the one chosen by the WEA hierarchy, lodged as it was in a high Anglicanism of university and church which they, as individuals, had either grown up to know or joined over time. Working class nonconformity had its living roots in the workplace, whereas the middle class Anglican world of Temple and Gore was cloistered by the university and the public school. Yet bridges seem to have been built between the two. The liberal reach between that world and the nonconformity of Clover Street Unitarian Church is indeed ecumenical and post-denominational, finding common cause in the relief of poverty and ignorance within a struggle against the human exigencies of capitalism.

Goffman's sociological frame analysis (1974), or Bourdieu's concept of habitus (1990) whereby individuals or groups construct a meaning for themselves to account for social experiences, is illuminating here in that those with the centralised power in the WEA and who had followed an established upper middle class route starting, possibly, with public school (Temple, Rugby School ; Gore, Harrow School ; Tawney, Rugby School) and progressing seamlessly to university, would build a cultural edifice and a language which supported or 'framed' their understanding of the world. This set of perceptions may well include a high church formulation of sacred views. Others, those working people with minimal schooling and experiences only of labour, would see their religio-cultural representation framed by low-church nonconformity with its emphasis on a Christ for the poor and a plain speaking litany. Yet, the bridge that brought the two groups together was formed by a secondary 'frame,' one which concerned a secular rather than a sacred calling and which foregrounded social justice. Small wonder then that Mansbridge was anxious to 'unframe' as far as possible the classroom experiences of the WEA students and thereby maintain a position outside of the determinism of religious and political ideology.

Most worker students remained in their faith of origin although there were exceptions. Wadsworth, initially from a Congregational family brought up his daughter in the Church of England and shifted habitus or frame, possibly as he achieved status and social standing. Mansbridge similarly, with beginnings in congregationalism (he had been a Sunday School teacher in that chapel) was drawn into the Church of England, eventually having a memorial set in his spiritual home of Gloucester Cathedral.

An escape from their conditions

In the 'Cambridge Essays on Adult Education' (Parry 1920 p219) there was a telling word used by Alfred Cobham, a WEA student, which sheds a little light on certain perceptions of the time. Cobham expresses his delight that members of the tutorial classes were 'allowed to peep in,' during University Summer Schools, 'at the banqueting halls of intellectual life and traditional glory.' 'Allowed' is probably the right word if we concede that there existed only token access for the worker students to these same inner halls of academic life. Given Marriott's concerns about the intellectual abilities of workers and his reservations about their right to choose their own subject to study, it would seem that whilst University Extension offered knowledge to a wider outreach population, when it came to its expansion through the tutorial classes, there remained a sense of unease. This 'experiment' might be going too far. Too much, it may have been felt, was being given away to a social class ill-suited and ill-prepared for the rigours of higher education.

The fact that outreach came to mean, in many ways, 'at arm's length' is reflected in the fact that so few individuals actually did go on to enter the lecture halls of the universities. This was limited access, partial inclusion, some might suggest token liberalism.

One senses that Tawney and Mansbridge knew this and trimmed the aspirations of the students accordingly. Mansbridge's own personal rejection in his early attempt at entering university may have set him on a disappointed trajectory towards an auto-didacticism that he came to feel, in some ways, to be the more honourable route. Knowledge for its own sake, knowledge to become better citizens and leaders of labour rather than graduating, would have to do. Better that, than set out on a potentially disillusioning ascent into the middle classes. It would not be for another 50 years that the Open University flung open its doors to widen access substantially and another thirty again before the Polytechnics as 'new universities' would target what came to be known as 'non-traditional' entrants into higher education.

And if university was not a possibility following the first tutorial class, why not a better job ? The debate between whether it was preparation for life or for livelihood is not answerable here or definitively. Some students saw it one way, some the other but few of them would have suggested that the tutorial class provided them with an exit from their origins in the working class. Fred Hall was already taking a B Com whilst (at weekends) studying under Tawney. A P Wadsworth's contributions to the Rochdale Observer and then to the Manchester Guardian were not a product of the WEA, he was doing these things already and his family knew the editor who gave him his first job ! Those who went on to teach or on to clerical employment (Ethel Kershaw, Lord, Briggs, Lees, Turner and Wilkinson) may have done so regardless of their attendance at the Saturday class. Only those who took teaching and organising jobs with the WEA itself (Price, Pearce, Cryer) or students who rose within the trades union movement (Binns, Collinge, Lees and Nuttall) may be said to have channelled their work with Tawney – and even then tentatively - into their future careers.

The tutorial class was not, then, an escape in its own right. What it did was inspire individuals to reach out for more knowledge than would normally have been the case and nurture an unquenchable desire to enrich their personal lives no matter which course that life took. In that sense they contributed to an enhancement of the communities in which they lived and worked, raising their class but not necessarily raising individuals out of their class. In fact it seems that most stayed in the community of their birth. Post World War II generations have grown accustomed to a meritocratic urgency, a drive for the right qualification and certification and acquiescence before the commodification of learning. In many ways it has become education's sole and substantive rationale with league tables and over-assessment regimes contributing towards it. It is difficult then, to imagine a time in the past when qualifications were far from everything and that personal 'enrichment' was not simply an add-on to the timetable in a secondary school but was itself a reason for study. The 20th century striving towards individual social mobility has led to an educational ladder leaning all too often against a job-shaped cloud which the students in 1908 would neither have recognised nor attempted to climb.

A special group of people ?

When Tom Price wrote that 'we have the right kind of men and women in the class' (TUC Library : Ref WEA CENTRAL/3/6/1) he was calling to mind not only their social status and their commitment to learning and personal development but also their tenacity in making a success of Albert Mansbridge's great 'experiment.' These were people who were going to complete the course.

But if this was an experiment, and it was a word used frequently by Mansbridge, a legitimate question might be to ask : were these people experimented 'upon' or (more probably) was the experiment an investigation into the educational possibilities for working people more generally ? If this latter was the case then a supplementary question arises : just how representative was <u>this</u> particular group of people within the working class ?

The answer to this has to be that they were far from representative. We have already seen that Rochdale as a town had long been recognised for its radicalism and its propensity for self-mobilisation (Gill 1986 ; Mitchell 1892 ; Rose in Donajgrodzki 1977 ; Wiggins 1995). In addition, at many points in this text it has been shown that a significant number of this group were already involved in adult education, often as lecturers themselves. It may be surmised then that those 'first five or six' which Tawney identified (1909) as being 'excellent' students from the tutorial class would have probably come from their ranks. Fred Hall, Stanley Dawson, Tom Price and A P Wadsworth were known across Rochdale as eminent local speakers, Joseph Binns, Harold Briggs and Amy Fozard were already adept and respected in their trades union and religious fields. Henighan was writing frequent articles for radical magazines. These were special people with particular educational interests and skills and came from that part of the working population unfairly and dismissively recognised by Orwell (1963 p144) as the ones who win scholarships and are :

> 'obviously not fitted for a life of manual labour'…. rising 'via Labour Party politics'….. to become 'a Labour MP or a high-up trade union official….. picked out to fight for his mates, and all it means to him is a soft job and the chance of bettering himself' (ibid p155).

This may have been so for Hall, Wadsworth and Dawson, much less for those who stayed in the town and battled for better working conditions and adequate pay in the textile industry.

But the group was unrepresentative for other reasons too. For one thing, on the whole they were young people, mostly between 21 and 35 years of age. One student was in his fifties but he was an exception. Wadsworth was only 17. It is difficult not to conclude that this age-group was chosen deliberately by the Education Guild or the WEA bearing in mind that between 60 and 70 students applied for the class and only 43 were picked to take part on the grounds that smaller numbers were more manageable. So in what ways were the students selected and were those rejected included in the following cohort in 1909 ? These questions will remain subject to speculation as no account of the selection procedure was recorded. What we do know is that a call went out from the Guild for 'young and energetic members of the manual working class who are keenly alive to civic questions,' so in this we have a clear indication as to who they would have preferred to take part. Young people with an already developed interest in social questions of the day were the ones most welcomed and one doubts that such stringent entry requirements went out for other courses. And their age might have made a difference to their motives for attending the class. Being at the beginning of their careers it could be argued that social mobility might have been something of a consideration for these students, whereas had they been older and occupationally settled, there would have been less of a vocational reason for attending. These were young people with the world before them and perhaps anxious to use the WEA in any way that they could. They, again, were in Price's words 'the right kind of men and women' and had something riding on the project's success.

Without clear evidence as to who initially applied it can only be an hypothesis, but given the WEA's enthusiasm to make it work, selection does seem to have taken place on age and ability grounds. As a critical aspect of the experiment therefore, this constitutes a purposive and determined sample, selected not only for their particular attributes but also to give the project every chance of success.

Less an experiment then, than a pilot case study in anticipation of the launch of a distinctive, national organisation.

So whilst the students were special because of their standing within the working class community, others with the same social status were **not** chosen to be a part of the experiment. There were no women from the factory floor, for example. Could this be because none applied ? This seems unlikely as later cohorts had working women coming forward and the one in Littleborough in 1910 certainly included them. The presence of Fanny Taylor in the class of 1908 – who was not working at all, and Amy Fozard working only intermittently at home – leads one to conclude that very few women of *any* occupational description must have applied and those that did were accepted unconditionally.

The situation with the men was different and Brooks (2000 p77) contends that there was, in this case, more than a suspicion of cherry-picking male students of ability, a consequence of which was that the class members were far from the romantic sons of manual labour but real labour aristocracy with feet firmly planted in the established decencies of the chapel or the ideological thought of emergent political parties. It might be added, with a certain amount of assured speculation, that at least two of the high flyers identified by Tawney came from and gravitated towards lower middle class occupational positions rather than from authentic working class communities – namely Wadsworth and Dawson with parents owning a tailoring and a printing business respectively in 1908, both living in good areas of the town and going on to careers in journalism and printing.

Brooks (2000) goes even further when he suggests, with ill-concealed and perhaps justifiable irritation, that Mansbridge protected this 'special group' in Rochdale at a time when Tawney sought to leave his tutoring post for a similar position in Wrexham, knowing that Rochdale was the WEA's flagship town and that much depended upon them. Brooks takes the argument to an extreme however, by reading Mansbridge's decision as one based on a form of social engineering or, as he sees it, eugenics, in that the Rochdale class of 1908 were thought intellectually purer than the one in Wrexham. Further, he records Tawney as having said that Rochdale people retained a distinctiveness and even a superiority to those living in the East End of London or in Glasgow because they had an 'underlying dignity which had not been crushed by their material surroundings' (Brooks 2000 p70). For Brooks, Tawney and Mansbridge could see in Rochdale a new moral society in microcosm (ibid p71) and wanted to protect it. Such alleged group segregation might be ignored if it were not for the fact that a similar distinction was made between the Rochdale class and one from nearby Littleborough which was assessed by Tawney as a 'little more backward' than its neighbouring tutor group. Sensibly, it could be argued that over the course of a hundred years such phrases have come to have more of a negative and political 'edge' than they might have had originally, but there is no denying, with Brooks, a tendency within the WEA hierarchy not only to evaluate groups cognitively but to elevate the Rochdale group above all others in so doing.

The tutorial class of 1908 were therefore far from an average cross section of the Rochdale working population. Their skills were better than most, their awareness of history, politics and literature had been honed in University Extension classes and they had the temperament (perhaps borne of engagement with related sacred and secular causes) to commit to serious study. In the light of changes in the make-up of subsequent WEA classes with fewer and fewer working class students attending as time went by, this special group of students is by no means typical either of the Rochdale population of workers in 1908 or of the type of 'workers' engaging with the WEA in years to come.

Change and the WEA

Much has changed in education in the United Kingdom over the hundred and seven years since the first WEA tutorial class in 1908. The structure of education itself through the development of a compulsory and sectorised national school system, the raising of the school leaving age, the introduction of comprehensivisation and the growing importance of certification being but snapshots of the many transformations affecting the experiences of children and young people.

But what of adults ? Certainly more knowledge pathways now exist through to further and higher education than in 1908 and these have been formalised and made accessible to a wider UK public than ever before albeit with fees and loans increasing in tandem. But whilst Access to Higher Education courses in Further Education colleges now offer tangible routes for non-traditional students to the universities, other adult education programmes – non-vocational, those not directly geared towards graduation, those which offer knowledge as a pastime, for its own sake or for enrichment – have been slashed by grant reductions and cut-backs since Further Education incorporation in the 1990's. The WEA still exists however, like a marooned voluntaristic island in an ocean of certificated award courses, although even the Association has changed in many ways, the 1980's for example witnessing a tapering-away of its links to the universities.

The early struggles to open up higher education for working people through the WEA were, in part, reflective of an era of contestation between policy makers, the church, trades unions, the universities and a certain concept of 'worker' which stood proud at the centre of the experiment. It goes without saying that none of these elements now remain as they once were. Due to successive amendments to Industrial Relations legislation, trades unions have been reduced in size and in potency. Steel , coal, ship building, textiles and most of the heavy industries no longer employ the thousands they once did and so gone is the 'Sing as you go' (fictionally) happy flow of workers through the mill gates led by that other Rochdale phenomenon, Gracie Fields. And disappeared with them is the early to mid 20th century identity of an industrial workforce in the sense of a mass working class many of whom, through changes in the labour market and a protracted era of consumer individualism, now seek to find their own material salvation within the promises of a putative classless, postmodern society. As technology and the service sector gather pace in replacing manual labour, the original concept of the industrial workforce recedes even further into the past. Gone too, to a large extent, is the moral foundation that might have been found in 1908 in the chapel and the church for as Gott (2003 p2) suggests, 'the semi-religious fervour with which Mansbridge extolled the virtues of education now seems quaint.' One wonders whether with its decline so too diminished a vital critical voice which at one time made pronouncements on the inequities of just such social change.

Curricular priorities have changed too along with society. The subjects of study for the students in 1908, history, economics and politics – a syllabus not necessarily designed or intended to provide for a better job but to shed light on their own lives - have been replaced in the main by a Gadarene dash for subjects which, through qualifications, promise to hike individuals up the job ladder. Politics as an academic subject of interest, like the trades union's power, has been trimmed and intellectually 'kettled' by succeeding education policies and as a result is perceived to be of diminishing importance within education and in terms of citizen participation. Neither the often-heard mantra : 'We can't change things' nor the poor voter turn-out in local and general elections – especially amongst the working class (Trickett 2015) - would have been welcomed or understood by the WEA or the CLC.

Alongside and perhaps related to the apparent decline in working class engagement with politics, the bigger picture has also shifted. At a time when global forces are pulling the strings of business, when banks are manipulating the finances which hold together employment and social security, when politics itself is pressed into the service of high finance, the study of history, politics and economics ought to be more important now than it ever was, but it is not. The students of 1908 lived through a time when radical thinking amongst key sections of the working population held out the prospect of better times for all. Now, just when it is needed, the radical is sidelined, the word 'radicalisation' a media slur saved for middle-eastern terrorists or urban bombers. The political spirit of 1908 has been submerged under not so much rational recreational activities as the passive and irrational recreation of consumerism. What chance a photograph in 2015 of 43 ardent and radically-minded young students in the centre of Rochdale ?

So because of all of these changes, it would seem anachronistic to keep the name 'Workers' in the title of the WEA. And the word 'fellowship' which once might have described its DNA seems no less bizarre, individualism and personal striving having undermined a communitarian search for equity, truth and fairness. And as for adult education, whilst the Open University, the University of the Air and distance learning certainly have their strengths and aim to reach out in the spirit of inclusivity, they do so for the increasingly isolated student. One fears that the community of learning that existed around the tutorial group of 1908 may have been lost forever notwithstanding the claims for ersatz 'communities' within social media.

But let us take care not to over-romanticise the past. Various 'communities' from the working population which were as separately distinct as the politically literate, the apathetic, the exhausted and the oppressed, existed side by side in the early years of the 20th century as they do today. They had different needs and ways of getting through difficult lives. The working class was never as homogenous a group as some idealistic political theorists might have supposed and in the opinion of Williams and Heath, in the 1930's (1936 p252) it was only the 'studious working class,' a small sub-section indeed, that was drawn into adult education. Perhaps it was ever thus. A significant number of the first tutorial class within a specially-selected group was distinct in exactly that way. That said, it could be argued that a truly mass movement for the emancipation of adult workers through education was more within reach in 1908 than in today's seeming-affluent society with its range of competing and comforting opiates.

So in some ways the tutorial class experiment was a success. It was the first step in setting up the national and international association of voluntary learners and teachers which provides, today, lifelong learning and nation-wide programmes for adults. Following its earliest precedence, the WEA in 2015 is vigorously student-centred and tutor-led, providing skills for employment, for well-being and for cultural development. It might be claimed, therefore, that the enthusiasm and commitment of the 43 pioneers of adult education in Rochdale helped to establish just such an association and ethos.

But in other ways the experiment failed in that those original students – drawn predominantly from one small corner of the worker population - constituted only a minority, elite section of the working population of Rochdale whilst many thousands of others were untouched by this initiative, were left outside of the experiment. Furthermore it could be argued that working class involvement in the WEA lasted for too short a space of time, perhaps two decades at the most, being eventually supplanted by subsequent waves of students from slightly more comfortable backgrounds as had been the case with the Mechanics Institutes. Unlike the Mechanics Institutes however, the WEA has survived and continues to do valuable work. Students joining classes within the WEA today are able to broaden their individual horizons through study or engage in the wider project of community enrichment. But regret remains that even though it had been an initial success, the tutorial class never really went on to raise large numbers from or out of the lower reaches of the working population, nor did it promise to do so. Rather, it largely confirmed their place in the social system, albeit at the same time enriching the lives of the few with knowledge and culture. But the few were familiar. They were those within the working class who *always had* looked to appreciate higher things, they were the ones who passed the 11+, those who squeezed into the grammar schools in the 1950's and 1960's. In tune with middle class aspirations, they were the decent worker students who recognised and enjoyed the benefits of what some thought to be a meritocracy. Many others, however, did not.

References

Ablett N (1912) The Miners' Next Step (Tonypandy : South Wales Miners Federation)

Adkins H (1908) Oxford and Working Class Education (*in Justice 19th December 1908*)

All The Year Round (*Co-operative Society Almanac February 29 1868*)

Ashworth J (1817) The Rise and Progress of the Unit Doctrine in the Societies of Rochdale, Newchurch in Rossendale and other places (Rochdale : J Westell)

Aspin C (1969) Lancashire, the first Industrial Society (Helmshore : Helmshore Historical Society)

Ball S (1907) What Oxford Want from Workpeople (Paper submitted to the National Conference of Working Class and Educational Organisations, London : WEA)

Bamford Keith, Gerald (no date) The Rise of Nonconformity in Rochdale 1750-1850 (*unpublished Dissertation for Masters in Theology at Kings College University of London*)

Bamford, Samuel (originally 1843, later edition 2005) Passages in the Life of a Radical (New York : Cosimo)

Barnard H C (1971) A History of English Education from 1760 (London : University of London Press)

Beaton Winifred (1918) The Tutorial Class Movement (in *The WEA Education Year Book p256*)

Bell T (1941) Pioneering Days (London : Lawrence and Wishart)

Bell T (1944) John Maclean : a fighter for freedom (Glasgow : Communist Party, Scottish Committee)

Berg M (1994) The Age of Manufactures 1700-1820 (London : Routledge)

Binns A (2013) Valley of a Hundred Chapels (Heptonstall : Grace Judson Press)

Birchall, J (1994) Co-op : the people's business (Manchester : Manchester University Press)

Blackburn Times 2nd October 1909 - Letter from Albert Mansbridge

Board of Education (1908) Reports of Lecturers (DES/R/3/37)

Board of Trade (1908a), Report of an Enquiry by the Board of Trade into Working Class Rents, Housing and Retail Prices together with the Standard Rates of Wages Prevailing in Certain Occupations in the Principal Industrial Towns of the United Kingdom (Cd 3864), (London: HMSO).

Bourdieu P (1990) The Logic of Practice (London : Polity Press)

Bourne G (1912) Change in the Village (New York : George H Doran)

Brooks R (2000) Rochdale, Wrexham and the University tutorial class movement 1907-1914 (*in Welsh History Review Vol 20 No 1 June*)

Burgess K (1975) The Origins of British Industrial Relations : the nineteenth century experience (London : Rowman and Littlefield)

Carpenter, Edward (new edition 2013, original 1916) My Days and Dreams : being autobiographical notes (new edition United States : Nabu Press)

Cartwright E S (1929) Looking Backwards ; a tutorial class anniversary by an old student (Oxford : Rewley House Papers ii)

Chadwick D (1857) On Free Public Libraries and Museums (*in Transactions of the National Association for the Promotion of Social Science No 575*)

Clarke Allen (new edition 1985 original 1899) The Effects of the Factory System (new edition Littleborough : George Kelsall)

Cole J (1986) The Power Game that gave us Education (*in The Rochdale Observer 19th April p57*)

Cole J (1984) Down Poorhouse Lane : the diary of a Rochdale workhouse (Rochdale : RAP)

Cole M (1948) Makers of the Labour Movement (London : Longmans, Green and Co)

Coneys M (no date) The Labour Movement and the Liberal Party in Rochdale 1890-1906 (unpublished Dissertation for MA : Huddersfield Polytechnic : Touchstones archives)

Craik W W (1964) Central Labour College 1909-29 (London : Lawrence and Wishart)

CRV (1908) The Ebbing Tide of Liberalism (*in Justice 1/2/1908*)

Currie R., Gilbert A. and Horsley L (1977) Churches and Churchgoers : patterns of church growth in the British Isles since 1700 (Oxford : Oxford University Press)

Curtis S J and Boultwood H E A (1967) An Introductory History of English Education since 1800 (London : University Tutorial Press)

Davies E (1975) An Examination of the development of the WEA : nationally and in the Rochdale and Oldham area (an unpublished Dissertation : Touchstones Local History Library, Rochdale)

Daily Chronicle (1903) The Educated Workman (in *The Daily Chronicle 14th December*)

Dickens C (1854 new edition 2003) Hard Times (new edition London : Penguin Classics)

Ditchfield G M (1991) Anti-Trinitarianism and Toleration in the late 18th century British Politics : the Unitarian petition of 1792' (*in Journal of Ecclesiastical History Vol 42 No 1*)

Donajgrodzki, A P (editor) (1977) Social Control in Nineteenth Century Britain. (London : Croom Helm)

Doyle M (2003) A Very Special Adventure : the illustrated history of the Workers' Educational Association (London : WEA)

Dyhouse C (2012) Girls Growing up in Victorian and Edwardian England (London : Routledge)

Evans J N (1966) Great Figures in the Labour Movement (London : Elsevier)

Foot M (1980) Debts of Honour (London : Picador)

Foster J (1977) Class Struggle and the Industrial Revolution in Three English Towns (London : Routledge)

Furniss Sanderson (1931) Memories of Sixty Years (London : Methuen)

Garrard J (1983) Leadership and Power in Victorian Industrial Towns 1830-1880 (Manchester : Manchester University Press)

Gibbons C L (1959) Recollections of the Movement for Independent Working Class Education 1909-1914 (unpublished : NCLC records)

Gill Helen (1986) From Adult Education in Victorian Rochdale (unpublished MA Dissertation for Huddersfield Polytechnic)

Goffman E (1974) Frame analysis: An essay on the organization of experience (New York : Harper and Row)

Gore A (2013) Estate in Rochdale where three out of four people are on benefits named as the most deprived area in England for the fifth year in a row (*in the Daily Mail 7th January 2013*)

Gott F (1990) Towards 2003 : an investigation into the relevance of the Workers Educational Association today (*in Studies in the Education of Adults Vol 22 Issue 1 April*)

Gowland D. A. (1979) Methodist Secessions : origins of free Methodism in 3 Lancashire Towns (Manchester : Manchester University Press)

Griffiths J (1969) Pages From Memory (London : J M Dent and Sons)

Hall F and Watkins A P (1937) Co-operation (Manchester : The Co-operative Union Ltd)

Hansard (12th March 1866) Parliamentary Debates (3rd series clxxxii)

Harrison J F C (1961) Learning and Living 1790-1960 (London : Routledge and Kegan Paul)

Harrison J F C (1990) Late Victorian Britain 1875-1901 (London : Fontana)

Harrison, Royden (1965) Before The Socialists : studies in Labour and politics 1861-1881 (London : Routledge and Kegan Paul)

Harrop S (ed) (1987) Oxford and Working Class Education (Nottingham : University of Nottingham Press)

Hempton D (2006) Methodism : empire of the spirit (Yale : Yale University Press)

Herford R Travers and Evans E D (eds) (1909) Historical Sketch of the North and East Lancashire Unitarian Mission and the Affiliated Churches (Bury : Fletcher and Speight)

Heywood T T (1931) The New Annals of Rochdale (Rochdale : Rochdale Times Ltd)

Hinden R (ed) (1964) The Radical Tradition (London : Minerva Press)

Hirst, Joseph Crowther (1881) Hiram Greg (London : Kessinger Press)

Hitchens C (2007) Thomas Paine's Rights of Man (London : Atlantic Books)

Horrabin J F and Horrabin W (1924) Working Class Education (London : The Labour Party Publishing Company)

Inglis K S (1963) Churches and the Working Classes in Victorian England (London : Routledge and Kegan Paul)

Jackson T (no date) A Brief History of the Early Years of the WEA : the partnership between labour and learning (London : WEA)

Jennings B (1979) Knowledge is Power : a short history of the WEA 1903-78 (Hull : Department of Adult Education, University of Hull)

Jennings B (1976) Albert Mansbridge and English Adult Education (Hull : University of Hull, Dept of Adult Education)

Joint Committee of University and Working Class Representatives (1909) Oxford and Working Class Education (Oxford : Clarendon Press)

Joyce Patrick (1982) Society and Politics : the culture of the factory in later Victorian England (London : The Harvester Press)

Justice (16 November 1907) – Editorial : The Education System in England

Justice (25 January 1908) – pleas from a Christian Socialist

Justice (15 August 1908) – assertion of un-representative Joint Committee

Justice (5 September 1908) – Price's defence of the Joint Committee

Justice (21 November 1908) – The Socialist Sunday School in Rochdale

Kershaw H (1910) Outline for Labour College Study (*in Plebs Vol 11 No 9*)

Kirk N (1985) The Growth of Working Class Reformism in mid-Victorian England (London : Croom Helm)

Kramer A (2015) Conscientious Objectors of the First World War: A determined resistance (Barnsley : Pen Sword Books)

Lansbury G (1918) Your Part in Poverty (London : Allen and Unwin)

Lawson J (1946) A Man's Life (London : Hodder and Stoughton)

Lee Mervyn L (1987) The Development of the Education Service in Rochdale from 1902 to 1965 (Manchester : Manchester University of Manchester : Med thesis)

Linehan J L (1977) The Industrial and Commercial Growth of Rochdale (Rochdale : Touchstones NO 1)

Living History Group (1975) Do You Remember ? (Rochdale : RAP)

Lyster-Jameson H (1927) An Outline of Psychology (*in Plebs League pviii*)

Maclure S (1970) One Hundred Years of London Education 1870-1970 (London : Allen Lane/The Penguin Press)

Maltby J B (1882) History of the Wesley Methodist Sunday School (Rochdale : The Local History Centre, Touchstones)

Manchester and Salford Co-operative Herald (*Volume 21 1909*)

Manchester Guardian 5th April 1844 - Rochdale's Board of Guardians (p7)

Manchester Guardian (1956) Wadsworth Retires (in *Manchester Guardian 31st October 1956*)

Mansbridge A and Halstead R (1903) Co-operation, Trade Unionism and University Extension (London : Association to Promote the Higher Education of Working Men)

Mansbridge A and Temple W (1909) Oxford University Tutorial Classes : Report of First Years Working (British Library Add 65215, fo 7)

Mansbridge A (1913) University Tutorial Classes : a study in the development of higher education (London : Longmans, Green and Co)

Mansbridge A (1920) An Adventure in WC Education : being the story of the WEA 1903-1915 (London : Longmans and Co)

Mansbridge A (1924) The Beginning of the WEA (*in The Highway xvi no 3 Summer p135*)

Mansbridge A (1940) The Trodden Road : an autobiography (London : Dent)

Mansbridge A (1944) The Kingdom of the Mind (London : Meridian Press)

Marriott S (1998) From University Extension to Extramural Studies : conflict and adjustment in English adult education 1917-1939 (*in Journal of Educational Administration and History Vol 30 No 1*)

Marsh G (2002) Mansbridge: A Life; A Biographical Note to Celebrate the Centenary of the WEA (London : WEA)

McLachan H (1919) The Methodist Unitarian Movement (Manchester : Manchester University Press)

McLeod H (1984) Religion and the Working Class in 19th Century Britain (London : Palgrave Macmillan)

McLeod H (1986) New Perspectives on Victorian Class Religion (*in Oral History Vol 14 No 35*)

Methodist Preachers (1807) Genuine Methodism Acquitted (Rochdale : J Hartley)

Millar J P M (1979) The Labour College Movement (London : National Council of Labour Colleges)

Mitchell J T W (1892) <u>Address to the Rochdale Co-operative Congress</u> (Rochdale : Rochdale Co-operative Society)

Monthly Messenger (1902) A Journal of the Unitarian Church, Rochdale (*February 1902 Vol XVI No 185*)

Monthly Messenger (1903) A Journal of the Unitarian Church, Rochdale (*November 1903 Vol XVIII No 206*)

Monthly Messenger (1910) A Journal of the Unitarian Church, Rochdale (*April 1910 Vol XXIV No 283*)

Monthly Messenger (1912) A Journal of the Unitarian Church, Rochdale (*June 1912 Vol XXVI No 309*)

Moran K (no date) <u>A Study of Aspects of Working Class Housing in 19th century Rochdale</u> (Manchester : Manchester College of Education unpublished thesis)

Morton Ann (1997) <u>Education and the State 1833-1966</u> (London : Public Record Office Publications)

Munby Z (2003) <u>Raising Our Voices : 100 years of women in the WEA</u> (London : WEA Women's Education Committee)

Neild W (1907) <u>What Workpeople Want Oxford to do</u> (Paper submitted to the National Conference of Working Class and Educational Organisations, London : WEA)

Nordinger E (1967) <u>The Working Class Tories</u> (London : MacGibbon and Kee)

Ormrod D (1984) R H Tawney and the Origins of Capitalism (*in History Workshop No 18, Autumn*)

Orwell G (1937, later edition 1963) <u>The Road to Wigan Pier</u> (Harmondsworth : Penguin Books)

Oxford University Delegacy (1910) <u>Tutorial Classes Committee : second annual report</u> (Oxford : Oxford University Press)

Parry R St John (1920) <u>Cambridge Essays on Adult Education</u> (Cambridge : Cambridge University Press)

Pedley F (1974) Rochdale's Worker Education (*in Rochdale Observer 12th October*)

Plebs (1910) A Prospectus for the Rochdale Labour College Class (*in Plebs Magazine October Vol 11 No 9*)

Price T W (1907) University Tutorial Classes (*in Oxford Chronicle 6th August*)

Price T W (1908) The Rochdale Tutorial Class (*in TUC Archives WEA CENTRAL/3/6/7*)

Price T W (1909) The Rochdale Tutorial Class (*in The Highway, February*)

Price T W (1924) <u>The Story of the WEA</u> (London : The Labour Publications Co Ltd)

Prynn D (1976) The Clarion Clubs, Rambling and the Holiday Associations in Britain since the 1890s (*in The Journal of Contemporary History, 11*)

Quinney V (1983) Workers' Education : a confrontation at Ruskin College (*in American Journal of Education Vol 92 No 1*)

Report of the Royal Commission (The Cross Report : 1887) Appointed to Enquire into the working of the Elementary Education Act, England and Wales (London : Hansard)

Riboud G (1910) Through French Spectacles : a visitor's impressions of the Rochdale Education Guild (*in Rochdale Observer July 9th 1910*)

Roberts K (ed) (2003) A Ministry of Enthusiasm : centenary essays on the Workers Educational Association (London : Pluto Press)

Rochdale Education Guild (1906) A Chapter in the History of Voluntary Educational Effort (Rochdale : Rochdale Education Guild)

Rochdale Education Guild (1909) Fourth Annual Handbook and Calendar (Rochdale : Ormerod Bros)

Rochdale Borough Council (1900) Rochdale Medical Officer of Health Report (Rochdale Borough Council)

Rochdale Housing Reform Council (1911) Dr Anderson's Housing Report on Rochdale (Rochdale : Rochdale Observer)

Rochdale Municipal Borough Council (1906) A Souvenir of the Rochdale Municipal Jubilee (Rochdale : Rochdale Borough Council)

Rochdale Observer March 8th 1937 – Thomas Binns' Obituary

Rochdale Observer 24th September 1890 – criticisms of the SDF

Rochdale Observer April 17th 1909 – Report of Maude Royden's speech to the Guild

Rochdale Observer 11th January 1911 – New Labour Exchange manager

Rochdale Observer 22nd July 1914   - Charles Hewitt's Tribunal hearing

Rochdale Observer 1st August 1914   - Castlemere chapel's call for a calm regarding the war

Rochdale Spectator 3rd August 1880 - School Board Work in Rochdale

Rochdale Times 3rd November 1894 – Rochdale Workmen forsaking Liberalism

Rochdale Times 13th April 1895 – New Premises for the SDF and the ILP

Rochdale Times 2nd March 1908 – letters concerning the WEA

Rochdale Unitarian Church : (ed) Diane Bennett (2014) All in Clover (Rochdale : Rochdale Unitarian Church)

Roper R S (1993) The Co-operative Chapel of Rochdale (Rochdale : Touchstones M861)

Rose J (2010) The Intellectual Life of the British Working Class (London : Yale University Press)

Rowntree B. Seebohm (1899 new edition 2001) <u>Poverty : a study of town life</u> (London : Policy Press)

Royden M (1947) <u>A Threefold Cord</u> (London : Victor Gollanz Ltd)

Ruskin College (1949) <u>The Story of Ruskin College</u> (Oxford : Oxford University Press)

Russell D (1997) <u>Football and the English</u> (Preston : Carnegie Publishing Ltd)

Samuelson Report (1884) <u>Report of the Royal Commission on Technical Instruction</u> (London : HMSO)

Savage M (1988) <u>The Dynamics of Working-class Politics: The Labour Movement in Preston, 1880-1940</u> (Cambridge : Cambridge University Press)

Simon Brian (1965) <u>Education and the Labour Movement 1870-1920</u> (London : Lawrence and Wishart)

Smith H P (1956) <u>Labour and Learning</u> (London : Basil Blackwell)

Spates J (2012) The Caretaker (in *The Friends of Ruskin's Brantwood Newsletter : Spring pp25-28*).

Stephens W B (1998) <u>Education in Britain 1750-1914</u> (London : Macmillan Press)

Stocks, Mary (1953) <u>The Workers Educational Association : the first fifty years</u> (London : Allen and Unwin)

Styler W E (1953) Manual Workers and the Workers Educational Association (*in The British Journal of Sociology Vol 4 No 1 March pp 79-83*)

Tawney R H (1909) Tutorial History Class (*in The Rochdale Observer 22nd September*)

Tawney R H (1912 new edition 1972) <u>R H Tawney's Commonplace Book</u> (new edition : Cambridge : Cambridge University Press)

Tawney R H (1912) Education and Social Progress (*Paper to the Co-operative Congress 28/5/12 Manchester*)

Tawney R H (1914) An Experiment in Democratic Education (in *The Political Quarterly, May*)

Tawney R H (1940) <u>Religion and the Rise of Capitalism</u> (London : Penguin)

Tawney R H (1953) <u>The WEA and Adult Education</u> (London : The Athlone Press)

Temple W (no date) <u>The Place of the WEA in English Education</u> (Manchester : WEA)

Thompson E P (1991) <u>The Making of the English Working Class</u> (Harmondsworth : Penguin)

Thompson E P (1993) <u>Witness Against the Beast : William Blake and the moral law</u> (New York : The New Press)

Travers Herford R and Evans E D (eds) (1909) <u>Historical Sketch of the North and East Lancashire Unitarian Mission and the Affiliated Churches</u> (Bury : Fletcher and Speight)

Trickett J (2015) It was the working class, not the middle class that sunk Labour (*in The New Statesman May 13th*)

Twigg H J (1924) An Outline History of Co-operative Education (Manchester : Manchester Co-operative Union)

Unitarian Church (1897) Constitution and by-Laws for North and East Lancashire Unitarian Mission (Accrington : Hepworth and Webster)

Wadsworth A P (1932) The Cotton Trade and Industrial Lancashire (Manchester : Manchester University Press)

Wadsworth A P (1958) The Strutts and the Arkwrights 1758-1830 : a study of the early factory system (Manchester : Manchester University Press)

Waters C (1990) British Socialists and the Politics of Popular Culture 1884-1914 (Stanford : Stanford University Press)

WEA (1905) Second Annual Report (London : WEA Publications)

WEA (1906) First Years Work of the Rochdale Education Guild (London : WEA Publications)

WEA (1907) Fourth Annual Report (London : WEA Publications)

WEA (1909) Reports on Tutorial Classes (London : WEA Publications)

WEA (1911) Eighth Annual Report (London : WEA Publications)

WEA/University of Oxford (1908) Oxford and Working Class Education : being a Report of a Joint Committee of University and Working Class Representatives on the relation of the University to the Higher Education of Workpeople (Oxford : Clarendon Press)

Webb B (1926) My Apprenticeship (London : Longmans, Green and Co)

Wiggins M J (1995) The Seeds of Industrialisation : Rochdale and Proto-Industry 1660-1760 (Rochdale : Touchstones Archive)

Williams W E and Heath A E (1936) Learn and Live : the consumer's view of adult education (London : Methuen)

Williams M and Farnie D A (1992) Cotton Mills in Greater Manchester (Preston : Carnegie Publishing Ltd)

Whitman Walt (1855) Leaves of Grass (New York : Dover Thrift Editions)

Wood George Henry (1910) The History of Wages in the Cotton Industry (Manchester : Sherratt and Hughes)

Archives

Bolton Central Library Attendance Register for Mission Churches 1872-76

Bolton Central Library Constitution and by-Laws for North and East Lancashire Unitarian Mission (First printed 1897 by Accrington : Hepworth and Webster)

John Rylands Library : letters and documents of A P Wadsworth

Rochdale Touchstones : Education Provision in Rochdale and District (news cuttings 1896-1986 : TO1)

Rochdale Touchstones : Co-operative Society News (news cuttings Ref M 861)

Rochdale Touchstones : Inkster I (no date) Science, Steam, Intellect and Social Class in R 1833-1900 (Reference : R91)

TUC Library, London Metropolitan University : Student essays and letters (Ref : WEA CENTRAL/3/6/2)

London School of Economics (1905) William Beveridge Papers (London School of Economics 20/9/05)

Working Class Movement Library, Salford (1909) Minutes of the Rochdale Women's Social and Political Union

Websites

Jefferies J (2005) The UK Population : Past Present and Future at : http://www.google.co.uk/url?sa=t&rct=j&q=&esrc=s&source=web&cd=1&ved=0CCEQFjAA&url=http%3A%2F%2Fwww.ons.gov.uk%2Fons%2Frel%2Ffertility-analysis%2Ffocus-on-people-and-migration%2Fdecember-2005%2Ffocus-on-people-and-migration---focus-on-people-and-migration---chapter-1.pdf&ei=uJpgVMWmIsSBsQT-roLADg&usg=AFQjCNG-6OubO6MlJqsymyrP-jFNW5YVOQ&sig2=1DvtA-VQVLiRO4SYx3gkqg&bvm=bv.79189006,d.ZGU (accessed September 18th 2015).

Office for National Statistics (2012) Chapter 4 at :

http://www.google.co.uk/url?sa=t&rct=j&q=&esrc=s&source=web&cd=2&sqi=2&ved=0CCcQFjAB&url=http%3A%2F%2Fwww.ons.gov.uk%2Fons%2Fdcp171776_253938.pdf&ei=Mu_1VKuDKs7taoT6gcAL&usg=AFQjCNERae2aArr9abphyjSZ7V4XomFqNw&sig2=Nz3r6x1nCWKdaKPc6Ld1Qw&bvm=bv.87269000,d.d2s (accessed September 18th 2015).

Royden, Mike : The Roydens of Frankby at :

www.roydenhistory.co.uk (accessed September 24th 2015)

Index

A	Pages
Affiliation to the Rochdale Education Guild	43, 141
Assessment	177-178, 185, 187, 208
Association to Promote the Higher Education of Working Men	34, 38-39
B	
Band of Hope	87, 89
Bloomsbury Group	123
Board Schools	18
Brighton Co-operative Society	69
C	
Catiline Club	38
Central Labour College (CLC)	22, 28, 112-113, 151, 198-204, 203, 217
Chartism	20, 22, 24-25, 28, 65, 200-201
Child labour	17-18, 23-24, 117
Christian Economic Society	35
Christian Socialism	28, 31-34, 37-39, 54, 102, 149, 210
The Clarion	23-24, 157, 200
Clover Street Unitarian Church	40, 43, 59, 65-68, 74, 86-87, 89, 95-96, 98, 101-102, 109-110, 125, 150, 152, 205, 211
Cockerton Judgement (1901)	35
Conscientious objectors	91, 107-108, 113-114
Co-operative College	15, 102, 167, 198
Co-operative movement and education	28-29, 31-32, 54, 59, 68-71, 73-74, 84, 102, 146, 153, 167, 181, 198
Co-operative Union	68, 70, 90, 102
Compulsory school attendance	18-20, 216
Cotton processing in Rochdale	9-12, 14, 17, 56, 58, 69, 86-87, 90, 92-96, 98-99, 106-107, 112, 115-117, 120-121, 127-129, 134, 137, 140-141, 145-146, 149,
Cross Commission (1890)	170
Course duration	18, 53, 80
Curriculum of the tutorial class	47, 50, 52, 54, 75-78, 165-167, 192, 201, 209-210
D	
Difficulties in study	157-158, 173, 176-179, 181, 187
Disease	14, 87
E	
Economic conditions	9-14
Education Act (1870)	16-18, 145, 152, 192
Education and the church	59-68
Educational change	16-20
Elementary Education Act (1891)	18
Elitism and the university	45, 202
Essays of the tutorial class	8, 20, 45, 55, 78, 147, 153, 166, 169, 172-173, 174-178, 180, 182, 184, 186, 203
Evaluations of the class	180-187

F	
Factory Acts	16, 18, 24
Fees and the curriculum	31, 47-48, 55, 71, 76, 102, 177, 201, 216
Fellowship of Reconciliation	107
franchise and the vote	15, 21, 56, 154, 157
G	
German tour from Rochdale Educational Guild	90-91, 97-98, 106, 110-111, 121, 135, 172
Great Public Health Act of 1875	14
H	
Half-time system	16-17, 19, 117
'Hiram Greg'	66
Housing conditions in Rochdale	11-12, 158-164
I	
ILP	19, 21, 26, 57, 90-91, 108, 128, 149, 151, 194, 197, 205
Industry in Rochdale	9-14
Inspection of the tutorial class	82, 180
J	
Justice magazine	19-20, 23, 32, 52-53, 68, 105, 202
L	
Labour exchanges	116-117, 139, 173, 192, 198-199
the Labour movement	22-27
library support	73, 76, 179, 181, 187, 190
life expectancy	12, 14, 63, 163
literacy	17, 62, 191
Littleborough WEA	10, 42, 48, 101, 175-176, 187, 215
London Co-operative Society (1825)	69
London Working Man's Association	29
Longton	79, 146, 148-149, 169, 171, 175-176, 186, 206-207
M	
The Manchester Guardian	25, 136-138, 166, 198, 212
Marx	9, 11, 15, 22, 27, 32, 112-113, 150-151, 154, 168, 200-201
Mechanics Institutes	28, 46, 69, 76, 154, 201, 208, 219
Methodism	60-65, 94, 107, 136
monitorial system	19-20, 192, 209
motives and motivation	188-207
N	
No-Conscription Fellowship League	106-108
nonconformity	59-68, 151-152, 210-211
O	
Occupations of the students	81, 97, 145-149, 156, 163-164, 178, 191-194, 214-215
Organisation of the tutorials	75-83
Overcrowded housing	14, 159-163
Overtime	75, 172, 176-177, 186
Oxford Conference (1907)	45, 50-53, 55, 75, 77, 198, 201
P	
paternalism	14, 25
Pay in the cotton industry	10

Peterloo	25
Pickhill All Saints Church	129-131
Plebs Magazine	113, 201, 203-204
Political affiliations of students	149-151, 168, 170, 175, 177, 199-200
Population in Rochdale	12
Poverty	11-12
R	
School leaving age	18-19, 217
Resources	178-179, 181, 187
Rochdale	
Co-operators	20, 39-40, 59, 65, 71, 149, 167
Economic characteristics and Independence	58-59
networks	42, 68, 71, 149, 189, 191, 205
Radical history	24-25, 56-59
Religious influences	59-68
Religion and party politics	63-64
University Extension (evening) Lecture Committee	39-40, 72
Ruskin College	31, 45, 51-52, 74, 112, 195, 198, 203
S	
Samuelson Report (1884)	18
sanitation in Rochdale	13
SDF	19, 26, 32, 43, 50, 52-53, 57, 121, 125, 149, 151, 205
Shawclough United Methodists	94
Search for a tutor	77-81
Sheffield People's College	29
Social class of the students	145-148, 169, 181, 184-185
Social mobility	35, 159, 164, 190-193, 195, 213-214
Socialist Sunday Schools	22, 63-64, 69
Student homes and houses	158-164
Students in the class	84, 144
Subject to be studied	50, 55-56, 75-78, 80, 90, 165, 179, 181-182, 187-188, 203
Sunday School movement	16, 40, 43, 61-63, 66, 68-69, 89, 96, 101, 146
T	
Taff Vale	24
Teaching and learning in class	68-69, 72. 76, 79, 82, 167-175, 180-181, 185, 202, 209-210
Teaching style	80, 169-169, 174
Tutorial class size	51-52, 81, 184, 208
Tutor's fee	79-81
U	
Unitarian church	61-62, 64-67, 76, 86, 89, 95, 144, 151, 185
organisation	66-67
V	
Student values and beliefs	149-151
voluntarism	75, 209
W	
WEA Women's Officer	157
Women in the tutorial class	152-157, 215
Women's Social and Political Union	73, 90, 113, 115-116, 154

Rochdale's Pioneers of Worker Education

At the beginning of the 20th century, many working men and women in Rochdale, as in so many industrial towns across the United Kingdom, were eager to build on the knowledge they had of the world. They wanted to learn, not just about science or literature but about their immediate industrial experience and their social and political place in it.

Their cries for knowledge were heard, and men of learning from the Co-operative Movement and from the universities came forward to help them with educational courses that met their intellectual, spiritual and political needs. At the forefront of this support rose the Workers Educational Association (the WEA) but it needed a town and a group of students to carry out its great 'experiment.'

Rochdale was chosen, for its radical history, its network of educational organisations, its nonconformist zeal and its commitment to learning. In 1908 the town hosted the first WEA tutorial class in the country and recruited one of the great socialist thinkers of the day in R H Tawney to lead, and in the end to be led by its worker students.

This book tells the story of how the WEA tutorial class came into being, the social situation faced by those who came forward for study, who the students were and what they went on to become. Drawn from the mills and often the poorest neighbourhoods in Rochdale, this first group of students were indeed pioneers of worker education.

From a photograph of the first tutorial class of 1908, Gary Heywood-Everett has identified and celebrated individual students, discussed their aspirations, looked at what they did for a living and interviewed some of their relatives. Not only does he discuss the reason why Rochdale was chosen as the site for this great experiment in worker education but also asks what motivated the first students to join and, following their experiences, how they used their knowledge.

Printed in Great Britain
by Amazon